Learning Object-Oriented Programming

Explore and crack the OOP code in Python, JavaScript, and C#

Gastón C. Hillar

BIRMINGHAM - MUMBAI

Learning Object-Oriented Programming

First published: July 2015

Production reference: 1100715

Published by Packt Publishing Ltd.
Livery Place
35 Livery Street
Birmingham B3 2PB, UK.

ISBN 978-1-78528-963-7

www.packtpub.com

Credits

Author
Gastón C. Hillar

Reviewers
Róman Joost
Hugo Solis

Commissioning Editor
Sarah Croufton

Acquisition Editor
Nadeem Bagban

Content Development Editor
Divij Kotian

Technical Editor
Parag Topre

Copy Editor
Relin Hedly

Project Coordinator
Nikhil Nair

Proofreader
Safis Editing

Indexer
Monica Ajmera Mehta

Graphics
Disha Haria

Production Coordinator
Arvindkumar Gupta

Cover Work
Arvindkumar Gupta

About the Author

Gastón C. Hillar is an Italian and has been working with computers since he was 8 years old. In the early 80s, he began programming with the legendary Texas TI-99/4A and Commodore 64 home computers. Gaston has a bachelor's degree in computer science and graduated with honors. He also holds an MBA, in which he graduated with an outstanding thesis. At present, Gaston is an independent IT consultant and a freelance author who is always looking for new adventures around the world.

He has been a senior contributing editor at Dr. Dobb's and has written more than a hundred articles on software development topics. Gatson was also a former Microsoft MVP in technical computing. He has received the prestigious Intel® Black Belt Software Developer award seven times.

He is a guest blogger at Intel® Software Network (`http://software.intel.com`). You can reach him at `gastonhillar@hotmail.com` and follow him on Twitter at `http://twitter.com/gastonhillar`. Gastón's blog is `http://csharpmulticore.blogspot.com`.

He lives with his wife, Vanesa, and his two sons, Kevin and Brandon.

Acknowledgments

At the time of writing this book, I was fortunate to work with an excellent team at Packt Publishing. Their contributions vastly improved the presentation of this book. James Jones gave me a brilliant idea that led me to jump into the exciting project of teaching object-oriented programming in three popular, yet heterogeneous, programming languages. Divij Kotian helped me realize my vision for this book and provided many sensible suggestions regarding the text, format, and flow of the book, which is quite noteworthy. I would like to thank my technical reviewers and proofreaders for their thorough reviews and insightful comments. I was able to incorporate some of the knowledge and wisdom that they have gained in their many years in the software development industry. This book was possible because of their valuable feedback.

The entire process of writing a book requires a huge number of lonely hours. I couldn't have written an entire book without dedicating some time to play soccer with my sons, Kevin and Brandon, and my nephew, Nicolas. Of course, I never won a match.

About the Reviewers

Róman Joost first learned about open source software in 1997. He has contributed to multiple open source projects in his professional career. Roman is currently working at Red Hat in Brisbane, Australia. In his leisure time, he enjoys photography, spending time with his family, and digital painting with GIMP.

Hugo Solis is an assistant professor in the physics department at the University of Costa Rica. His current research interests include computational cosmology, complexity, and the influence of hydrogen on material properties. Hugo has vast experience in languages, including C, C++, and Python for scientific programming and visualization. He is a member of the Free Software Foundation and has contributed code to some free software projects. Hugo has contributed to *Mastering Object-oriented Python and Kivy: Interactive Applications in Python* as a technical reviewer and is the author of *Kivy Cookbook, Packt Publishing*. He is currently in charge of the IFT, a Costa Rican scientific nonprofit organization for the multidisciplinary practice of physics (`http://iftucr.org`).

I'd like to thank my beloved mother, Katty Sanchez, for her support and vanguard thoughts.

---

www.PacktPub.com

Support files, eBooks, discount offers, and more

For support files and downloads related to your book, please visit www.PacktPub.com.

Did you know that Packt offers eBook versions of every book published, with PDF and ePub files available? You can upgrade to the eBook version at www.PacktPub.com and as a print book customer, you are entitled to a discount on the eBook copy. Get in touch with us at service@packtpub.com for more details.

At www.PacktPub.com, you can also read a collection of free technical articles, sign up for a range of free newsletters and receive exclusive discounts and offers on Packt books and eBooks.

https://www2.packtpub.com/books/subscription/packtlib

Do you need instant solutions to your IT questions? PacktLib is Packt's online digital book library. Here, you can search, access, and read Packt's entire library of books.

Why subscribe?

- Fully searchable across every book published by Packt
- Copy and paste, print, and bookmark content
- On demand and accessible via a web browser

Free access for Packt account holders

If you have an account with Packt at www.PacktPub.com, you can use this to access PacktLib today and view 9 entirely free books. Simply use your login credentials for immediate access.

To my sons, Kevin and Brandon, and my wife, Vanesa

Table of Contents

Preface

Object-oriented programming, also known as OOP, is a required skill in absolutely any modern software developer job. It makes a lot of sense because object-oriented programming allows you to maximize code reuse and minimize the maintenance costs. However, learning object-oriented programming is challenging because it includes too many abstract concepts that require real-life examples to make it easy to understand. In addition, object-oriented code that doesn't follow best practices can easily become a maintenance nightmare.

Nowadays, you need to work with more than one programming language at the same time to develop applications. For example, a modern Internet of Things project may require the Python code running on a board and a combination of C#, JavaScript, and HTML code to develop both the web and mobile apps that allow users to control the Internet of Things device. Thus, learning object-oriented programming for a single programming language is usually not enough.

This book allows you to develop high-quality reusable object-oriented code in Python, JavaScript, and C#. You will learn the object-oriented programming principles and how they are or will be used in each of the three covered programming languages. You will also learn how to capture objects from real-world elements and create object-oriented code that represents them. This book will help you understand the different approaches of Python, JavaScript, and C# toward object-oriented code. You will maximize code reuse in the three programming languages and reduce maintenance costs. Your code will become easy to understand and it will work with representations of real-life elements.

What this book covers

Chapter 1, Objects Everywhere, covers the principles of object-oriented paradigms and some of the differences in the approaches toward object-oriented code in each of the three covered programming languages: Python, JavaScript, and C#. You will understand how real-world objects can become part of fundamental elements in the code.

Chapter 2, Classes and Instances, tells you how to generate blueprints in order to create objects. You will understand the difference between classes, prototypes, and instances in object-oriented programming.

Chapter 3, Encapsulation of Data, teaches you how to organize data in the blueprints that generate objects. You will understand the different members of a class, learn the difference between mutability and immutability, and customize methods and fields to protect them against undesired access.

Chapter 4, Inheritance and Specialization, explores how to create a hierarchy of blueprints that generate objects. We will take advantage of inheritance and many related features to specialize behavior.

Chapter 5, Interfaces, Multiple Inheritance, and Composition, works with more complex scenarios in which we have to use instances that belong to more than one blueprint. We will use the different features included in each of the three covered programming languages to code an application that requires the combination of multiple blueprints in a single instance.

Chapter 6, Duck Typing and Generics, covers how to maximize code reuse by writing code capable of working with objects of different types. In this chapter, you will learn parametric polymorphism, generics, and duck typing.

Chapter 7, Organization of Object-Oriented Code, provides information on how to write code for a complex application that requires dozens of classes, interfaces, and constructor functions according to the programing language that you use. It will help you understand the importance of organizing object-oriented code and think about the best solution to organize object-oriented code.

Chapter 8, Taking Full Advantage of Object-Oriented Programming, talks about how to refactor existing code to take advantage of all the object-oriented programming techniques that you learned so far. The difference between writing object-oriented code from scratch and refactoring existing code is explained in this chapter. It will also help you prepare object-oriented code for future requirements.

What you need for this book

You will need a computer with at least an Intel Core i3 CPU or equivalent with 4 GB RAM, running on Windows 7 or a higher version, Mac OS X Mountain Lion or a higher version, or any Linux version that is capable of running Python 3.4, and a browser with JavaScript support.

You will need Python 3.4.3 installed on your computer. You can work with your favorite editor or use any Python IDE that is compatible with the mentioned Python version.

In order to work with the C# examples, you will need Visual Studio 2015 or 2013. You can use the free Express editions to run all the examples. If you aren't working on Windows, you can use Xamarin Studio 5.5 or higher.

In order to work with the JavaScript examples, you will need web browsers such as Chrome 40.x or higher, Firefox 37.x or higher, Safari 8.x or higher, Internet Explorer 10 or higher that provides a JavaScript console.

Who this book is for

If you're a Python, JavaScript, or C# developer and want to learn the basics of object-oriented programming with real-world examples, this book is for you.

Conventions

In this book, you will find a number of text styles that distinguish between different kinds of information. Here are some examples of these styles and an explanation of their meaning.

Code words in text, database table names, folder names, filenames, file extensions, pathnames, dummy URLs, user input, and Twitter handles are shown as follows: "We can use a `rectangle` class as a blueprint to generate the four different `rectangle` instances."

A block of code is set as follows:

```
function calculateArea(width, height) {
  return new Rectangle(width, height).calculateArea();
}

calculateArea(143, 187);
```

When we wish to draw your attention to a particular part of a code block, the relevant lines or items are set in bold:

```
function Mammal() {}
Mammal.prototype = new Animal();
Mammal.prototype.constructor = Mammal;
Mammal.prototype.isPregnant = false;
Mammal.prototype.pairsOfEyes = 1;
```

Any command-line input or output is written as follows:

```
Rectangle {width: 293, height: 117}
Rectangle {width: 293, height: 137}
```

New terms and **important words** are shown in bold. Words that you see on the screen, for example, in menus or dialog boxes, appear in the text like this: "The following line prints **"System.Object"** as a result in the **Immediate Window** in the IDE."

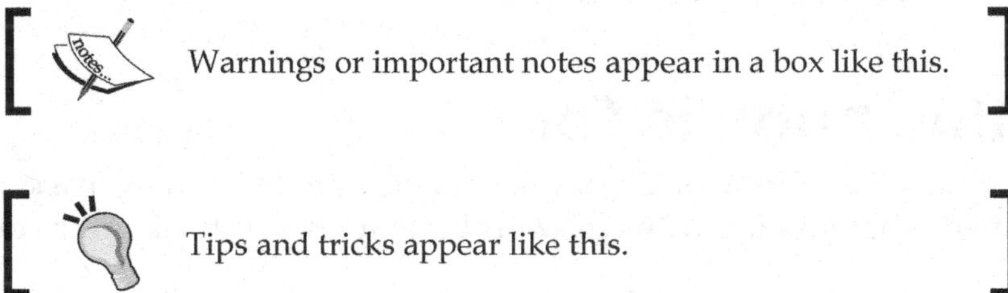

Warnings or important notes appear in a box like this.
Tips and tricks appear like this.

Reader feedback

Feedback from our readers is always welcome. Let us know what you think about this book—what you liked or disliked. Reader feedback is important for us as it helps us develop titles that you will really get the most out of.

To send us general feedback, simply e-mail `feedback@packtpub.com`, and mention the book's title in the subject of your message.

If there is a topic that you have expertise in and you are interested in either writing or contributing to a book, see our author guide at `www.packtpub.com/authors`.

Customer support

Now that you are the proud owner of a Packt book, we have a number of things to help you to get the most from your purchase.

Downloading the example code

You can download the example code files from your account at `http://www.packtpub.com` for all the Packt Publishing books you have purchased. If you purchased this book elsewhere, you can visit `http://www.packtpub.com/support` and register to have the files e-mailed directly to you.

Errata

Although we have taken every care to ensure the accuracy of our content, mistakes do happen. If you find a mistake in one of our books—maybe a mistake in the text or the code—we would be grateful if you could report this to us. By doing so, you can save other readers from frustration and help us improve subsequent versions of this book. If you find any errata, please report them by visiting `http://www.packtpub.com/submit-errata`, selecting your book, clicking on the **Errata Submission Form** link, and entering the details of your errata. Once your errata are verified, your submission will be accepted and the errata will be uploaded to our website or added to any list of existing errata under the Errata section of that title.

To view the previously submitted errata, go to `https://www.packtpub.com/books/content/support` and enter the name of the book in the search field. The required information will appear under the **Errata** section.

Piracy

Piracy of copyrighted material on the Internet is an ongoing problem across all media. At Packt, we take the protection of our copyright and licenses very seriously. If you come across any illegal copies of our works in any form on the Internet, please provide us with the location address or website name immediately so that we can pursue a remedy.

Please contact us at `copyright@packtpub.com` with a link to the suspected pirated material.

We appreciate your help in protecting our authors and our ability to bring you valuable content.

eBooks, discount offers, and more

Did you know that Packt offers eBook versions of every book published, with PDF and ePub files available? You can upgrade to the eBook version at `www.PacktPub.com` and as a print book customer, you are entitled to a discount on the eBook copy. Get in touch with us at `customercare@packtpub.com` for more details.

At `www.PacktPub.com`, you can also read a collection of free technical articles, sign up for a range of free newsletters, and receive exclusive discounts and offers on Packt books and eBooks.

Questions

If you have a problem with any aspect of this book, you can contact us at `questions@packtpub.com`, and we will do our best to address the problem.

1
Objects Everywhere

Objects are everywhere, and therefore, it is very important to recognize elements, known as objects, from real-world situations. It is also important to understand how they can easily be translated into object-oriented code. In this chapter, you will learn the principles of object-oriented paradigms and some of the differences in the approaches towards object-oriented code in each of the three programming languages: Python, JavaScript, and C#. In this chapter, we will:

- Understand how real-world objects can become a part of fundamental elements in the code
- Recognize objects from nouns
- Generate blueprints for objects and understand classes
- Recognize attributes to generate fields
- Recognize actions from verbs to generate methods
- Work with UML diagrams and translate them into object-oriented code
- Organize blueprints to generate different classes
- Identify the object-oriented approaches in Python, JavaScript, and C#

Recognizing objects from nouns

Let's imagine, we have to develop a new simple application, and we receive a description with the requirements. The application must allow users to calculate the areas and perimeters of squares, rectangles, circles, and ellipses.

It is indeed a very simple application, and you can start writing code in Python, JavaScript, and C#. You can create four functions that calculate the areas of the shapes mentioned earlier. Moreover, you can create four additional functions that calculate the perimeters for them. For example, the following seven functions would do the job:

- `calculateSquareArea`: This receives the parameters of the square and returns the value of the calculated area for the shape
- `calculateRectangleArea`: This receives the parameters of the rectangle and returns the value of the calculated area for the shape
- `calculateCircleArea`: This receives the parameters of the circle and returns the value of the calculated area for the shape
- `calculateEllipseArea`: This receives the parameters of the ellipse and returns the value of the calculated area for the shape
- `calculateSquarePerimeter`: This receives the parameters of the square and returns the value of the calculated perimeter for the shape
- `calculateRectanglePerimeter`: This receives the parameters of the rectangle and returns the value of the calculated perimeter for the shape
- `calculateCirclePerimeter`: This receives the parameters of the circle and returns the value of the calculated perimeter for the shape

However, let's forget a bit about programming languages and functions. Let's recognize the real-world objects from the application's requirements. It is necessary to calculate the areas and perimeters of four elements, that is, four nouns in the requirements that represent real-life objects:

- Square
- Rectangle
- Circle
- Ellipse

We can design our application by following an object-oriented paradigm. Instead of creating a set of functions that perform the required tasks, we can create software objects that represent the state and behavior of a square, rectangle, circle, and an ellipse. This way, the different objects mimic the real-world shapes. We can work with the objects to specify the different attributes required to calculate their areas and their perimeters.

Now, let's move to the real world and think about the four shapes. Imagine that you have to draw the four shapes on paper and calculate both their areas and perimeters. What information do you require for each of the shapes? Think about this, and then, take a look at the following table that summarizes the data required for each shape:

Shape	Required data
Square	Length of side
Rectangle	Width and height
Circle	Radius (usually labeled as *r*)
Ellipse	Semi-major axis (usually labeled as *a*) and semi-minor axis (usually labeled as *b*)

The data required by each of the shapes is going to be encapsulated in each object. For example, the object that represents a rectangle encapsulates both the rectangle's width and height. *Data encapsulation* is one of the major pillars of object-oriented programming.

The following diagram shows the four shapes drawn and their elements:

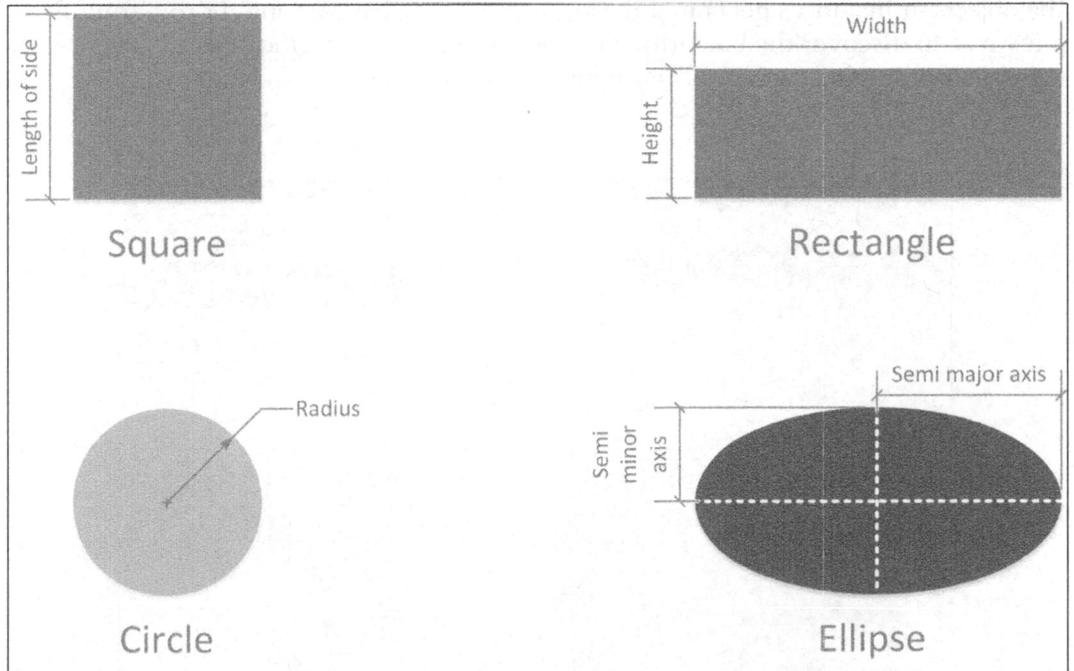

Generating blueprints for objects

Imagine that you want to draw and calculate the areas of four different rectangles. You will end up with four rectangles drawn, with their different widths, heights, and calculated areas. It would be great to have a blueprint to simplify the process of drawing each rectangle with their different widths and heights.

In object-oriented programming, a class is a blueprint or a template definition from which the objects are created. Classes are models that define the state and behavior of an object. After defining a class that defines the state and behavior of a rectangle, we can use it to generate objects that represent the state and behavior of each real-world rectangle.

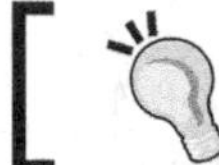

Objects are also known as instances. For example, we can say each rectangle object is an instance of the rectangle class.

The following image shows four rectangle instances drawn, with their widths and heights specified: Rectangle #1, Rectangle #2, Rectangle #3, and Rectangle #4. We can use a `rectangle` class as a blueprint to generate the four different `rectangle` instances. It is very important to understand the difference between a class and the objects or instances generated through its usage. Object-oriented programming allows us to discover the blueprint we used to generate a specific object. Thus, we are able to infer that each object is an instance of the `rectangle` class.

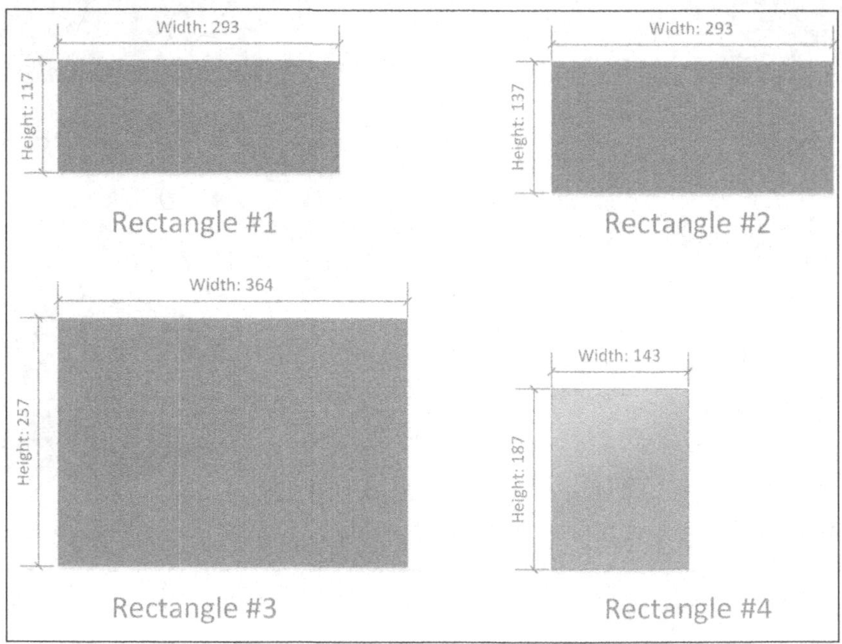

We recognized four completely different real-world objects from the application's requirements. We need classes to create the objects, and therefore, we require the following four classes:

- Square
- Rectangle
- Circle
- Ellipse

Recognizing attributes/fields

We already know the information required for each of the shapes. Now, it is time to design the classes to include the necessary attributes that provide the required data to each instance. In other words, we have to make sure that each class has the necessary variables that encapsulate all the data required by the objects to perform all the tasks.

Let's start with the **`Square`** class. It is necessary to know the length of side for each instance of this class, that is, for each `square` object. Thus, we need an encapsulated variable that allows each instance of this class to specify the value of the length of side.

> The variables defined in a class to encapsulate data for each instance of the class are known as **attributes** or **fields**. Each instance has its own independent value for the attributes or fields defined in the class.

The `Square` class defines a floating point attribute named `LengthOfSide` whose initial value is equal to `0` for any new instance of the class. After you create an instance of the `Square` class, it is possible to change the value of the `LengthOfSide` attribute.

For example, imagine that you create two instances of the `Square` class. One of the instances is named **`square1`**, and the other is **`square2`**. The instance names allow you to access the encapsulated data for each object, and therefore, you can use them to change the values of the exposed attributes.

Imagine that our object-oriented programming language uses a dot (`.`) to allow us to access the attributes of the instances. So, `square1.LengthOfSide` provides access to the length of side for the `Square` instance named `square1`, and `square2.LengthOfSide` does the same for the `Square` instance named `square2`.

You can assign the value `10` to `square1.LengthOfSide` and `20` to `square2.LengthOfSide`. This way, each `Square` instance is going to have a different value for the `LengthOfSide` attribute.

Now, let's move to the **`Rectangle`** class. We can define two floating-point attributes for this class: `Width` and `Height`. Their initial values are also going to be `0`. Then, you can create two instances of the `Rectangle` class: `rectangle1` and **`rectangle2`**.

You can assign the value `10` to `rectangle1.Width` and `20` to `rectangle1.Height`. This way, `rectangle1` represents a 10 x 20 rectangle. You can assign the value `30` to `rectangle2.Width` and `50` to `rectangle2.Height` to make the second `Rectangle` instance, which represents a 30 x 50 rectangle.

The following table summarizes the floating-point attributes defined for each class:

Class name	Attributes list
Square	LengthOfSide
Rectangle	Width Height
Circle	Radius
Ellipse	SemiMajorAxis

The following image shows a **UML** (**Unified Modeling Language**) diagram with the four classes and their attributes:

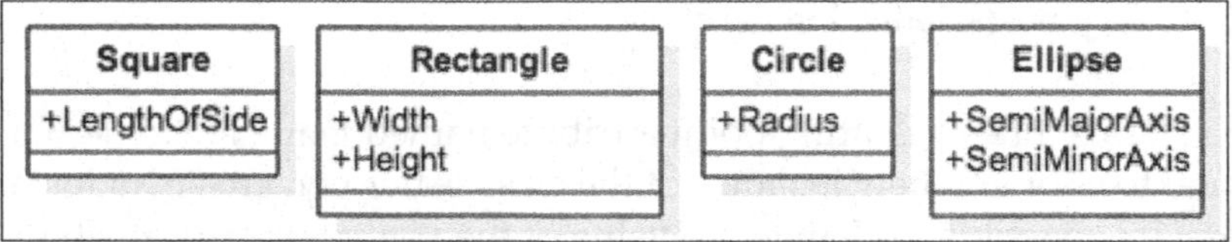

Recognizing actions from verbs – methods

So far, we have designed four classes and identified the necessary attributes for each of them. Now, it is time to add the necessary pieces of code that work with the previously defined attributes to perform all the tasks. In other words, we have to make sure that each class has the necessary encapsulated functions that process the attribute values specified in the objects to perform all the tasks.

Let's start with the **Square** class. The application's requirements specified that we have to calculate the areas and perimeters of squares. Thus, we need pieces of code that allow each instance of this class to use the **LengthOfSide** value to calculate the area and the perimeter.

The functions or subroutines defined in a class to encapsulate the behavior for each instance of the class are known as **methods**. Each instance can access the set of methods exposed by the class. The code specified in a method is able to work with the attributes specified in the class. When we execute a method, it will use the attributes of the specific instance. A good practice is to define the methods in a logical place, that is, in the place where the required data is kept.

The `Square` class defines the following two parameterless methods. Notice that we declare the code for both methods in the definition of the `Square` class:

- `CalculateArea`: This returns a floating-point value with the calculated area for the square. The method returns the square of the `LengthOfSide` attribute value ($LengthOfSide^2$ or *LengthOfSide ^ 2*).
- `CalculatePerimeter`: This returns a floating-point value with the calculated perimeter for the square. The method returns the `LengthOfSide` attribute value multiplied by `4` (*4 * LengthOfSide*).

Imagine that, our object-oriented programming language uses a dot (`.`) to allow us to execute methods of the instances. Remember that we had two instances of the `Square` class: `square1` with `LengthOfSide` equal to `10` and `square2` with `LengthOfSide` equal to `20`. If we call `square1.CalculateArea`, it would return the result of 10^2, which is `100`. On the other hand, if we call `square2.CalculateArea`, it would return the result of 20^2, which is `400`. Each instance has a diverse value for the `LengthOfSide` attribute, and therefore, the results of executing the `CalculateArea` method are different.

If we call `square1.CalculatePerimeter`, it would return the result of *4 * 10*, which is `40`. On the other hand, if we call `square2.CalculatePerimeter`, it would return the result of *4 * 20*, which is `80`.

Now, let's move to the **`Rectangle`** class. We need exactly two methods with the same names specified for the `Square` class. However, they have to calculate the results in a different way.

- `CalculateArea`: This returns a floating-point value with the calculated area for the rectangle. The method returns the result of the multiplication of the `Width` attribute value by the `Height` attribute value (*Width * Height*).
- `CalculatePerimeter`: This returns a floating-point value with the calculated perimeter for the rectangle. The method returns the sum of two times the `Width` attribute value and two times the `Height` attribute value (*2 * Width + 2 * Height*).

Remember that, we had two instances of the `Rectangle` class: `rectangle1` representing a 10 x 20 rectangle and `rectangle2` representing a 30 x 50 rectangle. If we call `rectangle1.CalculateArea`, it would return the result of *10 * 20*, which is `200`. On the other hand, if we call `rectangle2.CalculateArea`, it would return the result of *30 * 50*, which is `1500`. Each instance has a diverse value for both the `Width` and `Height` attributes, and therefore, the results of executing the `CalculateArea` method are different.

If we call `rectangle1.CalculatePerimeter`, it would return the result of *2 * 10 + 2 * 20*, which is `60`. On the other hand, if we call `rectangle2. CalculatePerimeter`, it would return the result of *2 * 30 + 2 * 50*, which is `160`.

The **`Circle`** class also needs two methods with the same names. The two methods are explained as follows:

- `CalculateArea`: This returns a floating-point value with the calculated area for the circle. The method returns the result of the multiplication of π by the square of the `Radius` attribute value ($\pi * Radius^2$ or $\pi * (Radius \wedge 2)$).
- `CalculatePerimeter`: This returns a floating-point value with the calculated perimeter for the circle. The method returns the result of the multiplication of π by two times the `Radius` attribute value.

Finally, the **`Ellipse`** class defines two methods with the same names but with different code and a specific problem with the perimeter. The following are the two methods:

- `CalculateArea`: This returns a floating-point value with the calculated area for the ellipse. The method returns the result of the multiplication of π by the square of the `Radius` attribute value ($\pi * SemiMajorAxis * SemiMinorAxis$).

- `CalculatePerimeter`: This returns a floating-point value with the calculated approximation of the perimeter for the ellipse. Perimeters are very difficult to calculate for ellipses, and therefore, there are many formulas that provide approximations. An exact formula needs an infinite series of calculations. Thus, let's consider that the method returns the result of a formula that isn't very accurate and that we will have to improve on it later. The method returns the result of $2 * \pi * SquareRoot((SemiMajorAxis^2 + SemiMinorAxis^2) / 2)$.

The following figure shows an updated version of the UML diagram with the four classes, their attributes, and their methods:

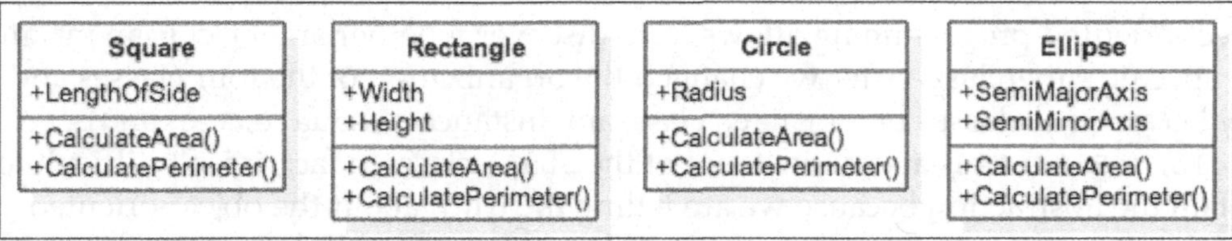

Organizing the blueprints – classes

So far, our object-oriented solution includes four classes with their attributes and methods. However, if we take another look at these four classes, we would notice that all of them have the same two methods: `CalculateArea` and `CalculatePerimeter`. The code for the methods in each class is different, because each shape uses a different formula to calculate either the area or the perimeter. However, the declarations or the contracts for the methods are the same. Both methods have the same name, are always parameterless, and both return a floating-point value.

When we talked about the four classes, we said we were talking about four different geometrical shapes or simply, shapes. Thus, we can generalize the required behavior for the four shapes. The four shapes must declare the `CalculateArea` and `CalculatePerimeter` methods with the previously explained declarations. We can create a contract to make sure that the four classes provide the required behavior.

The contract will be a class named `Shape`, and it will generalize the requirements for the geometrical shapes in our application. The `Shape` class declares two parameterless methods that return a floating-point value: `CalculateArea` and `CalculatePerimeter`. Then, we can declare the four classes as subclasses of the **`Shape`** class that inherit these definitions, but provide the specific code for each of these methods.

> We can define the `Shape` class as an abstract class, because we don't want to be able to create instances of this class. We want to be able to create instances of `Square`, `Rectangle`, `Circle`, or `Ellipse`. In this case, the `Shape` abstract class declares two abstract methods. We call `CalculateArea` and `CalculatePerimeter` abstract methods because the abstract class declares them without an implementation, that is, without code. The subclasses of `Shape` implement the methods because they provide code while maintaining the same method declarations specified in the `Shape` superclass. *Abstraction* and *hierarchy* are the two major pillars of object-oriented programming.

Object-oriented programming allows us to discover whether an object is an instance of a specific superclass. After we changed the organization of the four classes and they became subclasses of the `Shape` class, any instance of `Square`, `Rectangle`, `Circle`, or `Ellipse` is also an instance of the `Shape` class. In fact, it isn't difficult to explain the abstraction because we are telling the truth about the object-oriented model that represents the real world. It makes sense to say that a rectangle is indeed a shape, and therefore, an instance of a `Rectangle` class is a `Shape` class. An instance of a `Rectangle` class is both a `Shape` class (the superclass of the `Rectangle` class) and a `Rectangle` class (the class that we used to create the object).

When we were implementing the `Ellipse` class, we discovered a specific problem for this shape; there are many formulas that provide approximations of the perimeter value. Thus, it makes sense to add additional methods that calculate the perimeter using other formulas.

We can define the following two additional parameterless methods, that is, two methods without any parameter. These methods return a floating-point value to the `Ellipse` class to solve the specific problem of the ellipse shape. The following are the two methods:

- `CalculatePerimeterWithRamanujanII`: This uses the second version of a formula developed by Srinivasa Aiyangar Ramanujan
- `CalculatePerimeterWithCantrell`: This uses a formula proposed by David W. Cantrell

This way, the `Ellipse` class implements the methods specified in the `Shape` superclass. The `Ellipse` class also adds two specific methods that aren't included in any of the other subclasses of `Shape`.

The following diagram shows an updated version of the UML diagram with the abstract class, its four subclasses, their attributes, and their methods:

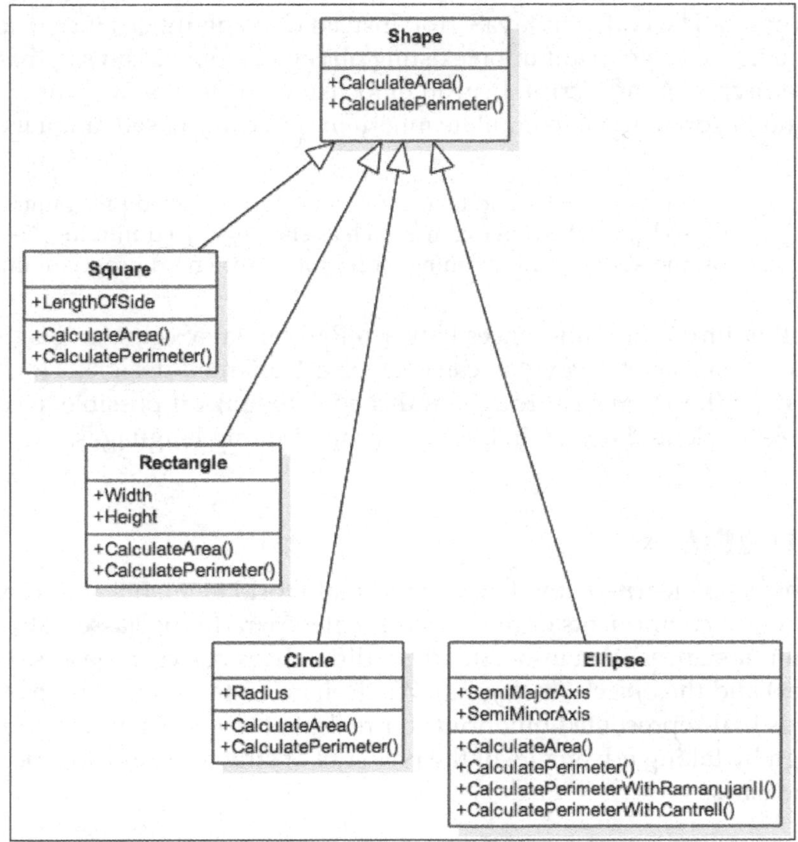

Object-oriented approaches in Python, JavaScript, and C#

Python, JavaScript, and C# support object-oriented programming, also known as OOP. However, each programming language takes a different approach. Both Python and C# support classes and inheritance. Therefore, you can use the different syntax provided by each of these programming languages to declare the `Shape` class and its four subclasses. Then, you can create instances of each of the subclasses and call the different methods.

On the other hand, JavaScript uses an object-oriented model that doesn't use classes. This object-oriented model is known as **prototype-based programming**. However, don't worry. Everything you have learned so far in your simple object-oriented design journey can be coded in JavaScript. Instead of using inheritance to achieve behavior reuse, we can expand upon existing objects. Thus, we can say that objects serve as prototypes in JavaScript. Instead of focusing on classes, we work with instances and decorate them to emulate inheritance in class-based languages.

The object-oriented model known as prototype-based programing is also known by other names such as classless programming, instance-based programming, or prototype-oriented programming.

There are other important differences between Python, JavaScript, and C#. They have a great impact on the way you can code object-oriented designs. However, you will learn different ways throughout this book to make it possible to code the same object-oriented design in the three programming languages.

Summary

In this chapter, you learned how to recognize real-world elements and translate them into the different components of the object-oriented paradigm: classes, attributes, methods, and instances. You understood the differences between classes (blueprints or templates) and the objects (instances). We designed a few classes with attributes and methods that represented blueprints for real-life objects. Then, we improved the initial design by taking advantage of the power of abstraction, and we specialized in the `Ellipse` class.

Now that you have learned some of the basics of the object-oriented paradigm, you are ready to start creating classes and instances in Python, JavaScript, and C# in the next chapter.

2
Classes and Instances

In this chapter, we will start generating blueprints to create objects in each of the three programming languages: Python, JavaScript, and C#. We will:

- Understand the differences between classes, prototypes, and instances in object-oriented programming
- Learn an object's lifecycle and how object constructors and destructors work
- Declare classes in Python and C# and use workarounds to have a similar feature in JavaScript
- Customize the process that takes place when you create instances in Python, C#, and JavaScript
- Customize the process that takes place when you destroy instances in Python, C#, and JavaScript
- Create different types of objects in Python, C#, and JavaScript

Understanding classes and instances

In the previous chapter, you learned some of the basics of the object-oriented paradigm, including classes and objects, also known as instances. Now, when you dive deep into the programming languages, the class is always going to be the type and the blueprint. The object is the working instance of the class, and one or more variables can hold a reference to an instance.

Let's move to the world of our best friends, the dogs. If we want to model an object-oriented application that has to work with dogs and about a dozen dog breeds, we will definitely have a `Dog` abstract class. Each dog breed required in our application will be a subclass of the `Dog` superclass. For example, let's assume that we have the following subclasses of `Dog`:

- `TibetanSpaniel`: This is a blueprint for the dogs that belong to the Tibetan Spaniel breed
- `SmoothFoxTerrier`: This is a blueprint for the dogs that belong to the Smooth Fox Terrier breed

So, each dog breed will become a subclass of `Dog` and a type in the programming language. Each dog breed is a blueprint that we will be able to use to create instances. `Brian` and `Merlin` are two dogs. `Brian` belongs to the Tibetan Spaniel breed, and `Merlin` belongs to the Smooth Fox Terrier breed. In our application, `Brian` will be an instance of the `TibetanSpaniel` subclass, and `Merlin` will be an instance of the `SmoothFoxTerrier` subclass.

As both `Brian` and `Merlin` are dogs, they will share many attributes. Some of these attributes will be initialized by the class, because the dog breed they belong to determines some features, for example, the area of origin, the average size, and the watchdog ability. However, other attributes will be specific to the instance, such as the name, weight, age, and hair color.

Understanding constructors and destructors

When you ask the programming language to create an instance of a specific class, something happens under the hood. The programming language runtime creates a new instance of the specified type, allocates the necessary memory, and then executes the code specified in the constructor. When the runtime executes the code within the constructor, there is already a live instance of the class. Thus, you have access to the attributes and methods defined in the class. However, as you might have guessed, you must be careful with the code you put within the constructor, because you might end up generating large delays when you create instances of the class.

Constructors are extremely useful to execute setup code and properly initialize a new instance.

So, for example, before you can call the `CalculateArea` method, you want the `Width` and `Height` attributes for each new `Rectangle` instance to have a value initialized to `0`. Constructors are extremely useful when we want to define the attributes of the instances of a class right after their creation.

Sometimes, we need specific arguments to be available when we are creating an instance. We can design different constructors with the necessary arguments and use them to create instances of a class. This way, we can make sure that there is no way of creating specific classes without using the authorized constructors that ask for the necessary arguments.

At some point, your application won't need to work with an instance anymore. For example, once you calculate the perimeter of an ellipse and display the results to the user, you don't need the specific `Ellipse` instance anymore. Some programming languages require you to be careful about leaving live instances alive. You have to explicitly destroy them and de-allocate the memory that it was consuming.

The runtimes of Python, C#, and JavaScript use a garbage-collection mechanism that automatically de-allocates memory used by instances that aren't referenced anymore. The garbage-collection process is a bit more complicated, and each programming language and runtime has specific considerations that should be taken into account to avoid unnecessary memory pressure. However, let's keep our focus on the object's life cycle. In these programming languages, when the runtime detects that you aren't referencing an instance anymore and when a garbage collection occurs, the runtime executes the code specified within the instance's destructor.

You can use the destructor to perform any necessary cleanup before the object is destroyed and removed from memory. However, take into account that JavaScript doesn't provide you with the possibility to customize a destructor.

For example, think about the following situation. You need to count the number of instances of a specific class that are being kept alive. You can have a variable shared by all the classes. Then, you customize the class constructor to atomically increase the value for the counter, that is, increase the value of the variable shared by all the classes of the same time. Finally, you customize the class destructor to automatically decrease the value for the counter. This way, you can check the value of this variable to know the objects that are being referenced in your application.

Declaring classes in Python

Throughout this book, we will work with Python 3.4.3. However, all the explanations and code samples are compatible with Python 3.x.x. Therefore, you can work with previous Python versions as long as the major version number is 3. We will use JetBrains PyCharm Community Edition 4 as the main Python IDE and the supplier of an interactive Python console. However, you can use your favorite Python IDE or just the Python console.

Everything is a class in Python, that is, all the elements that can be named in Python are classes. Guido van Rossum designed Python according to the first-class everything principle. Thus, all the types are classes, from the simplest types to the most complex ones: integers, strings, lists, dictionaries, and so on. This way, there is no difference between an integer (`int`), a `string`, and a `list`. Everything is treated in the same way. Even functions, methods, and modules are classes.

For example, when we enter the following lines in a Python console, we create a new instance of the `int` class. The console will display `<class 'int'>` as a result of the second line. This way, we know that `area` is an instance of the `int` class:

```
area = 250
type(area)
```

When we type the following lines in a Python console, we create a new instance of the `function` class. The console will display `<class 'function'>` as a result of the second line. Thus, `calculateArea` is an instance of the `function` class:

```
def calculateArea(width, height):
    return width * height

type(CalculateArea)
```

Let's analyze the simple `calculateArea` function. This function receives two arguments: width and height. It returns the width value multiplied by the height value. If we call the function with two `int` values, that is, two `int` instances, the function will return a new instance of `int` with the result of `width` multiplied by `height`. The following lines call the `calculateArea` function and save the returned `int` instance in the `rectangleArea` variable. The console will display `<class 'int'>` as a result of the third line. Thus, `rectangleArea` is an instance of the `int` class:

```
rectangleArea = calculateArea(300, 200)
print(rectangleArea)
type(rectangleArea)
```

The following lines create a new minimal `Rectangle` class in Python:

```
class Rectangle:
    pass
```

The `class` keyword followed by the class name (`Rectangle`) and a colon (`:`) composes the header of the class definition. In this case, the class doesn't have a parent class or a superclass. Therefore, there aren't superclasses enclosed in parentheses after the class name and before the colon (`:`). The indented block of statements that follows the class definition composes the body of the class. In this case, there is just a single statement, `pass`, and the class doesn't define either attributes or methods. The `Rectangle` class is the simplest possible class we can declare in Python.

Any new class you create that doesn't specify a superclass will be a subclass of the `builtins.object` class. Thus, the `Rectangle` class is a subclass of `builtins.object`.

The following line prints `True` as a result in a Python console, because the `Rectangle` class is a subclass of `object`:

```
issubclass(Rectangle, object)
```

The following lines represent an equivalent way of creating the `Rectangle` class in Python. However, we don't need to specify that the class inherits from an object because it adds unnecessary boilerplate code:

```
class Rectangle(object):
    pass
```

Customizing constructors in Python

We want to initialize instances of the `Rectangle` class with the values of both `width` and `height`. After we create an instance of a class, Python automatically calls the `__init__` method. Thus, we can use this method to receive both the `width` and `height` arguments. We can then use these arguments to initialize attributes with the same names. We can think of the `__init__` method as the equivalent of a constructor in other object-oriented programming languages.

The following lines create a `Rectangle` class and declare an `__init__` method within the body of the class:

```
class Rectangle:
    def __init__(self, width, height):
        print("I'm initializing a new Rectangle instance.")
        self.width = width
        self.height = height
```

This method receives three arguments: `self`, `width`, and `height`. The first argument is a reference to the instance that called the method. We used the name `self` for this argument. It is important to notice that `self` is not a Python keyword. It is just the name for the first argument, and it is usually called `self`. The code within the method prints a message indicating that the code is initializing a new `Rectangle` instance. This way, we will understand when the code within the `__init__` method is executed.

Then, the following two lines create the `width` and `height` attributes for the instance and assign them the values received as arguments with the same names. We use `self.width` and `self.height` to create the attributes for the instance. We create two attributes for the `Rectangle` instance right after its creation.

The following lines create two instances of the `Rectangle` class named `rectangle1` and `rectangle2`. The Python console will display `I'm initializing a new Rectangle instance.` after we enter each line in the Python console:

```
rectangle1 = Rectangle(293, 117)
rectangle2 = Rectangle(293, 137)
```

```
Python 3.4.3 (v3.4.3:9b73f1c3e601, Feb 23 2015, 02:52:03)
[GCC 4.2.1 (Apple Inc. build 5666) (dot 3)] on darwin
>>> class Rectangle:
    def __init__(self, width, height):
        print("I'm initializing a new Rectangle instance.")
        self.width = width
        self.height = height
>>> rectangle1 = Rectangle(293, 117)
rectangle2 = Rectangle(293, 137)
I'm initializing a new Rectangle instance.
I'm initializing a new Rectangle instance.

>>>
```

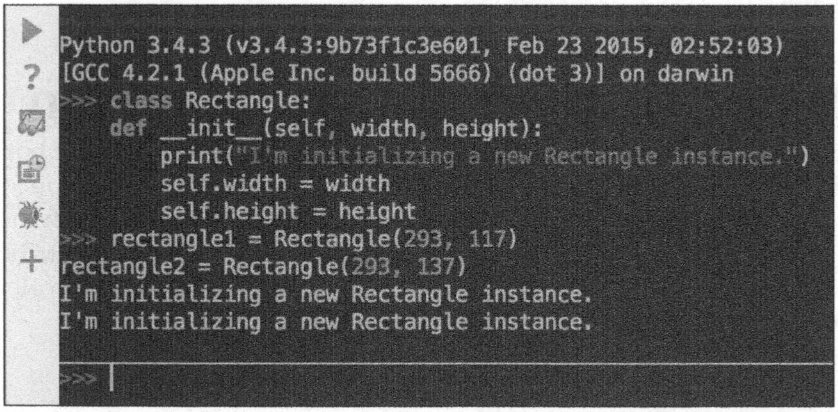

The preceding screenshot shows the Python console. Each line that creates an instance specifies the class name followed by the desired values for both the `width` and the `height` as arguments enclosed in parentheses. If we take a look at the declaration of the `__init__` method within the `Rectangle` class, we will notice that we just need to specify the second and third arguments (`width` and `height`). Also, we just need to skip the required first parameter (`self`). Python resolves many things under the hood. We just need to make sure that we specify the values for the required arguments after `self` to successfully create and initialize an instance of `Rectangle`.

After we execute the previous lines, we can check the values for `rectangle1.width`, `rectangle1.height`, `rectangle2.width`, and `rectangle2.height`.

The following line will generate a `TypeError` error and won't create an instance of `Rectangle` because we missed the two required arguments: `width` and `height`. The specific error message is `TypeError: __init__() missing 2 required positional arguments: 'width' and 'height'`. The error message is shown in the following screenshot:

```
rectangleError = Rectangle()
```

```
>>> rectangle1.width
293
>>> rectangle1.height
117
>>> rectangle2.width
293
>>> rectangle2.height
137
>>> rectangleError = Rectangle()
Traceback (most recent call last):
  File "<input>", line 1, in <module>
TypeError: __init__() missing 2 required positional arguments: 'width' and 'height'

>>>
```

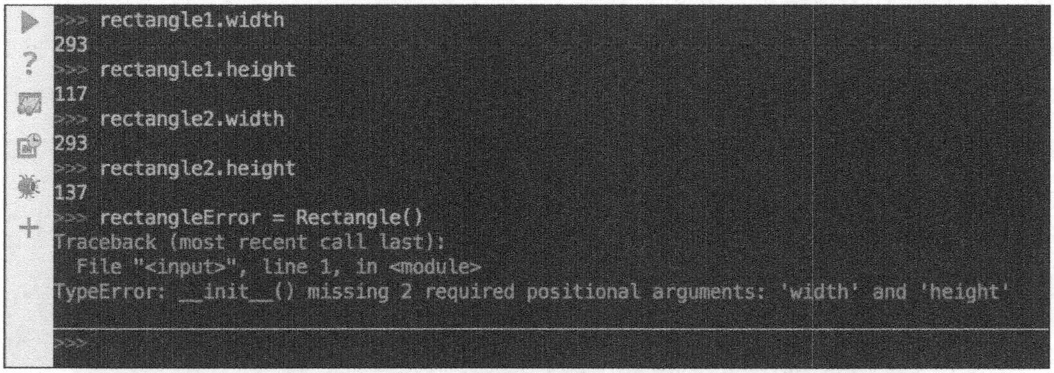

Customizing destructors in Python

We want to know when the instances of the `Rectangle` class are removed from memory, that is, when the objects become inaccessible and get deleted by the garbage-collection mechanism. However, it is very important to notice that the ways in which garbage collection works depends on the implementation of Python. Remember that, Python runs on a wide variety of platforms.

Before Python removes an instance from memory, it calls the `__del__` method. Thus, we can use this method to add any code we want to run before the instance is destroyed. We can think of the `__del__` method as the equivalent of a destructor in other object-oriented programming languages.

The following lines declare a `__del__` method within the body of the `Rectangle` class. Remember that Python always receives `self` as the first argument for any instance method:

```
def __del__(self):
        print('A Rectangle instance is being destroyed.')
```

The following lines create two instances of the `Rectangle` class: `rectangleToDelete1` and `rectangleToDelete2`. Then, the next lines assign `None` to both variables. Therefore, the reference count for both objects reaches `0`, and the garbage-collection mechanism deletes them. The Python console will display `I'm initializing a new Rectangle instance.` and then `A Rectangle instance is being destroyed.` twice in the Python console. Python executes the code within the `__del__` method after we assign `None` to each variable that had the only reference to an instance of the `Rectangle` class:

```
rectangleToDestroy1 = Rectangle(293, 117)
rectangleToDestroy2 = Rectangle(293, 137)
rectangleToDestroy1 = None
rectangleToDestroy2 = None
```

```
>>> class Rectangle:
    def __init__(self, width, height):
        print("I'm initializing a new Rectangle instance.")
        self.width = width
        self.height = height
    def __del__(self):
        print('A Rectangle instance is being destroyed.')
>>> rectangleToDestroy1 = Rectangle(293, 117)
rectangleToDestroy2 = Rectangle(293, 137)
rectangleToDestroy1 = None
rectangleToDestroy2 = None
I'm initializing a new Rectangle instance.
I'm initializing a new Rectangle instance.
A Rectangle instance is being destroyed.
A Rectangle instance is being destroyed.
>>>
```

6: TODO   Python Console   Terminal

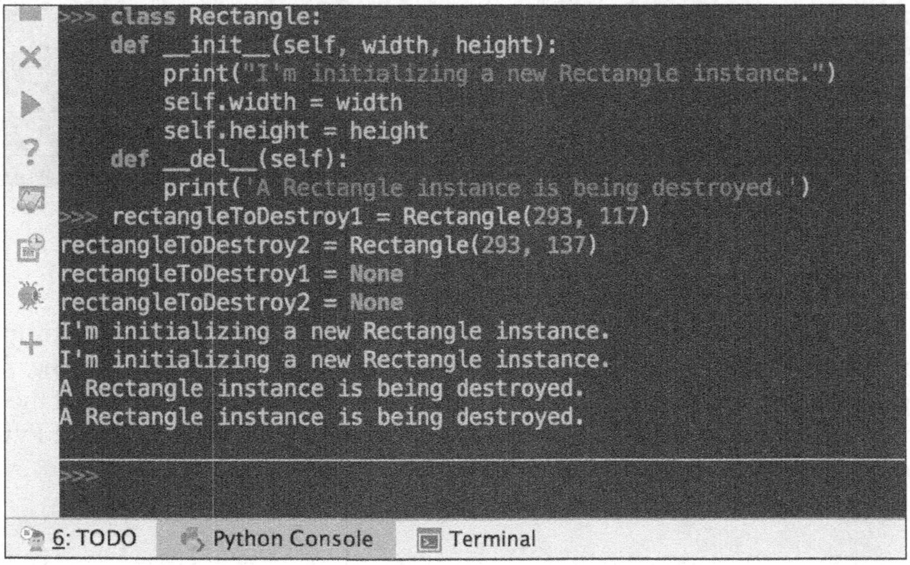

You can add some cleanup code within the `__del__` method. However, take into account that most of the time, you can follow best practices to release resources without having to add code to the `__del__` method. Remember that you don't know exactly when the `__del__` method is going to be executed. Even when the reference count reaches `0`, the Python implementation might keep the resources until the appropriate garbage collection destroys the instances.

The following lines create a `rectangle3` instance of the `Rectangle` class and then assign a `referenceToRectangle3` reference to this object. Thus, the reference count to the object increases to `2`. The next line assigns `None` to `rectangle3`, and therefore, the reference count for the object goes down from `2` to `1`. As the `referenceToRectangle3` variable stills holds a reference to the `Rectangle` instance, Python doesn't destroy the instance, and we don't see the results of the execution of the `__del__` method:

```
rectangle3 = Rectangle(364, 257)
referenceToRectangle3 = rectangle3
rectangle3 = None
```

Python destroys the instance if we add a line that assigns `None` to `referenceToRectangle3`:

```
referenceToRectangle3 = None
```

However, it is very important to know that you don't need to assign `None` to a reference to force Python to destroy objects. In the previous examples, we wanted to understand how the `__del__` method worked. Python will automatically destroy the objects when they aren't referenced anymore.

Creating instances of classes in Python

We already created instances of the simple `Rectangle` class. We just needed to use the class name, specify the required arguments enclosed in parentheses, and assign the result to a variable.

The following lines declare a `calculate_area` method within the body of the `Rectangle` class:

```
def calculate_area(self):
    return self.width * self.height
```

The method doesn't require arguments to be called from an instance because it just declares the previously explained `self` parameter. The following lines create an instance of the `Rectangle` class named `rectangle4` and then print the results of the call to the `calculate_area` method for this object:

```
rectangle4 = Rectangle(143, 187)
print(rectangle4.calculate_area())
```

Now, imagine that we want to have a function that receives the width and height values of a rectangle and returns the calculated area. We can take advantage of the `Rectangle` class to code this new function. We just need to create an instance of the `Rectangle` class with the `width` and `height` received as parameters and return the result of the call to the `calculate_area` method. Remember that we don't have to worry about releasing the resources required by the `Rectangle` instance, because the reference count for this object will become `0` after the function returns the result. The following lines show the code for the `calculateArea` independent function, which isn't part of the `Rectangle` class body:

```
def calculateArea(width, height):
    return Rectangle(width, height).calculate_area()

print(calculateArea(143, 187))
```

Notice that the Python console displays the following messages. Thus, we can see that the instance is destroyed and the code within the `__del__` method is executed. The messages are shown in the following screenshot:

```
I'm initializing a new Rectangle instance.
A Rectangle instance is being destroyed.
26741
```

```
>>> rectangle4 = Rectangle(143, 187)
rectangle4.calculate_area()
I'm initializing a new Rectangle instance.
>>> print(rectangle4.calculate_area())
26741
>>> def calculateArea(width, height):
    return Rectangle(width, height).calculate_area()

print(calculateArea(143, 187))
I'm initializing a new Rectangle instance.
A Rectangle instance is being destroyed.
26741
>>>
```

6: TODO Python Console Terminal

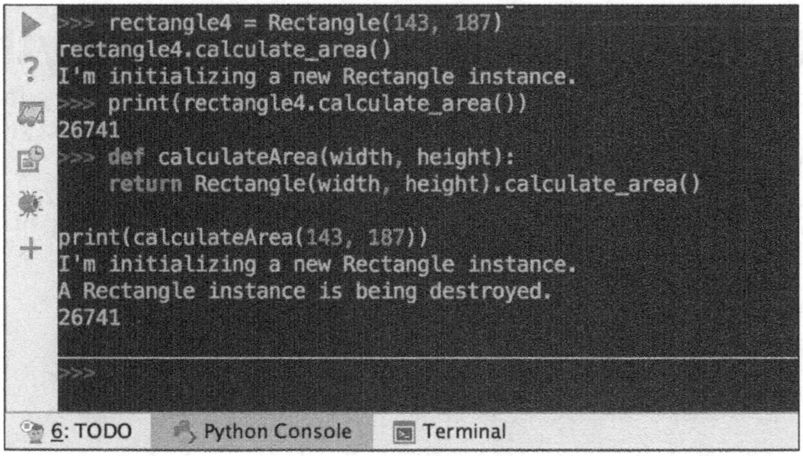

Declaring classes in C#

Throughout this book, we will work with C# 6.0 (introduced in Microsoft Visual Studio 2015). However, most of the explanations and code samples are also compatible with C# 5.0 (introduced in Visual Studio 2013). If a specific example uses C# 6.0 syntax and isn't compatible with C# 5.0, the code will be properly labeled with the compatibility warning. We will use Visual Studio Community 2015 as the main IDE. However, you can also run the examples using Mono or Xamarin.

The following lines declare a new minimal `Circle` class in C#:

```
class Circle
{
}
```

The `class` keyword followed by the class name (`Circle`) composes the header of the class definition. In this case, the class doesn't have a parent class or a superclass. Therefore, there aren't any superclasses listed after the class name and a colon (:). A pair of curly braces ({}) encloses the class body after the class header. In this case, the class body is empty. The `Circle` class is the simplest possible class we can declare in C#.

> Any new class you create that doesn't specify a superclass will be a subclass of the `System.Object` class in C#. Thus, the `Circle` class is a subclass of `System.Object`.

The following lines represent an equivalent way of creating the `Circle` class in C#. However, we don't need to specify that the class inherits from `System.Object`, because it adds unnecessary boilerplate code:

```
class Circle: System.Object
{
}
```

Customizing constructors in C#

We want to initialize instances of the `Circle` class with the radius value. In order to do so, we can take advantage of the constructors in C#. Constructors are special class methods that are automatically executed when we create an instance of a given type. The runtime executes the code within the constructor before any other code within a class.

We can define a constructor that receives the radius value as an argument and use it to initialize an attribute with the same name. We can define as many constructors as we want. Therefore, we can provide many different ways of initializing a class. In this case, we just need one constructor.

The following lines create a `Circle` class and define a constructor within the class body.

```
class Circle
{
  private double radius;

  public Circle(double radius)
  {
    Console.WriteLine(String.Format("I'm initializing a new Circle
instance with a radius value of {0}.", radius));
    this.radius = radius;
  }
}
```

The constructor is a public class method that uses the same name as the class: `Circle`. The method receives a single argument: `radius`. The code within the method prints a message on the console, indicating that the code is initializing a new `Circle` instance with a specific radius value. This way, we will understand when the code within the constructor is executed. As the constructor has an argument, it is known as a parameterized constructor.

Then, the following line assigns the radius double value received as an argument to the private radius double field. We use `this.radius` to access the private radius attribute for the instance and `radius` to reference the argument. In C#, the `this` keyword provides access to the instance that has been created and the one we want to initialize. The line before the constructor declares the private `radius` double field. At this time, we won't pay attention to the difference between the `private` and `public` keywords. We will dive deep into the proper usage of these keywords in *Chapter 3, Encapsulation of Data*.

The following lines create two instances of the `Circle` class: `circle1` and `circle2`. The **Windows Console** application will display `I'm initializing a new Circle instance with a radius value of`, followed by the radius value specified in the call to the constructor of each instance:

```
class Chapter01
{
  public static void Main(string[] args)
  {
```

```
        var circle1 = new Circle(25);
        var circle2 = new Circle(50);
        Console.ReadLine();
    }
}
```

Each line that creates an instance uses the `new` keyword, followed by the desired value for the radius as an argument enclosed in parentheses. We used the `var` keyword to let C# automatically assign the `Circle` type for each of the variables. After we execute the two lines that create the instances of `Circle`, we can use an inspector, such as the **Autos Window**, the **Watch Window**, or the **Immediate Window**, to check the values for `circle1.radius` and `circle2.radius`.

The following line prints **"System.Object"** as a result in the **Immediate Window** in the IDE. This is because the `Circle` class is a subclass of `System.Object`:

```
circle1.GetType().BaseType.ToString()
```

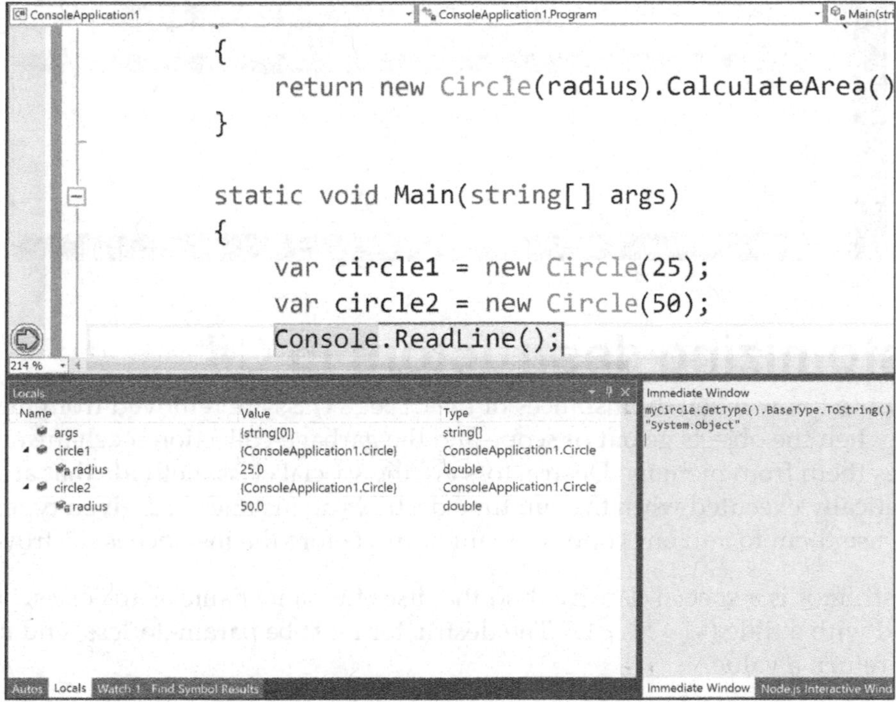

The following line won't allow the console application to compile and will display a build error. This is because the compiler cannot find a parameterless constructor declared in the `Circle` class. The specific error message is `ConsoleApplication does not contain a constructor that takes 0 arguments`. The following screenshot displays the `var circleError = new Circle();` error:

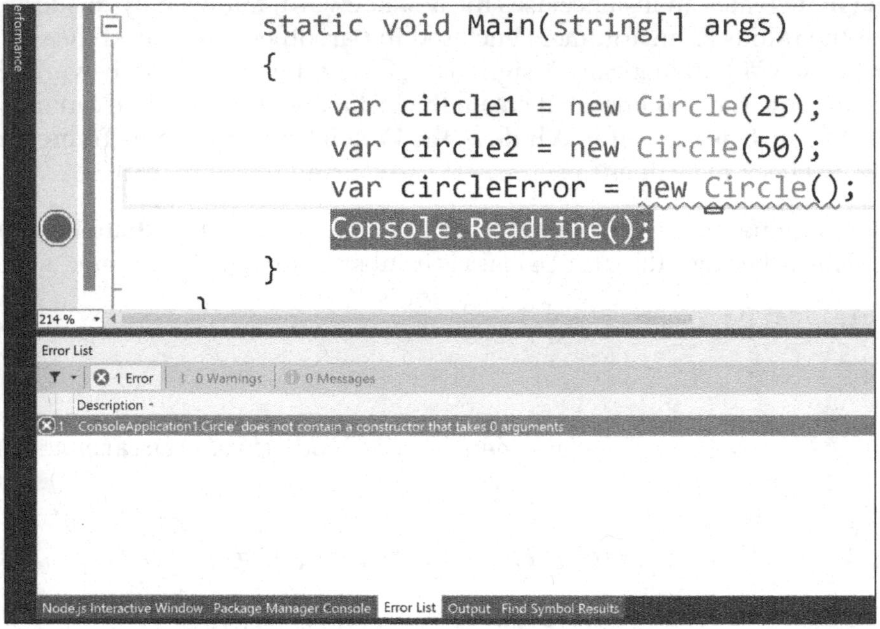

```
static void Main(string[] args)
{
    var circle1 = new Circle(25);
    var circle2 = new Circle(50);
    var circleError = new Circle();
    Console.ReadLine();
}
```

Error List

1 Error | 0 Warnings | 0 Messages

Description

1 'ConsoleApplication1.Circle' does not contain a constructor that takes 0 arguments

Customizing destructors in C#

We want to know when the instances of the `Circle` class are removed from memory, that is, when the objects go out of scope and the garbage-collection mechanism removes them from memory. Destructors are the special class methods that are automatically executed when the run time destroys an instance of a given type. Thus, we can use them to add any code we want to run before the instance is destroyed.

The destructor is a special class method that uses the same name as the class, but prefixed with a tilde (~): `~Circle`. The destructor must be parameterless, and it cannot return a value.

The following lines declare a destructor (a `~Circle` method) within the body of the `Circle` class:

```
~Circle()
{
  Console.WriteLine(String.Format("I'm destroying the Circle instance
with a radius value of {0}.", radius));
}
```

The code within the destructor prints a message on the console indicating that the runtime is destroying a `Circle` instance with a specific radius value. This way, we will understand when the code within the destructor is executed.

If we execute the console application after adding the code for the destructor to the `Circle` class, we will see the following lines in the console output. The first two lines will appear before we press a key. After we press a key, we will see the two lines indicating that the code within the destructor has been executed. This is because the two variables `circle1` and `circle2` have run out of scope and the garbage collector has destroyed the objects:

```
I'm initializing a new Circle instance with a radius value of 25.
I'm initializing a new Circle instance with a radius value of 50.

I'm destroying the Circle instance with a radius value of 50.
I'm destroying the Circle instance with a radius value of 25.
```

Creating instances of classes in C#

We already created instances of the simple `Circle` class. We just needed to use the `new` keyword followed by the class name, specify the required arguments enclosed in parentheses, and assign the result to a variable.

The following lines declare a public `CalculateArea` method within the body of the `Circle` class:

```
public double CalculateArea()
{
  return Math.PI * Math.Pow(this.radius, 2);
}
```

The method doesn't require arguments to be called. It returns the result of the multiplication of π by the square of the radius field value (`this.radius`). The following lines show a new version of the `Main` method. These lines create two instances of the `Circle` class: `circle1` and `circle2`. The lines then display the results of calling the `CalculateArea` method for the two objects. The new lines are highlighted, as follows:

```
class Chapter01
{
  public static void Main(string[] args)
  {
    var circle1 = new Circle(25f);
    var circle2 = new Circle(50f);
    Console.WriteLine(String.Format("The area for circle #1 is {0}",
circle1.CalculateArea()));
    Console.WriteLine(String.Format("The area for circle #2 is {0}",
circle2.CalculateArea()));
    Console.ReadLine();
  }
}
```

Now, imagine that we want to have a function that receives the radius value of a circle and has to return the calculated area. We can take advantage of the `Circle` class to code this new function. We just need to create an instance of the `Circle` class with the radius received as a parameter and return the result of the call to the `CalculateArea` method. Remember that, we don't have to worry about releasing the resources required by the `Circle` instance, because the object will go out of scope after the function returns the result. The following lines show the code for the new `CalculateCircleArea` function that isn't part of the `Circle` class body. The function is a method of the *Chapter 1, Objects Everywhere* class body, which also has the `Main` method:

```
class Chapter01
{
  private static double CalculateCircleArea(double radius)
  {
    return new Circle(radius).CalculateArea();
  }

  static void Main(string[] args)
  {
    double radius = 50;
    Console.WriteLine(String.Format("The area for a circle with a
radius of {0} is {1} ", radius, CalculateCircleArea(radius)));
    Console.ReadLine();
  }
}
```

The Windows command line displays the following messages. Thus, we can see that the instance is destroyed and the code within the destructor is executed:

```
I'm initializing a new Circle instance with a radius value of 50.
The area for a circle with a radius of 50 is 7853.98163397448
I'm destroying the Circle instance with a radius value of 50.
```

Understanding that functions are objects in JavaScript

We will use **Chrome Developer Tools** (CDT), as the main JavaScript console. However, you can run the examples in any other browser that provides a JavaScript console.

Functions are first-class citizens in JavaScript. In fact, functions are objects in JavaScript. When we type the following lines in a JavaScript console, we create a new function object. Thus, `calculateArea` is an object, and its type is `function`. Notice the results of writing the following lines in a JavaScript console. The displayed type for `calculateArea` is a function, as follows:

```
function calculateArea(width, height) { return width * height; }
typeof(calculateArea)
```

The `calculateArea` function receives two arguments: `width` and `height`. It returns the width value multiplied by the height value. The following line calls the `calculateArea` function and saves the returned number in the `rectangleArea` variable:

```
var rectangleArea = calculateArea(300, 200);
console.log(rectangleArea);
```

Functions are special objects in JavaScript that contain code and that you can invoke. They contain properties and methods. For example, if we type the following line, the JavaScript console will display the value for the `name` property of the function object, that is, the `calculateArea` function:

```
console.log(calculateArea.name);
```

Downloading the example code

You can download the example code files from your account at `http://www.packtpub.com` for all the Packt Publishing books you have purchased. If you purchased this book elsewhere, you can visit `http://www.packtpub.com/support` and register to have the files e-mailed directly to you.

Working with constructor functions in JavaScript

The following lines of code create an object named `myObject` without any specific properties or methods. This line checks the type of the variable (`myObject`) and then prints the key-value pairs that define the object on the JavaScript console:

```
var myObject = {};
typeof(myObject);
myObject
```

The preceding lines created an empty object. Therefore, the result of the last line shows `Object {}` on the console. There are no properties or methods defined in the object. However, if we enter `myObject.` (`myObject` followed by a dot) in a JavaScript console with autocomplete features, we will see many properties and methods listed, as shown in the following screenshot. The object includes many built-in properties and methods:

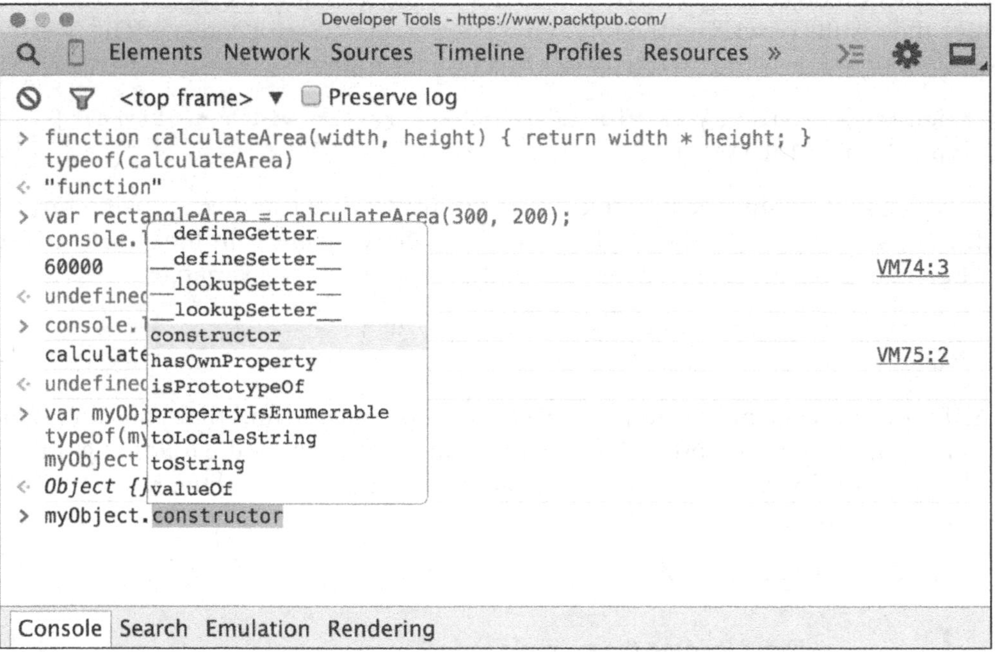

The following lines of code create an object named `myRectangle` with two key-value pairs enclosed within a pair of curly braces ({}). A colon (:) separates the key from the value and a comma (,) separates the key-value pairs. The next line checks the type of the variable (`object`) and prints the key-value pairs that define the object on the JavaScript console:

```
var myRectangle = { width: 300, height: 200 };
typeof(myRectangle);
myRectangle
```

The preceding lines created an object with two properties: `width` and `height`. The result of the last line shows `Object {width: 300, height: 200}` on the console. Thus, the `width` property has an initial value of `300`, and the `height` property has an initial value of `200`. If we enter `myRectangle.` (`myRectangle` followed by a dot) in a JavaScript console with autocomplete features, we will see the `width` and `height` properties listed with the built-in properties and methods, as shown in the following screenshot:

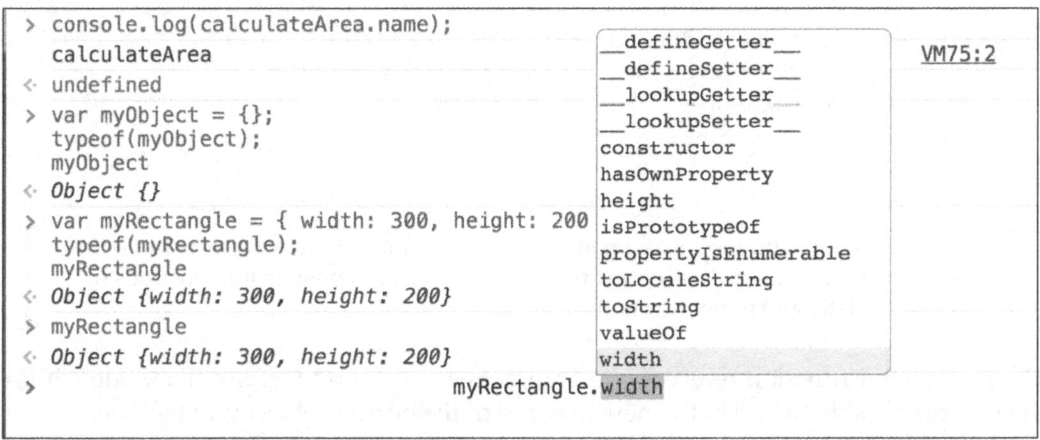

So far, we have been creating independent objects. The first example was an empty object, and the second case was an object with two properties with their initial values initialized. However, if we want to create another object with the same properties but different values, we would have to specify the property names again. For example, the following line creates another object named `myRectangle2`, with the same two keys, but different values:

```
var myRectangle2 = { width: 500, height: 150 };
```

However, we are repeating code and can have typos when we enter the key names, that is, the names for the future properties of the instance. Imagine that we had written the following line instead of the preceding line (notice that the code contains typos):

```
var myRectangle2 = { widh: 500, hight: 150 };
```

The previous line will generate `widh` and `hight` properties instead of `width` and `height`. Thus, if we want to retrieve the value from `myRectangle2.width`, we would receive `undefined` as a response. This is because `myRectangle2` created the `widh` property instead of `width`.

We want to initialize new rectangle objects with the values of both the width and the height. However, we don't want a typo to generate problems in our code. Thus, we need a blueprint that generates and initializes properties with the same names. In addition, we want to log a message to the console whenever we have a new rectangle object. In order to do so, we can take advantage of the constructor function. The following lines declare a `Rectangle` constructor function in JavaScript:

```
function Rectangle(width, height) {
  console.log("I'm creating a new Rectangle");
  this.width = width;
  this.height = height;
}
```

Notice the capitalized name of the function, `Rectangle` instead of `rectangle`. It is a good practice to capitalize constructor functions to distinguish them from the other functions.

The constructor function receives two arguments: `width` and `height`. The code within the function is able to access the new instance of the current object that has been created with the `this` keyword. Thus, you can translate `this` to the current object. The code within the function prints a message on the JavaScript console, indicating that it is creating a new rectangle. The code then uses the received `width` and `height` arguments to initialize properties with the same names. We use `this.width` and `this.height` to create the properties for the instance. We create two properties for the instance right after its creation. We can think of the constructor function as the equivalent of a constructor in other object-oriented programming languages.

The following lines create two `Rectangle` objects named `rectangle1` and `rectangle2`. Notice the usage of the `new` keyword to call the constructor function, with the `width` and `height` values enclosed in parentheses. The Python console will display `I'm initializing a new Rectangle instance.` after we enter each line in the Python console:

```
var rectangle1 = new Rectangle(293, 117);
var rectangle2 = new Rectangle(293, 137);
```

Each line that creates an instance uses the `new` keyword followed by the constructor function and the desired values for both the width and the height as arguments enclosed in parentheses. After we execute the previous lines, we can check the values for `rectangle1.width`, `rectangle1.height`, `rectangle2.width`, and `rectangle2.height`.

Enter the following two lines in the console:

```
rectangle1;
rectangle2;
```

The console will display the following two lines:

```
Rectangle {width: 293, height: 117}
Rectangle {width: 293, height: 137}
```

```
> function Rectangle(width, height) {
      console.log("I'm creating a new Rectangle");
      this.width = width;
      this.height = height;
  }
<· undefined
> var rectangle1 = new Rectangle(293, 117);
  var rectangle2 = new Rectangle(293, 137);
  I'm creating a new Rectangle                                VM231:3
  I'm creating a new Rectangle                                VM231:3
<· undefined
> rectangle1;
<· Rectangle {width: 293, height: 117}
> rectangle2;
<· Rectangle {width: 293, height: 137}
> |
```

It is very clear that we have created two `Rectangle` objects and not just two `Object` objects. We can see that the constructor function name appears before the key-value pairs.

Enter the following line in the console:

```
rectangle1 instanceof Rectangle
```

The console will display `true` as a result of the evaluation of the previous expression, because `rectangle1` is an instance of `Rectangle`. This way, we can determine whether an object is a `Rectangle` object, that is, an instance created using the `Rectangle` constructor function.

Creating instances in JavaScript

We already created instances with the simple `Rectangle` constructor function. We just needed to use the `new` keyword and the constructor function name. We then need to specify the required arguments enclosed in parentheses and assign the result to a variable.

The following lines declare a new version of the `Rectangle` constructor function that adds a `calculateArea` function to the blueprint:

```
function Rectangle(width, height) {
    console.log("I'm creating a new Rectangle");
    this.width = width;
    this.height = height;

    this.calculateArea = function() {
        return this.width * this.height;
    }
}
```

The new constructor function adds a parameterless `calculateArea` method to the instance. The following lines of code create a new `Rectangle` object named `rectangle3` and then print the results of the call to the `calculateArea` method for this object:

```
var rectangle3 = new Rectangle(143, 187);
rectangle3.calculateArea();
```

If we enter the following line, the JavaScript console will display the same code we entered to create the new version of the `Rectangle` constructor function. Thus, we might create a new `Rectangle` object by calling the `rectangle3.constructor` function in the next line. Remember that the `constructor` property is automatically generated by JavaScript, and this property in is a function:

```
var rectangle4 = new rectangle3.constructor(300, 200);
```

Now, imagine that we want to have a function that receives the width and height values of a rectangle and returns the calculated area. We can take advantage of a `Rectangle` object to code this new function. We just need to create a `Rectangle` object using the `Rectangle` constructor function with `width` and `height` received as parameters. We then need to return the result of the call to the `calculateArea` method. Remember that we don't have to worry about releasing the resources required by the `Rectangle` object, because the variable will go out of scope after the function returns the result. The following lines show the code for the `calculateArea` independent function, which isn't a part of the `Rectangle` constructor function:

```
function calculateArea(width, height) {
  return new Rectangle(width, height).calculateArea();
}

calculateArea(143, 187);
```

Summary

In this chapter, you learned about an object's life cycle. You also learned how object constructors and destructors work. We declared classes in Python and C# and used constructor functions in JavaScript to generate blueprints for objects. We customized constructors and destructors, and tested their personalized behavior in action. We understood different ways of generating instances in the three programming languages.

Now that you have learned to start creating classes and instances, we are ready to share, protect, and hide data with the data-encapsulation features of Python, JavaScript, and C#, which is the topic of the next chapter.

3
Encapsulation of Data

In this chapter, we will start organizing data in blueprints that generate objects. We will protect and hide data in each of the three covered programming languages: Python, JavaScript, and C#. We will:

- Understand the different members of a class
- Learn the difference between mutability and immutability
- Customize methods and fields to protect them against undesired access
- Work with access modifiers, naming conventions, and properties
- Customize getter and setter methods
- Create properties with getters and setters in Python, C#, and JavaScript

Understanding the different members of a class

So far, we have been working with simple classes and used them to generate instances in Python and C#. We also defined the functions of a constructor to generate objects based on prototypes in JavaScript. Now, it's time to dive deeper to understand the different members of a class.

The following list enumerates all the possible element types that you can include in a class definition. We already worked with many of these elements:

- Constructor
- Destructor
- Class fields or class attributes
- Class methods
- Nested classes

- Instance fields or instance attributes
- Properties with getters and/or setters
- Events

You already learned how constructors and destructors work in Python and C#. We also worked with constructor functions in JavaScript. So far, we have been using instance fields, also known as instance attributes, to encapsulate data in our instances. We can access these fields or attributes without any kind of restriction as variables within an instance. We also worked with instance methods that we could invoke without any kind of restrictions.

However, as happens in real-world situations, sometimes restrictions are necessary to avoid serious problems. Sometimes, we want to restrict access or transform-specific instance fields in read-only attributes. The different programming languages take different approaches that allow you to establish restrictions for the different members of a class. We can combine these restrictions with properties that can define getters and/or setters.

Properties can define get and/or set methods, also known as **getters** and **setters**. Setters allow you to control how values are set to protected instance attributes, that is, these methods are used to change the values of underlying instance attributes. Getters allow you to control how values are returned. Getters don't change the values of the underlying attributes.

Sometimes, all the members of a class share the same field or attribute, and we don't need to have a specific value for each instance. For example, the dog breeds have some profile values, such as the average size of males (width and height) and the average size of females (width and height). We can define the following class fields to store the values that are shared by the `averageMaleWidth`, `averageMaleHeight`, `averageFemaleWidth`, and `averageFemaleHeight` instances. All these instances have access to the same class field and their values. However, it's also possible to apply restrictions to their access.

Events allow instances to notify other objects when an event takes place. A publisher instance raises or sends an event, whereas a subscriber instance receives or handles the event. Instances can subscribe to events to add the necessary code to be executed when an event is raised, that is, when something of interest occurs. You can think about events as a mechanism to generate subscriber-publisher relationships between instances. For example, you can use events to make a dog bark when another dog arrives near it.

It's also possible to define methods that don't require an instance of a specific class to be called; therefore, you can invoke them by specifying the class name and the method name. These methods are known as class methods; they operate on a class as a whole and have access to class fields, but they don't have access to any instance members (such as instance fields, properties, or methods) because there is no instance at all. The class methods are useful when you want to include methods related to a class; you don't want to generate an instance to call them.

Protecting and hiding data

When we design classes, we want to make sure that all the necessary data is available to the methods that will operate on this data; therefore, we encapsulate the data. However, we just want the relevant information to be visible to the users of our classes that will create instances, change values of accessible attributes or properties, and call the available methods. Therefore, we want to hide or protect some data that is just needed for internal use. We don't want accidental changes to sensitive data.

For example, when we create a new instance of any dog breed, we can use its name and birth date as two parameters for a constructor. The constructor initializes the values of two internal fields: `m_name` and `m_birthDate`.

We don't want a user of our dog breed class to be able to change a dog's name after an instance has been initialized because the name is not supposed to change. Thus, we define a property called `Name` with a getter method, but without a setter method. This way, it's possible to retrieve the dog's name, but we cannot change it because there isn't a setter method defined for the property. The getter method just returns the value of the `m_name` internal field. In addition, we can protect the internal `m_name` field to avoid the users of a class to access the `m_name` field from any instance of the class.

We don't want a user of our dog breed class to be able to change a dog's birth date after an instance has been initialized because the dog won't be born again on a different date. In fact, we just want to make the dog's age available to different users. Thus, we define a property called `Age` with a getter method, but without a setter method. This way, it's possible to retrieve the dog's age, but we cannot change it because there isn't a setter method defined for a property. The getter method returns the result of calculating the dog's age based on the current date and the value of the `m_birthDate` internal field. As in the previous example, we can also protect the internal `m_birthDate` field to prevent the users of a class to access a field from any instance of a class.

This way, our class can make two read-only properties, Name and Age, public. The m_name and m_birthDate internal fields aren't public and cannot be accessed from the instances of a class. The read-only properties expose the values of all internal fields.

Working with properties

It's possible to manually add getter and setter methods to emulate how properties work. For example, we can add a GetName method that just returns the value of the m_name internal field. Each time we want to retrieve a dog's name, it will be necessary to call the GetName method for that specific instance.

A dog's favorite toy may change over time. However, we still want to use getter and setter methods to keep control over the procedure of retrieving and setting the value of an underlying m_favoriteToy internal field. We always want users to change the values of a field using the getter and setter methods, just in case we need to add some code within these methods in the future. For example, we can decide that whenever a dog's favorite toy changes, it's necessary to update the dog's playfulness score. If we force the user to use the setter method whenever he/she needs to update the dog's favorite toy, we can easily add the necessary code that updates the dog's playfulness score within this setter method.

We can manually add both getter and setter methods to emulate how properties work for the m_favoriteToy internal field. We have to add a GetFavoriteToy getter method and a SetFavoriteToy setter method. This way, whenever we want to retrieve a dog's favorite toy, it will be necessary to call the GetFavoriteToy method for a specific instance. Whenever we want to specify a new value to a dog's favorite toy, it will be necessary to call the SetFavoriteToy method with the new favorite toy as an argument.

The getter and setter methods combined with the access protection of the m_favoriteToy internal field make it possible to have absolute control over the way in which the dog's favorite toy is retrieved and set. However, it would be nicer to define a public property named FavoriteToy. Whenever we assign a value to the FavoriteToy property, the SetFavoriteToy setter method is called under the hood with the value to be assigned as an argument. Whenever we specify the FavoriteToy property in any expression, the GetFavoriteToy getter method is called under the hood to retrieve the actual value.

Each programming language provides a different mechanism and syntax to define properties and customize the getter and setter methods. Based on our goals, we can combine properties, getter and setters methods, the underlying fields, and the access protection mechanisms.

Understanding the difference between mutability and immutability

By default, any instance field or attribute works like a variable; therefore, we can change their values. When we create an instance of a class that defines many public instance fields, we are creating a mutable object, that is, an object that can change its state.

For example, let's think about a class named `MutableVector3D` that represents a mutable 3D vector with three public instance fields: `X`, `Y`, and `Z`. We can create a new `MutableVector3D` instance and initialize the `X`, `Y`, and `Z` attributes. Then, we can call the `Sum` method with their delta values for `X`, `Y`, and `Z` as arguments. The delta values specify the difference between the existing value and the new or desired value. So, for example, if we specify a positive value of `20` in the `deltaX` parameter, it means that we want to add `20` to the `X` value.

The following lines show pseudocode in a neutral programming language that create a new `MutableVector3D` instance called `myMutableVector`, initialized with values for the `X`, `Y`, and `Z` fields. Then, the code calls the `Sum` method with the delta values for `X`, `Y`, and `Z` as arguments, as shown in the following code:

```
myMutableVector = new MutableVector3D instance with X = 30, Y = 50 and
Z = 70
myMutableVector.Sum(deltaX: 20, deltaY: 30, deltaZ: 15)
```

The initial values for the `myMutableVector` field are `30` for `X`, `50` for `Y`, and `70` for `Z`. The `Sum` method changes the values of all the three fields; therefore, the object state mutates as follows:

- `myMutableVector.X` mutates from `30` to `30 + 20 = 50`
- `myMutableVector.Y` mutates from `50` to `50 + 30 = 80`
- `myMutableVector.Z` mutates from `70` to `70 + 15 = 85`

The values for the myMutableVector field after the call to the Sum method are 50 for X, 80 for Y, and 85 for Z. We can say this method mutated the object's state; therefore, myMutableVector is a mutable object: an instance of a mutable class.

Mutability is very important in object-oriented programming. In fact, whenever we expose fields and/or properties, we will create a class that will generate mutable instances. However, sometimes a mutable object can become a problem. In certain situations, we want to avoid objects to change their state. For example, when we work with a concurrent code, an object that cannot change its state solves many concurrency problems and avoids potential bugs.

For example, we can create an immutable version of the previous MutableVector3D class to represent an immutable 3D vector. The new ImmutableVector3D class has three read-only properties: X, Y, and Z. Thus, there are only three getter methods without setter methods, and we cannot change the values of the underlying internal fields: m_X, m_Y, and m_Z. We can create a new ImmutableVector3D instance and initialize the underlying internal fields: m_X, m_Y, and m_Z. X, Y, and Z attributes. Then, we can call the Sum method with the delta values for X, Y, and Z as arguments.

The following lines show the pseudocode in a neutral programming language that create a new ImmutableVector3D instance called myImmutableVector, which is initialized with values for X, Y, and Z as arguments. Then, the pseudocode calls the Sum method with the delta values for X, Y, and Z as arguments:

```
myImmutableVector = new ImmutableVector3D instance with X = 30, Y = 50
and Z = 70
myImmutableSumVector = myImmutableVector.Sum(deltaX: 20, deltaY: 30,
deltaZ: 15)
```

However, this time the Sum method returns a new instance of the ImmutableVector3D class with the X, Y, and Z values initialized to the sum of X, Y, and Z and the delta values for X, Y, and Z. So, myImmutableSumVector is a new ImmutableVector3D instance initialized with X = 50, Y = 80, and Z = 85. The call to the Sum method generated a new instance and didn't mutate the existing object.

The immutable version adds an overhead as compared with the mutable version because it's necessary to create a new instance of a class as a result of calling the Sum method. The mutable version just changed the values for the attributes and it wasn't necessary to generate a new instance. Obviously, the immutable version has a memory and a performance overhead. However, when we work with the concurrent code, it makes sense to pay for the extra overhead to avoid potential issues caused by mutable objects.

Encapsulating data in Python

First, we will add attributes to a class in Python and then use prefixes to hide specific members of a class. We will use property getters and setters to control how we write and retrieve values to and from related attributes. We will use methods to add behaviors to classes, and we will create the mutable and immutable version of a 3D vector to understand the difference between an object that mutates state and an object that doesn't.

Adding attributes to a class

The `TibetanSpaniel` class is a blueprint for dogs that belong to the Tibetan Spaniel breed. This class should inherit from a `Dog` superclass, but we will forget about inheritance and other dog breeds for a while. We will use the `TibetanSpaniel` class to understand the difference between class attributes and instance attributes.

As happens with any other dog breed, Tibetan Spaniel dogs have some profile values. We will define the following class attributes to store the values that are shared by all the members of the Tibetan Spaniel breed. Note that the valid values for scores are from `0` to `10`; `0` is the lowest skill and `10` the highest.

- `family`: This is the family to which the dog breed belongs
- `area_of_origin`: This is the are a of origin of the dog breed
- `learning_rate`: This is the typical learning rate score for the members of this dog breed
- `obedience`: This is the average obedience score for the members of this dog breed
- `problem_solving`: This is the average problem solving score for the members of this dog breed

The following lines create a `TibetanSpaniel` class and declare the previously enumerated class attributes and a `__init__` method within the body of a class:

```
class TibetanSpaniel:
  family = "Companion, herding"
  area_of_origin = "Tibet"
  learning_rate = 9
  obedience = 3
  problem_solving = 8

  def __init__(self, name, favorite_toy, watchdog_ability):
    self.name = name
    self.watchdog_ability = watchdog_ability
    self.favorite_toy = favorite_toy
```

The preceding code assigns a value to each class variable after the class header within the class body and without `self.` as its prefix. This code assigns a value outside of any method because there is no need to create any instance to access the attributes of a class.

> It's common practice to place the class attributes at the top, right after the class header.

The following command prints the value of the previously declared `family` class attribute. Note that we didn't create any instance of the `TibetanSpaniel` class. Also, we specify an attribute after the class name and a dot:

```
print(TibetanSpaniel.family)
```

The following command creates an instance of the `TibetanSpaniel` class and then prints the value of the family class attribute. In this case, we will use an instance to access the class attribute:

```
brian = TibetanSpaniel("Brian", "Talking Minion", 4)
print(brian.family)
```

You can assign a new value to any class attribute. For example, the following command assigns `4` to the `obedience` class attribute:

```
TibetanSpaniel.obedience = 4
```

However, we must be very careful when we want to assign a new value to a class variable. We must address the class attribute through a class and not through an instance. If we assign a value to `obedience` through an instance named `brian`, Python will create a new instance attribute called `obedience`, instead of changing the value of the class attribute with the same name.

The following commands illustrate the problem. The first command creates a new instance attribute called `obedience` and sets its value to `8`; therefore, `brian.obedience` will be `8`. However, if we check the value of the `TibetanSpaniel.obedience` or `type(brian).obedience` class variable, the value continues to be `4`:

```
brian.obedience = 8

print(brian.obedience)
print(type(brian).obedience)
print(TibetanSpaniel.obedience)
```

Hiding data in Python using prefixes

The previously declared `TibetanSpaniel` class exposes the instance and class attributes without any kind of restriction. Thus, we can access these attributes and change their values. Python uses a special naming convention for attributes to control their accessibility. So far, we have been using attribute names without any kind of prefix; therefore, we could access attribute names within a class definition and outside of a class definition. These kinds of attributes are known as public attributes and are exposed without any restriction.

In Python, we can mark an attribute as protected by prefixing the attribute name with a leading underscore (_). For example, if we want to convert the name attribute from a public to a protected attribute, we just need to change its name from `name` to `_name`.

Whenever we mark an attribute as protected, we are telling the users of the class that they shouldn't use these attributes outside of the class definition. Thus, only the code written within the class definition and within subclasses should access attributes marked as protected. We say *should*, because Python doesn't provide a real shield for the attributes marked as protected; the language just expects users to be honest and take into account the naming convention. The following command shows a new version of the `__init__` method for the `TibetanSpaniel` class that declares three instance attributes as protected by adding a leading underscore (_) to names:

```
def __init__(self, name, favorite_toy, watchdog_ability):
    self._name = name
    self._watchdog_ability = watchdog_ability
    self._favorite_toy = favorite_toy
```

We can mark an attribute as private by prefixing the attribute name with two leading underscores (__). For example, if we want to convert the name attribute from a protected to a private attribute, we just need to change its name from `_name` to `__name`.

Whenever we mark an attribute as private, Python doesn't allow users to access the attribute outside of the class definition. The restriction also applies to subclasses; therefore, only the code written within a class can access attributes marked as private.

Python still provides access to these attributes outside of the class definition with a different name composed of a leading underscore (_), followed by the class name and the private attribute name. For example, if we use `__name` to mark name as a private attribute, it will be accessible with the `TibetanSpaniel__name` name. Obviously, the language expects users to be honest, take into account the naming convention, and avoid accessing the renamed private attribute. The following commands show a new version of the `__init__` method for the `TibetanSpaniel` class that declares three instance attributes as private by adding two leading underscores (__) to names:

```
def __init__(self, name, favorite_toy, watchdog_ability):
    self.__name = name
    self.__watchdog_ability = watchdog_ability
    self.__favorite_toy = favorite_toy
```

The same naming convention applies to instance attributes, class attributes, instance methods, and class methods.

Using property getters and setters in Python

Python provides a simple mechanism to define properties and specify the getter and/or setter methods. We want to make the following changes to our `TibetanSpaniel` class:

- Encapsulate the `name` attribute with a read-only `name` property
- Encapsulate the `__favorite_toy` attribute with a `favorite_toy` property
- Encapsulate the `__watchdog_ability` attribute with a `watchdog_ability` property and include the code in the setter method to assign `0` to the underlying attribute if the value specified is lower than `0` and `10` if the value specified is higher than `10`
- Define a `protection_score` read-only property with a getter method that calculates and returns a protection score based on the values of the `__watchdog_ability` private instance attribute, the `learning_rate` public class attribute, and the `problem_solving` public class attribute

We want a read-only `name` property; therefore, we just need to define a getter method that returns the value of the related `__name` private attribute. We just need to define a method named `name` and decorate it with `@property`. The following commands within the class body will do the job. Note that `@property` is included before the method's header:

```
@property
def name(self):
    return self.__name
```

After we add a getter method to define a read-only name property, we can create an instance of the edited class and try to change the value of the read-only property name, as shown in the following command:

```
merlin = TibetanSpaniel("Merlin", "Talking Smurf", 6)
merlin.name = "brian"
```

The Python console will display the following error because there is no setter method defined for the `name` property:

```
Traceback (most recent call last):
  File "<input>", line 1, in <module>
AttributeError: can't set attribute
```

We want to encapsulate the `__favorite_toy` private attribute with the `favorite_toy` property; therefore, we have to define both getter and setter methods. The getter method returns the value of the related `__favorite_toy` private attribute. The setter method receives the new favorite toy value as an argument and assigns this value to the related `__favorite_toy` private attribute. We have to decorate the setter method with `@favorite_toy.setter`, that is, `@`, followed by the property name and `.setter`. The following commands within the class body will do the job:

```
@property
def favorite_toy(self):
    return self.__favorite_toy

@favorite_toy.setter
def favorite_toy(self, favorite_toy):
    self.__favorite_toy = favorite_toy
```

The setter method for the `favorite_toy` property is very simple. The `watchdog_ability` property requires a setter method with more code to transform values lower than `0` in `0` and values higher than `10` in `10`. The following class body will do the job:

```
@property
def watchdog_ability(self):
    return self.__watchdog_ability

@watchdog_ability.setter
def watchdog_ability(self, watchdog_ability):
    if watchdog_ability < 0:
        self.__watchdog_ability = 0
    elif watchdog_ability > 10:
        self.__watchdog_ability = 10
    else:
        self.__watchdog_ability = watchdog_ability
```

After we add the `watchdog_ability` property, we will create an instance of the edited class and try to set different values to this property, as shown in the following code:

```
hugo = TibetanSpaniel("Hugo", "Tennis ball", 7)
hugo.watchdog_ability = -3
print(hugo.watchdog_ability)
hugo.watchdog_ability = 30
print(hugo.watchdog_ability)
hugo.watchdog_ability = 8
print(hugo.watchdog_ability)
```

In the preceding code, after we specified `-3` as the desired value for the `watchdog_ability` property, we printed its actual value and the result was `0`. After we specified `30`, the actual printed value was `10`. Finally, after we specified `8`, the actual printed value was `8`. The code in the setter method did its job. This is how we could control the values accepted for the underlying private instance attribute.

We want a read-only `protection_score` property. However, this time the getter method must calculate and return a protection score based on a private instance attribute and two public class attributes. Note that the code accesses the public class attributes through `type(self)`, followed by the attribute name. It's a safe way to access class attributes because we can change the class name or work with inheritance without unexpected issues. The following commands in the class body will do the job:

```
@property
def protection_score(self):
```

```
        return math.floor((self.__watchdog_ability + type(self).learning_
rate + type(self).problem_solving) / 3)
```

After we add the `protection_score` property, we will create an instance of the edited class and print the value of this read-only property:

```
cole = TibetanSpaniel("Cole", "Soccer ball", 4)
print(cole.protection_score)
```

Here is the complete code for the `TibetanSpaniel` class along with properties:

```
class TibetanSpaniel:
    family = "Companion, herding"
    area_of_origin = "Tibet"
    learning_rate = 9
    obedience = 3
    problem_solving = 8

    def __init__(self, name, favorite_toy, watchdog_ability):
        self.__name = name
        self.__watchdog_ability = watchdog_ability
        self.__favorite_toy = favorite_toy

    @property
    def name(self):
        return self.__name

    @property
    def favorite_toy(self):
        return self.__favorite_toy

    @favorite_toy.setter
    def favorite_toy(self, favorite_toy):
        self.__favorite_toy = favorite_toy

    @property
    def watchdog_ability(self):
        return self.__watchdog_ability

    @watchdog_ability.setter
    def watchdog_ability(self, watchdog_ability):
        if watchdog_ability < 0:
            self.__watchdog_ability = 0
        elif watchdog_ability > 10:
            self.__watchdog_ability = 10
        else:
```

```
            self.__watchdog_ability = watchdog_ability

    @property
    def protection_score(self):
        return math.floor((self.__watchdog_ability + type(self).
learning_rate + type(self).problem_solving) / 3)
```

Using methods to add behaviors to classes in Python

So far, we have added instance methods to classes and used getter and setter methods combined with decorators to define properties. Now, we want to generate a class to represent the mutable version of a 3D vector.

We will use properties with simple getter and setter methods for `x`, `y`, and `z`. The `sum` public instance method receives the delta values for `x`, `y`, and `z` and mutates an object, that is, the setter method changes the values of `x`, `y`, and `z`. Here is the initial code of the `MutableVector3D` class:

```
class MutableVector3D:
    def __init__(self, x, y, z):
        self.__x = x
        self.__y = y
        self.__z = z

    def sum(self, delta_x, delta_y, delta_z):
        self.__x += delta_x
        self.__y += delta_y
        self.__z += delta_z

    @property
    def x(self):
        return self.__x

    @x.setter
    def x(self, x):
        self.__x = x

    @property
    def y(self):
        return self.__y

    @y.setter
    def y(self, y):
```

```
        self.__y = y

    @property
    def z(self):
        return self.__z

    @z.setter
    def z(self, z):
        self.__z = z
```

It's a very common requirement to generate a 3D vector with all the values initialized to `0`, that is, `x = 0`, `y = 0`, and `z = 0`. A 3D vector with these values is known as an origin vector. We can add a class method to the `MutableVector3D` class named `origin_vector` to generate a new instance of the class initialized with all the values initialized to `0`. It's necessary to add the `@classmethod` decorator before the class method header. Instead of receiving `self` as the first argument, a class method receives the current class; the parameter name is usually named `cls`. The following code defines the `origin_vector` class method:

```
@classmethod
def origin_vector(cls):
    return cls(0, 0, 0)
```

The preceding method returns a new instance of the current class (`cls`) with `0` as the initial value for the three elements. The class method receives `cls` as the only argument; therefore, it will be a parameterless method when we call it because Python includes a class as a parameter under the hood. The following command calls the `origin_vector` class method to generate a 3D vector, calls the sum method for the generated instance, and prints the values for the three elements:

```
mutableVector3D = MutableVector3D.origin_vector()
mutableVector3D.sum(5, 10, 15)
print(mutableVector3D.x, mutableVector3D.y, mutableVector3D.z)
```

Now, we want to generate a class to represent the immutable version of a 3D vector. In this case, we will use read-only properties for `x`, `y`, and `z`. The `sum` public instance method receives the delta values for `x`, `y`, and `z` and returns a new instance of the same class with the values of `x`, `y`, and `z` initialized with the results of the sum. Here is the code of the `ImmutableVector3D` class:

```
class ImmutableVector3D:
    def __init__(self, x, y, z):
        self.__x = x
        self.__y = y
```

```
        self.__z = z

    def sum(self, delta_x, delta_y, delta_z):
        return type(self)(self.__x + delta_x, self.__y + delta_y,
self.__z + delta_z)

    @property
    def x(self):
        return self.__x

    @property
    def y(self):
        return self.__y

    @property
    def z(self):
        return self.__z

    @classmethod
    def equal_elements_vector(cls, initial_value):
        return cls(initial_value, initial_value, initial_value)

    @classmethod
    def origin_vector(cls):
        return cls.equal_elements_vector(0)
```

Note that the `sum` method uses `type(self)` to generate and return a new instance of the current class. In this case, the `origin_vector` class method returns the results of calling the `equal_elements_vector` class method with `0` as an argument. Remember that the `cls` argument refers to the actual class. The `equal_elements_vector` class method receives an `initial_value` argument for all the elements of the 3D vector, creates an instance of the actual class, and initializes all the elements with the received unique value. The `origin_vector` class method demonstrates how we can call another class method in a class method.

The following command calls the `origin_vector` class method to generate a 3D vector, calls the `sum` method for the generated instance, and prints the values for the three elements of the new instance returned by the `sum` method:

```
vector0 = ImmutableVector3D.origin_vector()
vector1 = vector0.sum(5, 10, 15)
print(vector1.x, vector1.y, vector1.z)
```

As explained previously, we can change the values of the private attributes; therefore, the `ImmutableVector3D` class isn't 100 percent immutable. However, we are all adults and don't expect the users of a class with read-only properties to change the values of private attributes hidden under difficult to access names.

Encapsulating data in C#

First, we will add fields to a class in C# and then use access modifiers to hide and protect a specific member of a class from unauthorized access. We will use property getters and setters to control how we write and retrieve values to and from related fields.

We will work with auto-implemented properties to reduce the boilerplate code. We will use methods to add behaviors to classes and create the mutable and immutable version of a 3D vector to understand the difference between an object that mutates state and an object that doesn't.

Adding fields to a class

The `SmoothFoxTerrier` class is a blueprint for dogs that belong to the Smooth Fox Terrier breed. This class should inherit from a `Dog` superclass, but we will forget about inheritance and other dog breeds for a while and use the `SmoothFoxTerrier` class to understand the difference between class fields and instance fields.

We will define the following class attributes to store the values that are shared by all the members of the Smooth Fox Terrier breed. The valid values for scores are from `0` to `10`; `0` is the lowest skill and `10` the highest:

- `Family`: This is the family to which the dog breed belongs
- `AreaOfOrigin`: This is the area of origin of the dog breed
- `Energy`: This is the average energy score for the dog breed
- `ColdTolerance`: This is the average cold tolerance score for the dog breed
- `HeatTolerance`: This is the average heat tolerance score for the dog breed

The following code creates the `SmoothFoxTerrier` class and declares the previously enumerated fields and a constructor in the body of the class:

```
class SmoothFoxTerrier
{
  public static string Family = "Terrier";
  public static string AreaOfOrigin = "England";
```

```
    public static int Energy = 10;
    public static int ColdTolerance = 8;
    public static int HeatTolerance = 8;

    public string Name;
    public int WatchdogAbility;
    public string FavoriteToy;

    public SmoothFoxTerrier(string name, int watchdogAbility, string
  favoriteToy)
    {
      this.Name = name;
      this.WatchdogAbility = watchdogAbility;
      this.FavoriteToy = favoriteToy;
    }
  }
```

The preceding code initializes each class field in the same line that declares the field. The only difference between a class field and an instance field is the inclusion of the `static` keyword. This indicates that we want to create a class field.

In C#, class fields are also known as static fields.

The following command prints the value of the previously declared `Family` static field. Note that we didn't create any instance of the `SmoothFoxTerrier` class, and we specify a field after the class name and a dot:

```
Debug.WriteLine(SmoothFoxTerrier.Family);
```

C# doesn't allow you to access a static field from an instance reference; therefore, we always require to use a class type to access a static field.

You can assign a new value to any static field declared as a variable. For example, the following command assigns `8` to the `Energy` static field:

```
SmoothFoxTerrier.Energy = 8;
```

We can easily convert a static field to a read-only static field by replacing the `static` keyword with the `const` one. For example, we don't want the users of a class to change the average energy score. Therefore, we can change the line that declared the static `Energy` field with the following command that creates a static constant or read-only field:

```
public const int Energy = 10;
```

Using access modifiers

The previously declared `SmoothFoxTerrier` class exposes the instance and static fields without any kind of restriction because we declared them with the `public` access modifier. Therefore, we can access these attributes and change their values, except for the static `Energy` field that we converted to a static constant.

C# uses type member access modifiers to control which code has access to a specific type member. So far, we have been declaring all the fields with the `public` access modifier. Therefore, we could access them in a class definition and outside of a class definition.

We can use any of the following access modifiers instead of `public` to restrict access to any field:

- `protected`: C# doesn't allow users to access a field outside of the class definition. Only the code in a class or its derived classes can access the field.
- `private`: C# doesn't allow users to access a field outside of the class definition. Only the code in the class can access the field. Its derived classes cannot access the field.
- `internal`: C# doesn't allow users to access a field outside of the assembly in which a class is included. The code within the same assembly can access the field. Its derived classes cannot access the field.
- `protected internal`: C# doesn't allow users to access a field outside of the assembly in which a class is included unless it's a derived class. The code within the same assembly can access the field. Its derived classes can access the field, as happens with `protected` fields without the addition of the `internal` modifier.

The following command shows how we can change the declaration of the public `Name` field to a `protected` field. We replace the public access modifier with `protected` and the name from `Name` to `_name`. As a naming convention, we will prefix the field name with a leading underscore (_) symbol for protected or private fields:

```
protected string _name;
```

Whenever we use the `protected` access modifier in a field declaration, we restrict access to this field to the code written within the class definition and within subclasses. C# generates a real shield for the fields marked as protected; there is no way to access them outside of the explained boundaries.

The following commands show a new version of the `SmoothFoxTerrier` class that declares three instance fields as `protected` by replacing the `public` access modifier with `protected`. In addition, field names add a leading underscore (_) as a prefix and use a lowercase first letter:

```
class SmoothFoxTerrier
{
  public static string Family = "Terrier";
  public static string AreaOfOrigin = "England";
  public static int Energy = 10;
  public static int ColdTolerance = 8;
  public static int HeatTolerance = 8;

  protected string _name;
  protected int _watchdogAbility;
  protected string _favoriteToy;

  public SmoothFoxTerrier(string name, int watchdogAbility, string
favoriteToy)
  {
    this._name = name;
    this._watchdogAbility = watchdogAbility;
    this._favoriteToy = favoriteToy;
  }
}
```

The following code shows how we can change the declaration of the `_name` protected field to a `private` field. We replace the `protected` access modifier with `private`:

```
private string _name;
```

Whenever we use the `private` access modifier in a field declaration, we restrict access to the field to the code written in the class definition and subclasses. C# generates a real shield for the fields marked as `private`; there is no way to access these outside of the class definition. The restriction also applies to subclasses; therefore, only the code written in a class can access attributes marked as private.

The following commands show a new version of the instance fields declaration for the `SmoothFoxTerrier` class that declares the three instance fields as `private`, replacing the `protected` keyword with `private`:

```
private string _name;
private int _watchdogAbility;
private string _favoriteToy;
```

After the previous changes are done, it's necessary to replace the code in the constructor with the following commands. This helps initialize new field names:

```
public SmoothFoxTerrier(string name, int watchdogAbility, string
favoriteToy)
{
  this._name = name;
  this._watchdogAbility = watchdogAbility;
  this._favoriteToy = favoriteToy;
}
```

We can use the same access modifiers for any type of member, including instance fields, static fields, instance methods, and static methods.

Using property getters and setters in C#

C# provides a simple yet powerful mechanism to define properties and specify the getter method and/or the setter method. We want to make the following changes to our `SmoothFoxTerrier` class:

- Encapsulate the `_name` field with a read-only `Name` property.
- Encapsulate the `_favoriteToy` attribute with a `FavoriteToy` property.
- Encapsulate the `_watchdogAbility` attribute with a `WatchdogAbility` property and include the code in the setter method to assign `0` to the underlying attribute if the value specified is lower than `0` and assign `10` when the value specified is higher than `10`.
- Define a `ProtectionScore` read-only property with a getter method that calculates and returns a protection score based on the values of the `_watchdogAbility` private instance field, the `ColdTolerance` public static field, and the `HeatTolerance` public static field.

We want a read-only `Name` property; therefore, we just need to define a getter method that returns the value of the related `_name` private field. We just need to add some code in the class body. We declare the `Name` property as a `public` field of the `string` type, followed by the definition of the getter method enclosed within a pair of curly braces ({ }). This encloses the definition of the getter method and/or the setter method. In this case, we just need a getter method. The `get` keyword starts the definition of the getter method whose contents are enclosed within a pair of curly braces ({ }). The following code in the class body will do the job:

```
public string Name
{
  get
  {
    return _name;
  }
}
```

After we add a getter method to define a read-only `Name` property, we will create an instance of the edited class and write code that changes the value of the `Name` read-only property, as shown in the following command:

```
var jerry = new SmoothFoxTerrier("Jerry", 7, "Boomerang");
jerry.Name = "Tom";
```

The code that assigns a value to the read-only `Name` property won't allow the console application to compile. It will display a build error because the compiler cannot find a setter method declared for the `Name` property. The specific error message is `Property or indexer 'ConsoleApplication1.SmoothFoxTerrier.Name' cannot be assigned to -- it is read only`. The following screenshot shows the generated error in the IDE:

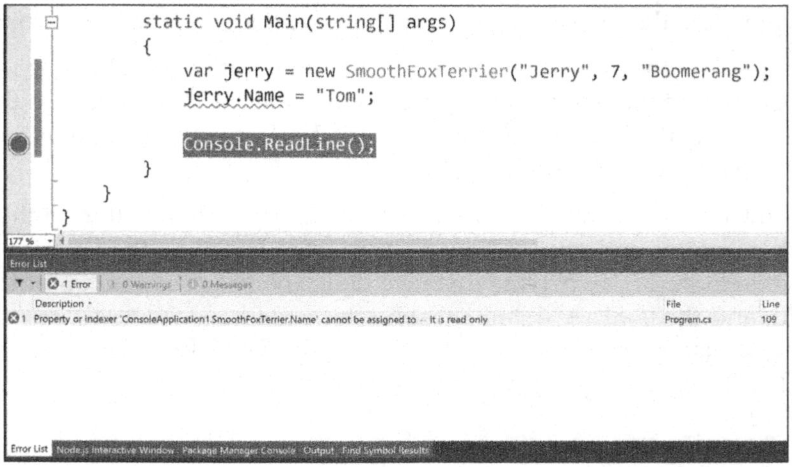

```
        static void Main(string[] args)
        {
            var jerry = new SmoothFoxTerrier("Jerry", 7, "Boomerang");
            jerry.Name = "Tom";

            Console.ReadLine();
        }
    }
}
```

We want to encapsulate the `_favoriteToy` private field with a `FavoriteToy` property; therefore, we have to define the getter method and the setter method. The getter method returns the value of the related `_favoriteToy` private field. The setter method receives the new favorite toy value as an argument named `value` and assigns this value to the related `__favoriteToy` private field. We declare the `FavoriteToy` property as a `public` field of the `string` type, followed by the definition of the getter method and the setter method enclosed in a pair of curly braces ({ }). The `get` keyword starts the definition of the getter method whose contents are enclosed within a pair of curly braces ({ }). The `set` keyword starts the definition of the setter method whose contents are enclosed within a pair of curly braces ({ }). The `set` keyword doesn't declare an argument named `value`. However, the code in this method receives the value assigned to the property in an implicit argument named `value`. The following code in the class body will do the job:

```
public string FavoriteToy
{
  get
  {
    return this._favoriteToy;
  }

  set
  {
    this._favoriteToy = value;
  }
}
```

The setter method for the `FavoriteToy` property is very simple because it just assigns the specified value to the related private field. The `WatchdogAbility` property requires a setter method with more code to transform values lower than `0` to `0` and values higher than `10` to `10`. The following code in the class body will do the job:

```
public string FavoriteToy
{
  get
  {
    return this._favoriteToy;
  }

  setpublic int WatchdogAbility
  {
    get
    {
      return this._watchdogAbility;
```

```
        }
        set
        {
          if (value < 0) {
            this._watchdogAbility = 0;
          } else if (value > 10) {
            this._watchdogAbility = 10;
          } else {
            this._watchdogAbility = value;
          }
        }
      }

      {
        this._favoriteToy = value;
      }
    }
```

After we add the `WatchdogAbility` property, we will create an instance of the edited class and try to set different values to this property, as shown in the following code:

```
var tom = new SmoothFoxTerrier("Tom", 8, "Boomerang");
tom.WatchdogAbility = -9;
Console.WriteLine(tom.WatchdogAbility);
tom.WatchdogAbility = 52;
Console.WriteLine(tom.WatchdogAbility);
tom.WatchdogAbility = 9;
Console.WriteLine(tom.WatchdogAbility);
```

After we specified `-9` as the desired value for the `WatchdogAbility` property, we printed its actual value to the console and the result was `0`. After we specified `52`, the actual printed value was `10`. Finally, after we specified `9`, the actual printed value was `9`. The code in the setter method did its job; we can control all the values accepted for the underlying private instance field.

We want a read-only `ProtectionScore` property. However, this time, the getter method must calculate and return a protection score based on a private instance field and two public static fields. Note that the code accesses all the public class fields through `SmoothFoxTerrier`, followed by the static field name. The following code in the class body will do the job:

```
public int ProtectionScore
{
  get
  {
```

```
    return (int)Math.Floor ((this._watchdogAbility + SmoothFoxTerrier.
ColdTolerance + SmoothFoxTerrier.HeatTolerance) / 3d);
  }
}
```

After we add the `ProtectionScore` property, we will create an instance of the edited class and print the value of this read-only property to the console:

```
var laura = new SmoothFoxTerrier("Laura", "Old sneakers", 9);
console.WriteLine(laura.ProtectionScore);
```

The following code shows the complete code for the `SmoothFoxTerrier` class with its properties:

```
class SmoothFoxTerrier
{
  public static string Family = "Terrier";
  public static string AreaOfOrigin = "England";
  public const int Energy = 10;
  public static int ColdTolerance = 8;
  public static int HeatTolerance = 8;

  private string _name;
  private int _watchdogAbility;
  private string _favoriteToy;

  public string Name
  {
    get
    {
      return this._name;
    }
  }

  public string FavoriteToy
  {
    get
    {
      return this._favoriteToy;
    }

    set
    {
      this._favoriteToy = value;
    }
```

```
    }

    public int WatchdogAbility
    {
      get
      {
        return this._watchdogAbility;
      }
      set
      {
        if (value < 0) {
          this._watchdogAbility = 0;
        } else if (value > 10) {
          this._watchdogAbility = 10;
        } else {
          this._watchdogAbility = value;
        }
      }
    }

    public int ProtectionScore
    {
      get
      {
        return Math.Floor ((this._watchdogAbility + SmoothFoxTerrier.
  ColdTolerance + SmoothFoxTerrier.HeatTolerance) / 3);
      }
    }

    public SmoothFoxTerrier(string name, int watchdogAbility, string
  favoriteToy)
    {
      this._name = name;
      this._watchdogAbility = watchdogAbility;
      this._favoriteToy = favoriteToy;
    }
  }
```

Working with auto-implemented properties

When we don't require any specific logic in the getter method or the setter method, we can take advantage of a simplified mechanism to declare properties called auto-implemented properties. For example, the following code use auto-implemented properties to simplify the declaration of the `FavoriteToy` property:

```
public string FavoriteToy { get; set; }
```

The previous code declares the `FavoriteToy` property with empty getter and setter methods. The compiler creates a private and anonymous field related to the defined property that only the property's automatically generated getters and setters access. If you need to customize either the getter method or the setter method in the future, you can replace the usage of auto-implemented properties with specific getter and setter methods and add your own private field to support a property if necessary.

If we use the previously defined `FavoriteToy` property with auto-implemented properties, we have to remove the `_favoriteToy` private field. In addition, we have to assign the `favoriteToy` private field received as an argument in the constructor to the `FavoriteToy` property instead of working with the private field, as shown in the following code:

```
this.FavoriteToy = favoriteToy;
```

We can also use auto-implemented properties when we want to create a read-only property that doesn't require any specific logic in the getter method. For example, the following code uses auto-implemented properties to simplify the declaration of the `Name` property:

```
public string Name { get; private set; }
```

The preceding code declares the setter method, also known as the **set accessor**, as private. This way, `Name` is a read-only property. As in the previous example, if we use the previously defined `Name` property with auto-implemented properties, we have to remove the `_name` private field. In addition, we have to assign the `name` property received as an argument in the constructor to the `Name` property instead of working with the private field, as shown in the following line of code:

```
this.Name = name;
```

The setter method is private; therefore, we can set the value for `Name` in the class. However, we cannot access the setter method outside of this class; therefore, it becomes a read-only property.

Using methods to add behaviors to classes in C#

So far, we have added instance methods to a class in C#, and used getter and setter methods to define properties. Now, we want to generate a class to represent the mutable version of a 3D vector in C#.

We will use auto-implemented properties for `X`, `Y`, and `Z`. The public `Sum` instance method receives the delta values for `X`, `Y`, and `Z` (`deltaX`, `deltaY`, and `deltaZ`) and mutates the object, that is, the method changes the values of `X`, `Y`, and `Z`. The following shows the initial code of the `MutableVector3D` class:

```
class MutableVector3D
{
  public double X { get; set; }
  public double Y { get; set; }
  public double Z { get; set; }

  public void Sum(double deltaX, double deltaY, double deltaZ)
  {
    this.X += deltaX;
    this.Y += deltaY;
    this.Z += deltaZ;
  }

  public MutableVector3D(double x, double y, double z)
  {
    this.X = x;
    this.Y = y;
    this.Z = z;
  }
}
```

It's a very common requirement to generate a 3D vector with all the values initialized to `0`, that is, `X = 0`, `Y = 0`, and `Z = 0`. A 3D vector with these values is known as an origin vector. We can add a class method to the `MutableVector3D` class named `OriginVector` to generate a new instance of the class initialized with all the values initialized to `0`. Class methods are also known as static methods in C#. It's necessary to add the `static` keyword after the public access modifier before the class method name. The following commands define the `OriginVector` static method:

```
public static MutableVector3D OriginVector()
{
  return new MutableVector3D(0, 0, 0);
}
```

The preceding method returns a new instance of the `MutableVector3D` class with `0` as the initial value for all the three elements. The following code calls the `OriginVector` static method to generate a 3D vector, calls the `Sum` method for the generated instance, and prints the values for all the three elements on the console output:

```
var mutableVector3D = MutableVector3D.OriginVector();
mutableVector3D.Sum(5, 10, 15);
Console.WriteLine(mutableVector3D.X, mutableVector3D.Y,
mutableVector3D.Z)
```

Now, we want to generate a class to represent the immutable version of a 3D vector. In this case, we will use read-only properties for `X`, `Y`, and `Z`. We will use auto-generated properties with `private set`. The `Sum` public instance method receives the delta values for `X`, `Y`, and `Z` (`deltaX`, `deltaY`, and `deltaZ`) and returns a new instance of the same class with the values of `X`, `Y`, and `Z` initialized with the results of the sum. The code for the `ImmutableVector3D` class is as follows:

```
class ImmutableVector3D
{
  public double X { get; private set; }
  public double Y { get; private set; }
  public double Z { get; private set; }

  public ImmutableVector3D Sum(double deltaX, double deltaY, double
deltaZ)
  {
    return new ImmutableVector3D (
    this.X + deltaX,
    this.Y + deltaY,
    this.Z + deltaZ);
  }

  public ImmutableVector3D(double x, double y, double z)
  {
    this.X = x;
    this.Y = y;
    this.Z = z;
  }

  public static ImmutableVector3D EqualElementsVector(double
initialValue)
  {
    return new ImmutableVector3D(initialValue, initialValue,
initialValue);
```

```
    }

    public static ImmutableVector3D OriginVector()
    {
      return ImmutableVector3D.EqualElementsVector(0);
    }
  }
```

In the new class, the `Sum` method returns a new instance of the `ImmutableVector3D` class, that is, the current class. In this case, the `OriginVector` static method returns the results of calling the `EqualElementsVector` static method with `0` as an argument. The `EqualElementsVector` class method receives an `initialValue` argument for all the elements of the 3D vector, creates an instance of the actual class, and initializes all the elements with the received unique value. The `OriginVector` static method demonstrates how we can call another static method in a static method.

The following code calls the `OriginVector` static method to generate a 3D vector, calls the `Sum` method for the generated instance, and prints all the values for the three elements of the new instance returned by the `Sum` method on the console output:

```
var vector0 = ImmutableVector3D.OriginVector();
var vector1 = vector0.Sum(5, 10, 15);
Console.WriteLine(vector1.X, vector1.Y, vector1.Z);
```

C# doesn't allow users of the `ImmutableVector3D` class to change the values of `X`, `Y`, and `Z` properties. The code doesn't compile if you try to assign a new value to any of these properties. Thus, we can say that the `ImmutableVector3D` class is 100 percent immutable.

Encapsulating data in JavaScript

First, we will add properties to a constructor function in JavaScript. Then, we will use local variables to hide and protect specific members of a class from unauthorized access. We will use property getters and setters to control how we write and retrieve values to and from related local variables.

We will use methods to add behaviors to objects. Also, we will create the mutable and immutable version of a 3D vector to understand the difference between an object that mutates state and an object that doesn't.

Adding properties to a constructor function

As it so happens with dogs, cats also have breeds. The `ScottishFold` constructor function provides a blueprint for cats that belong to the Scottish Fold breed. We will use the `ScottishFold` constructor function to understand how we can take advantage of the fact that a constructor function is an object in JavaScript.

As it so happens with any other cat breeds, Scottish Fold cats have some profile values. We will add the following properties to the constructor function to store the values that are shared by all the members of the Scottish Fold breed. Note that the valid values for scores range from `0` to `5`; `0` is the lowest skill and `5` the highest:

- `generalHealth`: This is a score based on the genetic illnesses that are common to the cat breed
- `affectionateWithFamily`: This is a score based on the probability for the cat to shower the whole family with affection
- `intelligence`: This is a score based on how smart the cats that belong to this breed are
- `kidFriendly`: This is a score based on how tolerant of children the cats that belong to this breed are
- `petFriendly`: This is a score based on the likeliness of the cats that belong to this breed are to accept other pets at home

The following code defines a `ScottishFold` constructor function and then adds the previously enumerated attributes as properties of the constructor function:

```
function ScottishFold(name, favoriteToy, energy) {
  this.name = name;
  this.favoriteToy = favoriteToy;
  this.energy = energy;
}

ScottishFold.generalHealth = 3;
ScottishFold.affectionateWithFamily = 5;
ScottishFold.intelligence = 4;
ScottishFold.kidFriendly = 5;
ScottishFold.petFriendly = 4;
```

The preceding code assigns a value to properties of the ScottishFold constructor function after the definition of the constructor function. The following line of code prints the value of the previously declared generalHealth property. Note that we didn't use the ScottishFold constructor function to create any instance; we specify an attribute after the constructor function name and a dot:

```
console.log(ScottishFold.generalHealth)
```

You can assign a new value to any constructor function property. For example, the following line of code assigns the value 4 to the generalHealth property:

```
ScottishFold.generalHealth = 4;
```

The following lines of code creates an instance with the ScottishFold constructor function and then prints the value of the generalHealth property. In this case, we can use an instance to access a property through the constructor function stored in the constructor property:

```
Var lucifer = new ScottishFold("Lucifer", "Tennis ball", 4);
console.log(lucifer.constructor.generalHealth);
```

Hiding data in JavaScript with local variables

The previously declared ScottishFold constructor function generates instances that expose the instance and constructor function properties without any kind of restriction. Thus, we can access these properties and change their values.

JavaScript doesn't provide access modifiers. However, we can declare local variables in constructor functions to protect them from being accessed outside of the object blueprint definition. Only functions that are declared in the constructor function will be able to access local variables. The following code shows a new version of the ScottishFold constructor function that declares three local variables using the var keyword instead of the this. prefix. In addition, the following code adds a leading underscore (_) to the names:

```
function ScottishFold(name, favoriteToy, energy) {
  var _name = name;
  var _favoriteToy = favoriteToy;
  var _energy = energy;
}
```

The constructor function saves the values of all the three arguments in local variables. Thus, if we create a `ScottishFold` instance, we won't be able to access these variables. The following code tries to retrieve the value of all the local variables from a `ScottishFold` instance. The three lines that use all the variable names display undefined because there is no property with specified names. Only functions that are defined in the constructor function can access all the local variables:

```
Var lucifer = new ScottishFold("Lucifer", "Tennis ball", 4);
console.log(lucifer._name);
console.log(lucifer._favoriteToy);
console.log(lucifer._energy);
```

Using property getters and setters in JavaScript

JavaScript provides a mechanism to specify the getter method and/or setter method for properties. We want to make the following changes to our `ScottishFold` class:

- Encapsulate the `_name` local variable with a read-only `name` property
- Encapsulate the `_favoriteToy` local variable with a `favoriteToy` property
- Encapsulate the `_energy` local variable with an `energy` property and include a code in the setter method to assign `0` to the underlying attribute if the value specified is lower than `0`, and assign `5` if the value specified is higher than `5`

We want a read-only `name` property; therefore, we just need to define a getter method that returns the value of the related `_name` local variable. We just need to add some code in the class function declaration:

```
function ScottishFold(name, favoriteToy, energy) {
  var _name = name;
  var _favoriteToy = favoriteToy;
  var _energy = energy;

Object.defineProperty(this, 'name', { get: function(){ return _name; }
});
}
```

The code calls the `Object.defineProperty` function with the following arguments:

- `this`: This is the instance.
- `'name'`: This is the desired name for the property as a string.
- This is an object with the getter function code specified in the `get` property. Note that the getter function can access the `_name` variable defined in the constructor function.

After we add a getter method to define a read-only `name` property, we can create an instance of the edited constructor function and write code that reads, tries to change, and reads again the value of the `name` read-only property, as shown in the following code:

```
var lucifer = new ScottishFold("Lucifer", "Tennis ball", 4);
console.log(lucifer.name);
lucifer.name = "Jerry";
console.log(lucifer.name);
```

After we change the value of the `name` property, we can print the value of this property on the JavaScript console. It's still the same value that we specified when calling the `Lucifer` constructor function. There is no setter method defined; therefore, `name` is a read-only property.

We want to encapsulate the `_favoriteToy` local variable with a `favoriteToy` property; therefore, we have to define getter and setter methods. The getter method returns the value of the related `_favoriteToy` local variable. The setter method receives the new favorite toy value as a `val` argument named and assigns this value to the related `_favoriteToy` local variable. The following code in the class function declaration will do the job:

```
function ScottishFold(name, favoriteToy, energy) {
  var _name = name;
  var _favoriteToy = favoriteToy;
  var _energy = energy;

  Object.defineProperty(this, 'name', { get: function(){ return _name;
} });
    Object.defineProperty(this, 'favoriteToy', { get: function(){
return _favoriteToy; }, set: function(val){ _favoriteToy = val; } });
}
```

The setter method for the `favoriteToy` property is very simple because it just assigns the specified value to the related local variable. The `energy` property requires a setter method with more code to transform values lower than `0` to `0` and values higher than `5` to `5`. The following code in the constructor function will do the job:

```
function ScottishFold(name, favoriteToy, energy) {
  var _name = name;
  var _favoriteToy = favoriteToy;
  var _energy = energy;

  Object.defineProperty(this, 'name', { get: function(){ return _name;
} });
```

```
  Object.defineProperty(this, 'favoriteToy', { get: function(){ return
_favoriteToy; }, set: function(val){ _favoriteToy = val; } });
  Object.defineProperty(
  this,
  'energy', {
    get: function(){ return _energy; },
    set: function(val){
      if (val < 0) {
        _energy = 0;
      } else if (val > 5) {
        _energy = 5;
      } else {
        _energy = val;
      }
    }
  });
}
```

After we add the `energy` property, we can create an instance of the edited class and try to set different values to this property, as shown in the following code:

```
var garfield = new ScottishFold("Garfield", "Pillow", 1);
garfield.energy = -7;
console.log(Garfield.energy);
garfield.energy = 35;
console.log(Garfield.energy);
garfield.energy = 3;
console.log(Garfield.energy);
```

In the preceding code, after we specified `-7` as the desired value for the `energy` property, we printed its actual value to the console. The result was `0`. After we specified `35`, the actual printed value was `5`. Finally, after we specified `3`, the actual printed value was `3`. The code in the setter method did its job; we could control the values accepted for the underlying local variable.

Using methods to add behaviors to constructor functions

So far, we have added methods to a constructor function that produced instance methods in a generated object. In addition, we used getter and setter methods combined with local variables to define properties. Now, we want to generate a constructor function to represent the mutable version of a 3D vector.

We will use properties with simple getter and setter methods for x, y, and z. The sum public instance method receives the delta values for x, y, and z and mutates an object, that is, the method changes the values of x, y, and z. The following code shows the initial code of the MutableVector3D constructor function:

```
function MutableVector3D(x, y, z) {
  var _x = x;
  var _y = y;
  var _z = z;

  Object.defineProperty(this, 'x', {
    get: function(){ return _x; },
    set: function(val){ _x = val; }
  });

  Object.defineProperty(this, 'y', {
    get: function(){ return _y; },
    set: function(val){ _y = val; }
  });

  Object.defineProperty(this, 'z', {
    get: function(){ return _z; },
    set: function(val){ _z = val; }
  });

  this.sum = function(deltaX, deltaY, deltaZ) {
    _x += deltaX;
    _y += deltaY;
    _z += deltaZ;
  }
}
```

It's a very common requirement to generate a 3D vector with all the values initialized to 0, that is, x = 0, y = 0, and, z = 0. A 3D vector with these values is known as an origin vector. We can add a function to the MutableVector3D constructor function named originVector to generate a new instance of a class with all the values initialized to 0. The following code defines the originVector function:

```
MutableVector3D.originVector = function() {
  return new MutableVector3D(0, 0, 0);
};
```

The method returns a new instance built in the `MutableVector3D` constructor function with `0` as the initial value for all the three elements. The following code calls the `originVector` function to generate a 3D vector, calls the `sum` method for the generated instance, and prints all the values for all the three elements:

```
var mutableVector3D = MutableVector3D.originVector();
mutableVector3D.sum(5, 10, 15);
console.log(mutableVector3D.x, mutableVector3D.y, mutableVector3D.z);
```

Now, we want to generate a constructor function to represent the immutable version of a 3D vector. In this case, we will use read-only properties for `x`, `y`, and `z`. In this case, we will use the `ImmutableVector3D.prototype` property to define the `sum` method. The method receives the values of delta for `x`, `y`, and `z`, and returns a new instance with the values of `x`, `y`, and `z` initialized with the results of the sum. The following code shows the `ImmutableVector3D` constructor function and the additional code that defines all the other methods:

```
function ImmutableVector3D(x, y, z) {
  var _x = x;
  var _y = y;
  var _z = z;

  Object.defineProperty(this, 'x', {
    get: function(){ return _x; }
  });

  Object.defineProperty(this, 'y', {
    get: function(){ return _y; }
  });

  Object.defineProperty(this, 'z', {
    get: function(){ return _z; }
  });
}

ImmutableVector3D.prototype.sum = function(deltaX, deltaY, deltaZ) {
  return new ImmutableVector3D(
  this.x + deltaX,
  this.y + deltaY,
  this.z + deltaZ);
};

ImmutableVector3D.equalElementsVector = function(initialValue) {
  return new ImmutableVector3D(initialValue, initialValue,
initialValue);
```

```
};

ImmutableVector3D.originVector = function() {
  return ImmutableVector3D.equalElementsVector(0);
};
```

Again, note that the preceding code defines the `sum` method in the `ImmutableVector3D.prototype` method. This method will be available to all the instances generated in the `ImmutableVector3D` constructor function. The `sum` method generates and returns a new instance of `ImmutableVector3D`. In this case, the `originVector` method returns the results of calling the `equalElementsVector` method with `0` as an argument. The `equalElementsVector` method receives an `initialValue` argument for all the elements of the 3D vector, creates an instance of the actual class, and initializes all the elements with the received unique value. The `originVector` method demonstrates how we can call another function defined in the constructor function.

The following code calls the `originVector` method to generate a 3D vector, calls the `sum` method for the generated instance, and prints the values for all the three elements of the new instance returned by the `sum` method:

```
var vector0 = ImmutableVector3D.originVector();
var vector1 = vector0.sum(5, 10, 15);
console.log(vector1.x, vector1.y, vector1.z);
```

In this case, we took advantage of the `prototype` property. We will dive deeper into the advantages of how to work with the prototype property through out the course of this book.

Summary

In this chapter, we looked at the different members of a class or a blueprint. We worked with naming conventions in Python to hide attributes, took advantage of access modifiers in C#, and worked with local variables in a constructor function in JavaScript. We declared properties in different programming languages and customized their getter and setter methods.

We worked with dogs and cats and defined the shared properties of their breeds in classes and constructor functions. We also worked with mutable and immutable versions of a 3D vector.

Now that you have learned how to encapsulate data, we are ready to work with inheritance and specialization in Python, JavaScript, and C#, which are the topics of the next chapter.

4
Inheritance and Specialization

In this chapter, we will create a hierarchy of blueprints that generate objects. We will take advantage of inheritance and many related features to specialize behavior in each of the three covered programming languages. We will:

- Use classes to abstract behavior
- Understand the concept of simple inheritance and design a hierarchy of classes
- Learn the difference between overloading and overriding methods
- Understand the concept of overloading operators
- Understand polymorphism
- Take advantage of the prototype chain to use inheritance in JavaScript

Using classes to abstract behavior

So far, we have been creating classes on Python and C# to generate blueprints for real-life objects. In JavaScript we have been using constructor functions to achieve the same goal. Now it is time to take advantage of more advanced features of object-oriented programming and start designing a hierarchy of classes instead of working with isolated classes. Based on our requirements we will first design all the classes that we need. Then we will use all the features available in each of the covered programming languages to code the design.

We worked with dogs, cats, and some of their breeds. Now let's imagine that we have to work with a more complex solution that requires us to work with hundreds of breeds. In addition, we already know that our application will start working with domestic cats and dogs, but in the future it will be necessary to work with other members of the cat family, other mammals, other domestic mammals, reptiles, and birds. Thus, our object-oriented design needs to be ready for expansion purposes if required. However, wait! The animal kingdom is extremely complex and we don't want to model a complete representation of the animal kingdom and its classification; we just want to create all the necessary classes to have a flexible model that can be easily expanded.

So, this time a few classes won't be enough to represent the breeds of cats and dogs. The following list enumerates the classes that we will create along with their descriptions:

- `Animal`: This is an abstract class that generalizes all the members of the animal kingdom. Dogs, cats, reptiles, and birds have one thing in common: they are animals. Thus it makes sense to create an abstract class that will be the baseline for all the different classes of animals that we will have to represent in our object-oriented design.
- `Mammal`: This is a class that generalizes mammals. They are different from reptiles, amphibians, birds, and insects. We already know that we will also have to model reptiles and birds; therefore, we will create a `Mammal` class at this level.
- `DomesticMammal`: The tiger (*Panthera tigris*) is the largest and heaviest living species of the cat family. A tiger is a cat but it is completely different from a domestic cat. Our initial requirements tell us that we will work with domestic and wild animals; therefore, we will create a class that generalizes domestic mammals. In the future, we will have `WildMammal` that will generalize wild mammals.
- `Dog`: We could go on specializing the `DomesticMammal` class with additional subclasses until we reach a `Dog` class. For example, we can create a `CanidCarnivorianDomesticMammal` subclass and then make the `Dog` class inherit from it. However, the kind of application we have to develop doesn't require any intermediary classes between `DomesticMammal` and `Dog`. At this level, we will also have a `Cat` class. The `Dog` class generalizes the properties and methods required for a dog in our application. Subclasses of the `Dog` class will represent the different families of the dog breeds. For example, one of the main differences between a dog and a cat in our application domain is that a dog barks and a cat meows.

- `TerrierDog`: Each dog breed belongs to a family. We will work with a large number of dog breeds, and some profile values determined by their family are very important for our application. Thus we will create a subclass of the `Dog` class for each family. In this case, the sample `TerrierDog` class represents the Terrier family.
- `SmoothFoxTerrier`: Finally, a subclass of the dog breed family class will represent a specific dog breed that belongs to a family. Its breed determines the dog's look and behavior. A dog that belongs to the Smooth Fox Terrier breed will look and behave completely different than a dog that belongs to the Tibetan Spaniel breed. Thus we will create instances of all the classes at this level to give life to each dog in our application. In this case, the `SmoothFoxTerrier` class models an animal, a mammal, a domestic mammal, a dog, and a terrier family dog, specifically, a dog that belongs to the Smooth Fox Terrier breed.

Each class listed in the preceding list represents a specialization of the previous class, that is, its superclass, parent class, or superset, as shown in the following table:

Superclass, parent class, or superset	**Subclass, child class, or subset**
`Animal`	`Mammal`
`Mammal`	`DomesticMammal`
`DomesticMammal`	`Dog`
`Dog`	`TerrierDog`
`TerrierDog`	`SmoothFoxTerrier`

Our application requires many members of the Terrier family; therefore, the `SmoothFoxTerrier` class isn't going to be the only subclass of `TerrierDog`. In the future, we will have the following three additional subclasses of `TerrierDog`:

- `AiredaleTerrier`: This subclass represents the Airedale Terrier breed
- `BullTerrier`: This subclass represents the Bull Terrier breed
- `CairnTerrier`: This subclass represents the Cairn Terrier breed

Understanding inheritance

When a class inherits from another class, it inherits all the elements that compose the parent class, also known as superclass. The class that inherits all the elements of the parent class is known as a subclass. For example, the `Mammal` subclass inherits all the properties, instance fields or attributes, and class fields or attributes defined in the `Animal` superclass.

You don't have to forget what you learned in *Chapter 3, Encapsulation of Data*, about access modifiers and naming conventions that restrict access to certain members. We must take them into account to determine the inherited members that we will be able to access in subclasses. Some access modifiers and naming conventions applied to members don't allow subclasses to access these members defined in superclasses.

The `Animal` abstract class is the baseline for our class hierarchy. We require each animal to specify its age; therefore, we will have to specify the age of the animal when we create an instance of the `Animal` class. This class will define an `age` property and display a message whenever an instance of an animal has been created. The `Animal` class defines two attributes that specify the number of legs and pair of eyes. Both these attributes will be initialized to `0`, but its subclasses will have to set a value for these attributes. The `Animal` class defines two instance methods:

- **Print legs and eyes**: This method prints the number of legs and eyes of an animal
- **Print age**: This method prints an animal's age

In addition, we want to be able to compare the age of the different `Animal` instances using the following comparison operators when the programming language allows you to do it. The following are the comparison operators:

- Less than (<)
- Less than or equal to (<=)
- Greater than (>)
- Greater than or equal to (>=)

If your programming language doesn't allow you to use the previously enumerated operators to compare the age of the `Animal` instances, we can define instance methods with their appropriate names in the `Animal` class to achieve the same goal.

Wait! We said that we had to print a message whenever we created an `Animal` instance. However, we want animal to be an abstract class; therefore, we aren't supposed to create instances of this class. Thus, it seems that it is completely impossible to achieve our goal. When we inherit from a class, we also inherit its constructor; therefore, we can call the inherited constructor to run the initialization code for the base class. This way, it is possible to know when an instance of `Animal` is being created even when it is an abstract class. In fact, all the instances of subclasses of the `Animal` class are going to be instances of `Animal` too.

The `Mammal` abstract class inherits from the `Animal` superclass and specifies `1` as the value for a pair of eyes. The `Animal` superclass defines this class attribute with `0` as the initial value, but the `Mammal` subclass overwrites it with `1`. So far, all the mammals discovered on earth have just one pair of eyes. If scientists discover evidence of a mammal with more than one pair of eyes, we don't need this weird animal in our application; therefore, we won't worry about it.

We require each mammal to specify its age and whether it is pregnant when you create an instance of a mammal. The `Mammal` class inherits the age property from the `Animal` superclass; therefore, it is only necessary to add a property that allows you to access the `is pregnant` attribute. Note that we don't specify the gender at any time in order to keep things simple. If we add a gender attribute, we will need a validation to avoid a male gender being pregnant. Right now, our focus is on inheritance. The `Mammal` class displays a message whenever a mammal is created.

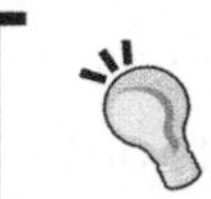

Each class inherits from one class; therefore, each new class that we will define has just one superclass. In this case, we will always work with *single inheritance*.

The `DomesticMammal` abstract class inherits from the `Mammal` class. We require each `DomesticMammal` abstract class to specify its name and favorite toy. Any domestic mammal has a name; it always picks a favorite toy. Sometimes, the favorite toy is not exactly the toy we would like them to pick (our shoes or sneakers), but let's keep the focus on our classes. It is necessary to add a read-only property that allows you to access the name attribute and the read/write property for the favorite toy. You cannot change the name of the domestic mammal, but you can force the mammal to change its favorite toy. The `DomesticMammal` class displays a message whenever a domestic mammal is created.

The `talk` instance method will display a message. This message indicates that the domestic mammal name is concatenated with the word `talk`. Each subclass must make the specific domestic mammal talk in a different way. A parrot can really talk but we will consider a dog's bark and a cat's meow as if they were talking.

The `Dog` class inherits from `DomesticMammal` and specifies `4` as the value for the number of legs. The `Animal` class, that is the `Mammal` superclass, defined this class attribute with `0` as its value, but `Dog` overwrites this inherited attribute with `4`. The `Dog` class displays a message whenever a dog instance is created.

We want dogs to be able to bark; therefore, we need a `bark` method. The `bark` method has to allow a dog to perform the following things:

- Bark happily just once
- Bark happily a specific number of times
- Bark happily to another domestic mammal with a name just once
- Bark happily to another domestic mammal with a name a specific number of times
- Bark angrily just once
- Bark angrily a specific number of times
- Bark angrily to another domestic mammal with a name just once
- Bark angrily to another domestic mammal with a name a specific number of times

We can have just one `bark` method or many `bark` methods. There are different mechanisms to solve the challenges of the different ways in which a dog must be able to bark. Not all the programming languages support the same mechanisms introduced in the classic object-oriented programming approach.

When we call the `talk` method for any dog, we want it to bark happily once. We don't want to display the message defined in the `talk` method introduced in the `DomesticMammal` class.

We want to know the breed and the breed family to which a dog belongs. Thus, we will define the dog's breed and breed family class attributes. Each subclass of the `Dog` superclass must specify the appropriate value for these class attributes. In addition, the two class methods will allow you to print the dog's breed and the dog's breed family.

The `TerrierDog` class inherits from `Dog` and specifies `Terrier` as the value for the breed family. This class displays a message whenever a `TerrierDog` class has been created.

Finally, the `SmoothFoxTerrier` class inherits from `TerrierDog` and specifies `Smooth Fox Terrier` as the value for the dog's breed. The `SmoothFoxTerrier` class displays a message whenever a `SmoothFoxTerrier` class has been created.

Understanding method overloading and overriding

Some programming languages allow you to define a method with the same name multiple times by passing different arguments. This feature is known as **method overloading**. In some cases, we can overload a constructor. However, it is very important to mention that a similar effect can be achieved with optional parameters or default values for specific arguments.

For example, we can take advantage of method overloading in a programming language that supports it to define multiple instances of the `bark` method. However, it is very important to avoid code duplication when we overload methods.

Sometimes, we define a method in a class and know that a subclass may need to provide a different instance of this method. When a subclass provides a different implementation of a method defined in a superclass with the same name, same arguments, and same return type, we say that we have overridden a method. When we override a method, the implementation in the subclass overwrites the code given in the superclass.

It is also possible to override properties and other members of a class in subclasses.

Understanding operator overloading

Some programming languages, such as C# and Python, allow you to redefine specific operators to work in a different way based on the classes in which we apply them. For example, we can use comparison operators—such as less than (<) and greater than (>)—to return the results of comparing the age value when they are applied to instances of `Dog`.

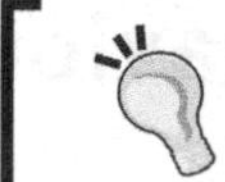

> The redefinition of operators to work in a specific way when applied to instances of specific classes is known as operator overloading.

An operator that works in one way when applied to an instance of a class may work differently on instances of another class. We can also override the overloaded operators in subclasses. For example, we can make comparison operators work in a different way in a superclass and its subclasses.

Taking advantage of polymorphism

We can use the same method, the same name, and same arguments to cause different things to happen according to the class in which we invoke a method. In object-oriented programming, this feature is known as *polymorphism*.

For example, consider that we define a `talk` method in the `Animal` class. The different subclasses of `Animal` must override this method to provide its own implementation of `talk`.

A `Dog` class will override this method to print the representation of a dog barking, that is, a `Woof` message. On the other hand, a `Cat` class will override this method to print the representation of a cat meowing, that is, a `Meow` message.

Now, let's think about a `CartoonDog` class that represents a dog that can really talk as part of a cartoon. The `CartoonDog` class will override the `talk` method to print a `Hello` message because the dog can really talk.

Thus, depending on the type of the instance, we will see a different result after invoking the same method along with the same arguments, even if all of them are subclasses of the same base class, that is, the `Animal` class.

Working with simple inheritance in Python

Firstly, we will create a base class in Python. Then we will use simple inheritance to create subclasses. We will then override methods and overload comparison operators to be able to compare different instances of a specific class and its subclasses. We will take advantage of this polymorphism.

Creating classes that specialize behavior in Python

Now it is time to code all the classes in Python. The following lines show the code for the `Animal` class in Python. The class header doesn't specify a base class; therefore, this class inherits from an object, that is, the most base type for any class in Python. Remember that we are working with Python 3.x and that the syntax to achieve the same goal in Python 2.x is different. In Python 3.x, a class that doesn't specify a base class implicitly inherits from an object:

```
class Animal:
    _number_of_legs = 0
```

```
    _pairs_of_eyes = 0

    def __init__(self, age):
        self._age = age
        print("Animal created")

    @property
    def age(self):
        return self._age

    @age.setter
    def age(self, age):
        self._age = age

    def print_legs_and_eyes(self):
        print("I have " + str(self._number_of_legs) + " legs and " +
str(self._pairs_of_eyes * 2) + " eyes.")

    def print_age(self):
        print("I am " + str(self._age) + " years old.")
```

The `Animal` class in the preceding code declares two protected class attributes initialized to `0`: `_number_of_legs` and `_pairs_of_eyes`. The `__init__` method requires an `age` value to create an instance of the `Animal` class and prints a message indicating that an animal has been created. This class encapsulates the `_age` protected instance attribute as an `age` property. In addition, the `Animal` class defines the following two instance methods:

- `print_legs_and_eyes`: This method displays the total number of eyes based on the `_pairs_of_eyes` value
- `print_age`: This method displays the age based on the `_age` value

We have to add more code to this class to be able to compare the age of all the different `Animal` instances using operators. We will add the necessary code to this class later.

Using simple inheritance in Python

The following lines show the code for the `Mammal` class that inherits from `Animal`. Note the `class` keyword followed by the class name: `Mammal`, the superclass from which it inherits enclosed in parenthesis `(Animal)`, and a colon (`:`) that contains the header of the class definition:

```
class Mammal(Animal):
```

```
    _pairs_of_eyes = 1

    def __init__(self, age, is_pregnant=False):
        super().__init__(age)
        self._is_pregnant = is_pregnant
        print("Mammal created")

    @property
    def is_pregnant(self):
        return self._is_pregnant

    @is_pregnant.setter
    def is_pregnant(self, is_pregnant):
        self._is_pregnant = is_pregnant
```

The `Mammal` class overwrites the value of the `_pairs_of_eyes` protected class attribute with `1`. Remember that the protected class attribute was present in the `Animal` class body, but initialized with `0`.

The `__init__` method requires an `age` value to create an instance of a class and specifies an additional optional argument, `is_pregnant`, whose default value is `False`. If we don't specify the value for `is_pregnant`, Python will use the default value indicated in the method declaration. We cannot declare multiple `__init__` method versions with a different number of parameters within a class in Python; therefore, we can take advantage of optional parameters.

The first line in the `__init__` method invokes the `__init__` method defined in the superclass, that is, the `Animal` class. This superclass defined the `__init__` method with just one argument: the `age` value; therefore, we call it using the `age` value received as an argument (`age`) in our `__init__` method:

```
super().__init__(age)
```

We use `super()` to reference the superclass of the current class.

The `__init__` method defined in the superclass initializes the value for the `_age` protected instance attribute and prints a message indicating that an `Animal` instance has been created. When the `__init__` method returns a value, the following code initializes the value of the `_is_pregnant` instance attribute and prints a message indicating that a mammal has been created:

```
self._is_pregnant = is_pregnant
print("Mammal created")
```

Overriding methods in Python

The following lines show the code for the DomesticMammal class that inherits from Mammal. The class keyword followed by the class name DomesticMammal, the superclass from which it inherits enclosed in parenthesis (Mammal), and a colon (:) that composes the header of the class definition is shown in the following code:

```
class DomesticMammal(Mammal):
    def __init__(self, name, age, favorite_toy, is_pregnant=False):
        super().__init__(age, is_pregnant)
        self._name = name
        self._favorite_toy = favorite_toy
        print("DomesticMammal created")


    @property
    def name(self):
        return self._name

    @property
    def favorite_toy(self):
        return self._favorite_toy

    @favorite_toy.setter
    def favorite_toy(self, favorite_toy):
        self._favorite_toy = favorite_toy

    def talk(self):
        print(self._name + ": talks")
```

The __init__ method requires a name, an age, and a favorite_toy to create an instance of a class. In addition, this method specifies an additional optional argument (is_pregnant) whose default value is False. As in the Mammal class, the first line in the __init__ method invokes the __init__ method defined in the superclass, that is, the Mammal class. The superclass defined the __init__ method with two arguments: age and is_pregnant. Thus, we call the __init__ method using arguments that have the same names in our __init__ method:

```
super().__init__(age, is_pregnant)
```

After it finishes initializing attributes, the __init__ method prints a message indicating that a DomesticMammal class has been created. This class defines a name read-only property and a favorite_toy property that encapsulate the _name and _favorite_toy protected instance attributes. The talk instance method displays a message with the _name value, followed by a colon (:) and talks.

The following lines of code show the code for the `Dog` class that inherits from `DomesticMammal`:

```
class Dog(DomesticMammal):
    _number_of_legs = 4
    _breed = "Just a dog"
    _breed_family = "Dog"

    def __init__(self, name, age, favorite_toy, is_pregnant=False):
        super().__init__(name, age, favorite_toy, is_pregnant)
        print("Dog created")

    def bark(self, times=1, other_domestic_mammal=None, is_
angry=False):
        message = self.name
        if other_domestic_mammal is not None:
            message += " to " + other_domestic_mammal.name + ": "
        else:
            message += ": "
        if is_angry:
            message += "Grr "
        message += "Woof " * times
        print(message)

    def talk(self):
        self.bark()

    @classmethod
    def print_breed(cls):
        print(cls._breed)

    @classmethod
    def print_breed_family(cls):
        print(cls._breed_family)
```

The `Dog` class in the preceding code overrides the `talk` method from **`DomesticMammal`** in **`Dog`**. As with the `__init__` method that has been overridden in all the subclasses we have been creating, we just declare this method with the same name. There is no need to add any decorator or keyword in Python to override a method defined in a superclass.

However, in this case the talk method doesn't invoke the __init__ method with the same name for its superclass, that is, we don't use super() to invoke the talk method defined in DomesticMammal. The talk method in the Dog class invokes the bark method without parameters because dogs bark and don't talk.

The **bark** method declaration includes three optional arguments. This way, we can call it without parameters or with values for different optional arguments. Python doesn't allow us to overload methods; therefore, we can take advantage of optional arguments. The **bark** method prints a message based on the specified number of times (times), the destination domestic mammal (other_domestic_mammal), and whether the dog is angry or not (is_angry).

The Dog class also declares two class attributes: _breed and _breed_family. We will override the values of these attributes in the subclasses of Dog. The print_breed class method displays the value of the _breed class attribute and the print_breed_family class method displays the value of the _breed_family class attribute. We won't override these class methods in our subclasses because we just need to override the values of the class attributes to achieve our goals. If we call these class methods from an instance of a subclass of Dog, these methods will execute the code specified in the Dog class, that is, the last class in the class hierarchy to override the talk method, but this code will use the value of the class attributes overridden in subclasses. Thus we will see a message that displays the values of all the class attributes as defined in our subclasses.

The following lines show the code for the TerrierDog class that inherits from Dog:

```
class TerrierDog(Dog):
    _breed = "Terrier dog"
    _breed_family = "Terrier"

    def __init__(self, name, age, favorite_toy, is_pregnant=False):
        super().__init__(name, age, favorite_toy, is_pregnant)
        print("TerrierDog created")
```

As happened in other subclasses that we have been coding, the __init__ method requires a name, an age, and a favorite_toy attribute to create an instance of the TerrierDog class; we also have the optional is_pregnant argument. The __init__ method invokes a method with the same name defined in the superclass, that is, the Dog class. Then the __init__ method prints a message indicating that a TerrierDog instance has been created. The Dog class sets "Terrier dog" and "Terrier" as _, which is the value for the breed and _breed_family class attributes defined in the superclass.

The following lines show the code for the `SmoothFoxTerrier` class that inherits from `TerrierDog`:

```
class SmoothFoxTerrier(TerrierDog):
    _breed = "Smooth Fox Terrier"

    def __init__(self, name, age, favorite_toy, is_pregnant=False):
        super().__init__(name, age, favorite_toy, is_pregnant)
        print("SmoothFoxTerrier created")
```

The `SmoothFoxTerrier` class sets `"Smooth Fox Terrier"` as the value for the `_breed` class attribute defined in the `Dog` class. The `__init__` method invokes a method with the same name defined in the superclass, that is the `TerrierDog` class and then prints a message. This message indicates that a `SmoothFoxTerrier` class instance has been created.

Overloading operators in Python

We want to be able to compare the age of different `Animal` instances using the following operators in Python:

- Less than (<)
- Less or equal than (<=)
- Greater than (>)
- Greater or equal than (>=)

We can overload operators in Python to achieve our goals by overriding special instance methods that Python invokes under the hood whenever we use all the operators to compare instances of `Animal`. We have to override the following methods in the **`Animal`** class:

- `__lt__`: This method gets invoked when we use the less than (<) operator
- `__le__`: This method gets invoked when we use the less than or equals to (<=) operator
- `__gt__`: This method gets invoked when we use the greater than (>) operator
- `__ge__`: This method gets invoked when we use the greater than or equals to (>=) operator

All the preceding instance methods have the same declaration. Python passes the instance specified at the right-hand side of the operator as an argument, which is usually named as `other`. Thus we have `self` and `other` as the arguments for the instance method, and we must return a `bool` value with the result of the application of the operator, in our case with the result of the comparison operator.

Let's consider that we have two instances of `Animal` or any of its subclasses named `animal1` and `animal2`. If we enter `print(animal1 < animal2)` on the Python console, Python will invoke the `animal1.__lt__` method with `self` equal to `animal1` and `other` equal to `animal2`. Thus we must return a Boolean value indicating that `self.age < other.age`, is equivalent to `animal1.age < animal2.age`.

We must add the following code to the body of the `Animal` class:

```
def __lt__(self, other):
    return self.age < other.age

def __le__(self, other):
    return self.age <= other.age

def __gt__(self, other):
    return self.age > other.age

def __ge__(self, other):
    return self.age >= other.age
```

Understanding polymorphism in Python

After we code all the classes, we will enter the following lines on a Python console:

```
SmoothFoxTerrier.print_breed()
SmoothFoxTerrier.print_breed_family()
```

The following lines show the messages displayed on the Python console after we enter the preceding lines of code:

```
Smooth Fox Terrier
Terrier
```

We coded the `print_breed` and `print_breed_family` class methods in the `Dog` class and didn't override these methods in any of the subclasses. However, we have overridden the values of the class attributes whose content these methods display: `_breed` and `_breed_family`. The former class attribute is overridden in the `SmoothFoxTerrier` class and the latter in the `TerrierDog` class.

We called the class methods from the `SmoothFoxTerrier` class; therefore, these methods took into account the values of the class attributes overridden in the `TerrierDog` and the `SmoothFoxTerrier` classes.

The following code creates an instance of the `SmoothFoxTerrier` class named `tom`:

```
tom = SmoothFoxTerrier("Tom", 5, "Sneakers")
```

The Python console will display the following messages as a result of all the `__init__` methods that have been called and prints a message indicating that an instance of a class has been created. Remember that we have overridden each `__init__` method in all the different classes up to `SmoothFoxTerrier` and its included code to call the `__init__` method of its superclass and display a message:

```
Animal created
Mammal created
DomesticMammal created
Dog created
TerrierDog created
SmoothFoxTerrier created
```

We don't have six different instances; we just have one instance that calls the `__init__` method of six different classes to perform all the necessary initialization in order to create an instance of `SmoothFoxTerrier`. If we execute the following code on the Python console, all of them will display `True` as the result because `tom` is an instance of `Animal`, `Mammal`, `DomesticMammal`, `Dog`, `TerrierDog`, and `SmoothFoxTerrier`:

```
print(isinstance(tom, Animal))
print(isinstance(tom, Mammal))
print(isinstance(tom, DomesticMammal))
print(isinstance(tom, Dog))
print(isinstance(tom, TerrierDog))
print(isinstance(tom, SmoothFoxTerrier))
```

The following code creates two additional instances of `SmoothFoxTerrier` named `pluto` and `goofy`:

```
pluto = SmoothFoxTerrier("Pluto", 6, "Tennis ball")
goofy = SmoothFoxTerrier("Goofy", 8, "Soda bottle")
```

The following code uses all the four operators that we overloaded in the `Animal` class: greater than (>), less than (<), greater than or equal to (>=), and less than or equal to (<=). Remember that we have overridden special instance methods in the `Animal` class that Python invokes under the hood whenever we use these operators. In this case, we apply these operators on instances of `SmoothFoxTerrier`, and the `Animal` class inherits the overridden special instance methods from the `Animal` base class. These four operators return the results of comparing the age value of all the different instances:

```
print(tom > pluto)
print(tom < pluto)
print(goofy >= tom)
print(tom <= goofy)
```

The following code calls the `bark` method for the instance named `tom` with a different number of arguments. This way, we can take advantage of all the optional arguments in Python. Remember that we coded the `bark` method in the `Dog` class, and the `SmoothFoxTerrier` class inherits the `bark` method from this superclass:

```
tom.bark()
tom.bark(2)
tom.bark(2, pluto)
tom.bark(3, pluto, True)
```

The following code shows the results of calling the `bark` method using different arguments:

```
Tom: Woof
Tom: Woof Woof
Tom to Pluto: Woof Woof
Tom to Pluto: Grr Woof Woof Woof
```

Working with simple inheritance in C#

First, we will create a base class in C#. Then we will use simple inheritance to create subclasses and specialize behavior. We will override methods and overload comparison operators to be able to compare different instances of a specific class and its subclasses. We will take advantage of this polymorphism.

Creating classes that specialize behavior in C#

Now it is time to code all the classes in C#. The following lines show the code for the `Animal` abstract class in C#. The class declaration doesn't specify a base class; therefore, this class inherits from `Object`, specifically `System.Object`. `System.Object` is the base class for all the classes included in .NET Framework. The usage of the `abstract` keyword before `class` makes this class an abstract class that we cannot use to create instances:

```
public abstract class Animal
{
  protected virtual int NumberOfLegs { get { return 0; } }
  protected virtual int PairsOfEyes { get { return 0; } }

  public int Age { get; set; }

  public Animal(int age)
```

```
    {
      this.Age = age;
      Console.WriteLine("Animal created.");
    }

    public void PrintLegsAndEyes()
    {
      Console.WriteLine(
        String.Format("I have {0} legs and {1} eyes.",
        this.NumberOfLegs,
        this.PairsOfEyes * 2));
    }

    public void PrintAge()
    {
      Console.WriteLine(
        String.Format("I am {0} years old."),
        this.Age);
    }
  }
```

The preceding class declares two read-only properties: `NumberOfLegs` and `PairsOfEyes`. Both these properties return `0` as its value. The usage of the `virtual` keyword allows you to override properties in any subclass of `Animal`.

In C#, we have to specify the properties or methods that we allow our subclasses to override by adding the `virtual` keyword. If we don't include the `virtual` keyword, a property or method cannot be overridden and we will see a compiler error if we try to do so.

The constructor requires an `age` value to create an instance of a class and prints a message indicating that an animal has been created. This class uses auto-implemented properties to generate the `Age` property. In addition, the `Animal` class defines the following two instance methods:

- `PrintLegsAndEyes`: This method displays the total number of eyes based on the `PairsOfEyes` value
- `PrintAge`: This method displays the age based on the `age` value

We have to add more code to this class to be able to compare the age of all the different `Animal` instances using operators. We will add the necessary code to this class later.

Using simple inheritance in C#

We will create many classes in C# which require the following `using` statements. We will dive deep into how the `using` statement works and the organization of object-oriented code in *Chapter 7, Organization of Object-Oriented Code*:

```
using System;
using System.Linq;
using System.Text;
```

The following lines show the code for the `Mammal` abstract class that inherits from `Animal`. Note the `class` keyword followed by the `Mammal` class name, a colon (`:`), and `Animal`: the superclass from which it inherits in the class definition:

```
public abstract class Mammal: Animal
{
    protected override int PairsOfEyes { get { return 1; } }
    public bool IsPregnant { get; set; }

    private void Init(bool isPregnant)
    {
        this.IsPregnant = isPregnant;
        Console.WriteLine("Mammal created.");
    }

    public Mammal(int age) : base(age)
    {
        this.Init(false);
    }

    public Mammal(int age, bool isPregnant) : base(age)
    {
        this.Init(isPregnant);
    }
}
```

The `Mammal` class name overrides the `PairsOfEyes` property and defines a new getter method that returns `1`. Remember that the protected class attribute was declared using the `virtual` keyword in the `Animal` class body, but the getter method returned `0`. In this case, the property declaration uses the `override` keyword to override the property declaration of the superclass.

We will use the `virtual` keyword to indicate that a property or method can be overridden in subclasses. Also, we will use the `override` keyword to override a property or method that was declared with the `virtual` keyword in a superclass.

Note that this `Animal` class declares two constructors. One of the constructors requires the `age` value to create an instance of a class. The other constructor requires the `age` and `isPregnant` value. If we create an instance of this class with just one `int` argument, C# will use the first constructor. If we create an instance of this class with two arguments: one `int` value and one `bool` value, C# will use the second constructor. Thus, we have overloaded the constructor and provided two different constructors. Of course, we can also take advantage of optional parameters. However, in this case we want to overload constructors.

The lines that declare two constructors are followed by a colon(`:`). A call to the constructor of the superclass with the `age` value is received as an argument. The `base` keyword enables you to call the superclass' constructor. Once the superclass' constructor finishes its execution, both constructors call the `Init` private method which initializes the `IsPregnant` property with a value received as an argument or the default `false` value in case it wasn't specified. The following code shows both constructor declarations:

```
public Mammal(int age) : base(age)
public Mammal(int age, bool isPregnant) : base(age)
```

We use `base` to reference the superclass' constructor.

The superclass' constructor initializes the value for the `Age` property and prints a message indicating that an `Animal` instance has been created. When a method returns, the `Init` private method defined in the `Mammal` class initializes the value of the `IsPregnant` property and prints a message indicating that a `Mammal` has been created. Don't forget that we cannot access private methods from subclasses; therefore, the `Init` method is only visible in the `Mammal` class.

Overloading and overriding methods in C#

The following lines show the code for the `DomesticMammal` class that inherits from `Mammal`. Note the `class` keyword followed by the `DomesticMammal` class name, a colon (`:`), and `Mammal`, the superclass from which it inherits in the class definition:

```
public abstract class DomesticMammal: Mammal
{
  public string Name { get; private set; }
  public string FavoriteToy { get; set; }

  private void Init(string name, string favoriteToy)
  {
    this.Name = name;
    this.FavoriteToy = favoriteToy;
    Console.WriteLine("DomesticMammal created.");
  }

  public virtual void Talk()
  {
    Console.WriteLine(String.Format("{0}: talks", this.Name));
  }

  public DomesticMammal(string name, int age, string favoriteToy)
    : base(age)
  {
    this.Init(name, favoriteToy);
  }

  public DomesticMammal(string name, int age, string favoriteToy, bool
isPregnant)
    : base(age, isPregnant)
  {
    this.Init(name, favoriteToy);
  }
}
```

The preceding class declares two constructors. The first constructor requires the `name`, `age`, and `favoriteToy` values to create an instance of a class. The other constructor adds the `isPregnant` argument. As in the `Mammal` class, the lines that declare both constructors are followed by a colon (`:`) and a call to the superclass' constructor. In one case, we just need the `age` value received as an argument, whereas in the other case, it is necessary to add the `isPregnant` value. Once the superclass' constructor finishes its execution, both constructors call the `Init` private method that initializes the properties of `Name` and `FavoriteToy`. After the `Init` method finishes initializing its properties, it prints a message indicating that `DomesticMammal` has been created. The following code shows the declarations of two constructors:

```
public DomesticMammal(string name, int age, string favoriteToy) :
base(age)
public DomesticMammal(string name, int age, string favoriteToy, bool
isPregnant) : base(age, isPregnant)
```

The class defines a `Name` read-only property and a `FavoriteToy` property with autoimplemented properties. The `Talk` instance method displays a message with the `Name` value. This is followed by a colon (`:`) and `talks`. Note that a method uses the `virtual` keyword in its declaration; therefore, we can override it in any subclass.

The following lines show the code for the `Dog` class that inherits from `DomesticMammal`:

```
public class Dog : DomesticMammal
{
  protected override int NumberOfLegs { get { return 4; } }
  public virtual string Breed { get { return "Just a dog"; } }
  public virtual string BreedFamily { get { return "Dog"; } }

  private void Init()
  {
    Console.WriteLine("Dog created.");
  }

  public Dog(string name, int age, string favoriteToy, bool
isPregnant): base(name, age, favoriteToy, isPregnant)
  {
    this.Init();
  }

  public Dog(string name, int age, string favoriteToy)
  : base(name, age, favoriteToy)
  {
```

```
        this.Init();
    }

    public void PrintBreed()
    {
      Console.WriteLine(this.Breed);
    }

    public void PrintBreedFamily()
    {
      Console.WriteLine(this.BreedFamily);
    }

    private void PrintBark(int times, DomesticMammal
  otherDomesticMammal, bool isAngry)
    {
      var sb = new StringBuilder();
      sb.Append(this.Name);
      if (otherDomesticMammal != null)
      {
        sb.Append(String.Format(" to {0}: ", otherDomesticMammal.Name));
      }
      else
      {
        sb.Append(": ");
      }

      if (isAngry)
      {
        sb.Append("Grr ");
      }
      sb.Append(string.Concat(Enumerable.Repeat("Woof ", times)));
      Console.WriteLine(sb.ToString());
    }

    public void Bark()
    {
      this.PrintBark(1, null, false);
    }

    public void Bark(int times)
```

```
    {
      this.PrintBark(times, null, false);
    }

    public void Bark(int times, DomesticMammal otherDomesticMammal)
    {
      this.PrintBark(times, otherDomesticMammal, false);
    }

    public void Bark(int times, DomesticMammal otherDomesticMammal, bool
  isAngry)
    {
      this.PrintBark(times, otherDomesticMammal, isAngry);
    }

    public override void Talk()
    {
      this.Bark();
    }
  }
```

The `Dog` class overrides the `Talk` method from `DomesticMammal` in `Dog`. As in the overridden properties of other subclasses, we just add the `override` keyword to the method declaration. This method doesn't invoke a method with the same name for its superclass, that is, we don't use the `base` keyword to invoke the `Talk` method defined in `DomesticMammal`. The `Talk` method in the `Dog` class invokes the `Bark` method without parameters because dogs bark and don't talk.

The `Bark` method is overloaded with four declarations with different arguments. The following lines show all the four different declarations included in the class body:

```
public void Bark()
public void Bark(int times)
public void Bark(int times, DomesticMammal otherDomesticMammal)
public void Bark(int times, DomesticMammal otherDomesticMammal, bool
isAngry)
```

This way, we can call any of the defined `Bark` methods based on the arguments that are provided. All the four methods end up invoking the `PrintBark` private method with different default values for all the arguments not provided in the call to `Bark`. The method uses `StringBuilder` to build and print a message based on the specified number of times (`times`), the destination domestic mammal (`otherDomesticMammal`), and whether the dog is angry or not (`isAngry`).

The Dog class also declares two read-only properties: Breed and BreedFamily. We will override the values of these properties in the subclasses of Dog so that they include the virtual keyword in their declaration. The PrintBreed instance method displays the value of the Breed property attribute, whereas the PrintBreedFamily instance method displays the value of the BreedFamily property. We won't override these instance methods in our subclasses because we just need to override the values of two read-only properties to achieve our goals. If we call these instance methods from an instance of a subclass of Dog, these methods will execute the code specified in the Dog class but this code will use the value of all the properties overridden in subclasses. Thus, we will see the messages that displays the values of all the properties as defined in subclasses.

The following lines show the code for the TerrierDog class that inherits from Dog:

```
public class TerrierDog : Dog
{
  public override string Breed { get { return "Terrier dog"; } }
  public override string BreedFamily { get { return "Terrier"; } }

  private void Init()
  {
    Console.WriteLine("TerrierDog created.");
  }

  public TerrierDog(string name, int age, string favoriteToy)
  : base(name, age, favoriteToy)
  {
    this.Init();
  }

  public TerrierDog(string name, int age, string favoriteToy, bool
isPregnant)
  : base(name, age, favoriteToy, isPregnant)
  {
    this.Init();
  }
}
```

As in the other subclasses that we have been coding, we have more than one constructor defined for a class. In this case, one of the constructors require the `name`, `age`, and `favoriteToy` values to create an instance of the `TerrierDog` class, and we also have a constructor that adds the `isPregnant` argument. Both constructors invoke the superclass' constructor and then call the private `Init` method. This method prints a message. This message indicates that `TerrierDog` has been created. The class sets `"Terrier dog"` and `"Terrier"` as the value for the properties of `Breed` and `BreedFamily` that were defined in the superclass and overridden in this `TerrierDog` class.

The following lines show the code for the `SmoothFoxTerrier` class that inherits from `TerrierDog`:

```
public class SmoothFoxTerrier : TerrierDog
{
  public override string Breed { get { return "Smooth Fox Terrier"; }
}

  private void Init()
  {
    Console.WriteLine("Smooth Fox Terrier created.");
  }

  public SmoothFoxTerrier(string name, int age, string favoriteToy)
  : base(name, age, favoriteToy)
  {
    this.Init();
  }

  public SmoothFoxTerrier(string name, int age, string favoriteToy,
bool isPregnant)
  : base(name, age, favoriteToy, isPregnant)
  {
    this.Init();
  }
}
```

The `SmoothFoxTerrier` class sets `"Smooth Fox Terrier"` as the value for the `Breed` property defined in the `Dog` class, which is overridden in this class. The `SmoothFoxTerrier` class defines two constructors with exactly the same parameters that were specified in the two constructors defined in the superclass. Both constructors invoke two constructors defined in the superclass and then call the `Init` private method. This method prints a message indicating that an instance of the `SmoothFoxTerrier` class has been created.

Overloading operators in C#

We want to be able to compare the age of different `Animal` instances using the following operators in C#:

- Less than (<)
- Less than or equal to (<=)
- Greater than (>)
- Greater than or equal to (>=)

We can overload the preceding operators in C# to achieve our goals by declaring operators in the `Animal` class that work as static methods that receive two arguments. C# will invoke operators under the hood whenever we use these operators to compare instances of `Animal`. We have to declare the following operators in the **`Animal`** class:

- <: This operator is invoked when we use the less than (<) operator
- <=: This operator is invoked when we use the less than or equal to (<=) operator
- >: This operator is invoked when we use the greater than (>) operator
- >=: This operator is invoked when we use the greater than or equal to (>=) operator

All the preceding operators have the same declaration. C# passes the instance specified at the left-hand side of the operator as the first argument and the instance specified at the right-hand side of the operator as the second argument. We will use names such as `self` and `other` for these arguments. Thus we have `self` and `other` as the arguments for operators, and we must return a `bool` value with the result of the application of the operator, in our case, with the result of the comparison operator.

Let's consider that we have two instances of `Animal` or any of its subclasses named `animal1` and `animal2`. If we enter `Console.WriteLine(animal1 < animal2);`, C# will invoke the **<** operator for the `Animal` class as a `static` method with `self` equal to `animal1` and `other` equal to `animal2`. Thus we must return a `bool` value indicating that `self.age < other.age` is equivalent to `animal1.age < animal2.age`.

We must add the following code to the body of the `Animal` class:

```
public static bool operator <(Animal self, Animal other)
{
  return self.Age < other.Age;
```

```
}

public static bool operator <=(Animal self, Animal other)
{
  return self.Age <= other.Age;
}

public static bool operator >(Animal self, Animal other)
{
  return self.Age > other.Age;
}

public static bool operator >=(Animal self, Animal other)
{
  return self.Age >= other.Age;
}
```

Understanding polymorphism in C#

After we code all the classes, we can write code in the `Main` method of a console application. The following are the first code of the `Main` method that create an instance of the `SmoothFoxTerrier` class named `tom`. Let's use one of its constructors that doesn't require the `isPregnant` argument:

```
var tom = new SmoothFoxTerrier("Tom", 5, "Sneakers");
tom.PrintBreed();
tom.PrintBreedFamily();
```

The following code shows the messages that will be displayed on the Windows console after we enter the preceding code:

```
Animal created.
Mammal created.
DomesticMammal created.
Dog created.
TerrierDog created.
Smooth Fox Terrier created.
Smooth Fox Terrier
Terrier
```

First, the Windows console displays the messages by each constructor that has been called. Remember that each constructor called its base class constructor and printed a message indicating that an instance of the class has been created. We don't have six different instances; we just have one instance that has been calling the chained constructors of six different classes to perform all the necessary initialization to create an instance of `SmoothFoxTerrier`. If we execute the following code in the **Immediate window** of Visual Studio, all of them will return `true` as the result because `tom` is an `Animal`, a `Mammal`, a `DomesticMammal`, a `Dog`, a `TerrierDog`, and a breed of `SmoothFoxTerrier`:

```
tom is Animal
tom is Mammal
tom is DomesticMammal
tom is Dog
tom is TerrierDog
tom is SmoothFoxTerrier
```

We coded the `PrintBreed` and `PrintBreedFamily` methods in the `Dog` class and we didn't override these methods in any of the subclasses. However, we have overridden the properties whose content these methods display: `Breed` and `BreedFamily`. The former property is overridden in the `SmoothFoxTerrier` class and the latter in the `TerrierDog` class.

The following code creates two additional instances of `SmoothFoxTerrier` named `pluto` and `goofy`. In this case, both code use the constructor that receives the `isPregnant` argument:

```
var pluto = new SmoothFoxTerrier("Pluto", 6, "Tennis ball", false);
var goofy = new SmoothFoxTerrier("Goofy", 8, "Soda bottle", false);
```

The following code uses the four operators that we have overloaded in the `Animal` class: greater than (>), less than (<), greater than or equal to (>=), and less than or equal to (<=). In this case, we apply these operators on instances of `SmoothFoxTerrier`, and the `Animal` class inherits the operators from the `Animal` base class. The four operators return the results of comparing the `age` value of the different instances:

```
Console.WriteLine(tom > pluto);
Console.WriteLine(tom < pluto);
Console.WriteLine(goofy >= tom);
Console.WriteLine(tom <= goofy);
```

The following code calls the `Bark` method for the `tom` instance with a different number of arguments. This way, we can take advantage of the `Bark` method that we overloaded four times with different arguments in C#. Remember that we coded the four `Bark` methods in the `Dog` class and the `SmoothFoxTerrier` class inherits the overloaded methods from this superclass:

```
tom.Bark();
tom.Bark(2);
tom.Bark(2, pluto);
tom.Bark(3, pluto, true);
```

The following code shows the results of calling the methods with the different arguments:

```
Tom: Woof
Tom: Woof Woof
Tom to Pluto: Woof Woof
Tom to Pluto: Grr Woof Woof Woof
```

Working with the prototype-based inheritance in JavaScript

First, we will create a constructor function in JavaScript and define properties and methods in its prototype. Then, we will take advantage of prototype-based inheritance in order to create objects that specialize the behavior defined in the baseline prototype. We will override methods and properties.

Creating objects that specialize behavior in JavaScript

Now it is time to code objects in JavaScript. The following code defines the `Animal` empty constructor function in JavaScript, followed by the declaration of properties and functions for the `Animal` prototype:

```
function Animal() {}

Animal.prototype.numberOfLegs = 0;
Animal.prototype.pairsOfEyes = 0;
Animal.prototype.age = 0;

Animal.prototype.printLegsAndEyes = function() {
```

```
  console.log("I have " + this.numberOfLegs + " legs and " + this.
pairsOfEyes * 2 + " eyes.");
}

Animal.prototype.printAge = function() {
  console.log("I am " + this.age + " years old.");
}
```

In this case, we will use an empty constructor function and then declare all the things that we want to share with the objects that will use `Animal` as its prototype in `Animal.prototype`. The prototype declares three properties initialized with `0` as its value: `age`, `numberOfLegs`, and `pairsOfEyes`.

In addition, the `Animal` prototype defines the following two methods:

- `printLegsAndEyes`: This method displays the total number of eyes based on the `pairsOfEyes` value
- `printAge`: This method displays the age based on the `age` value

We have to add more code to the object's prototype to be able to compare the age of the different `Animal` instances by calling methods. We will add the necessary code to the object's prototype later.

Using the prototype-based inheritance in JavaScript

The following is the code for the empty `Mammal` construction function. Now, let's set the `Mammal.prototype` property to a new instance of the previously defined `Animal` object. This way, we will be able to access the properties and methods defined in the `Animal` object in each `Mammal` instance:

```
function Mammal() {}
Mammal.prototype = new Animal();
Mammal.prototype.constructor = Mammal;
Mammal.prototype.isPregnant = false;
Mammal.prototype.pairsOfEyes = 1;
```

After we change the value of the `Mammal.prototype` property, we will assign the `Mammal` constructor function to the `Mammal.constructor` property in order to clean up the side effects on the constructor property when you change the value of a prototype. We add the `isPregnant` property initialized to `false`. Finally, we overwrite the value of the `pairsOfEyes` property with `1`. Remember that this property was declared in `Animal.prototype`.

Any instance of `Mammal` will be able to access the properties and methods declared in `Animal.prototype`.

Overriding methods in JavaScript

Here is the code for the empty `DomesticMammal` construction function. Here we will set the `DomesticMammal.prototype` property to a new instance of the previously defined `Mammal` object. This way, we will be able to access the properties and methods defined in both the `Mammal` and `Animal` objects in each `DomesticMammal` instance. The prototype chain makes it possible to access all the properties and methods defined in each `prototype` property of the different objects:

```
function DomesticMammal() {}

DomesticMammal.prototype = new Mammal();
DomesticMammal.prototype.constructor = DomesticMammal;
DomesticMammal.prototype.name = "";
DomesticMammal.prototype.favoriteToy = "";

DomesticMammal.prototype.talk = function() {
  console.log(this.name + ": talks");
}
```

We will use an empty constructor function again. Then we will declare all the things that we want to share with the objects that will use `DomesticMammal` as its prototype in `DomesticMammal.prototype`. This prototype declares two properties: `name` and `favoriteToy` initialized with an empty string as their value.

In addition, the preceding prototype defines the `talk` method that displays a message with the `name` value, followed by a colon (`:`) and `talks`. Note that this method will be overridden in the `Dog` object.

The following is the code for the empty `Dog` construction function. Then we set the `Dog.prototype` property to a new instance of the previously defined `DomesticMammal` object. This way, we will be able to access the properties and methods defined in the `DomesticMammal`, `Mammal`, and `Animal` objects in each `Dog` instance. We continue to grow the prototype chain:

```
function Dog() {}
Dog.prototype = new DomesticMammal();
Dog.prototype.constructor = Dog;
Dog.prototype.numberOfLegs = 4;
Dog.prototype.breed = "Just a dog";
Dog.prototype.breedFamily = "Dog";

Dog.prototype.printBreed = function() {
```

```
    console.log(this.breed);
}

Dog.prototype.printBreedFamily = function() {
    console.log(this.breedFamily);
}
```

The preceding code overwrites the value of the `numberOfLegs` inherited property with `4`. In addition, the code adds two new properties for `Dog.prototype`: `breed` and `breedFamily`. We will overwrite the values of these properties in the new objects that will have `Dog` as a prototype. The `printBreed` method displays the value of the `breed` property, and the `printBreedFamily` method displays the value of the `breedFamily` property. We won't override these methods in the objects that will have `Dog` as a prototype because we just need to overwrite the values of the properties to achieve our goals. If we call these methods from an instance of an object that includes `Dog` in its prototype chain, these methods will execute the function code declared in the `Dog` prototype, but the code will use the value of the properties overridden in specific objects. Thus, we will see messages that display the values of the properties as defined in the objects that include `Dog` in their prototype chain.

The following code declares a `bark` method and overrides the `talk` method inherited from `DomesticMammal` in `Dog`:

```
Dog.prototype.bark = function(times, otherDomesticMammal, isAngry) {
    var message = this.name;
    if (otherDomesticMammal) {
        message += " to " + otherDomesticMammal.name + ": ";
    }
    else {
        message += ": ";
    }
    if (isAngry) {
        message += "Grr ";
    }
    if (!times) {
        times = 1;
    }
    message += new Array(times + 1).join( "Woof " );
    console.log(message);
}

Dog.prototype.talk = function() {
    this.bark(1);
}
```

The `talk` method overridden in the `Dog` prototype invokes the `bark` method without parameters because dogs bark and don't talk. The `bark` method builds and prints a message according to the specified number of times (`times`), the destination of the domestic mammal (`otherDomesticMammal`), and whether the dog is angry or not (`isAngry`).

The following lines show the code for the `TerrierDog` constructor function and its prototype that inherits from `Dog`:

```
function TerrierDog() { }
TerrierDog.prototype = new Dog();
TerrierDog.prototype.constructor = TerrierDog;
TerrierDog.prototype.breed = "Terrier dog";
TerrierDog.prototype.breedFamily = "Terrier";
```

The `TerrierDog` class sets `"Terrier dog"` and `"Terrier"` as the value for the `breed` and `breedFamily` properties that were defined in `Dog`.

The following lines show the code for the `SmoothFoxTerrier` constructor function and its prototype that inherits from `TerrierDog`:

```
function SmoothFoxTerrier() { }
SmoothFoxTerrier.prototype = new TerrierDog();
SmoothFoxTerrier.prototype.constructor = TerrierDog;
SmoothFoxTerrier.prototype.breed = "Smooth Fox Terrier";

SmoothFoxTerrier.create = function (name, age, favoriteToy,
isPregnant) {
  var dog = new SmoothFoxTerrier();
  dog.name = name;
  dog.age = age;
  dog.favoriteToy = favoriteToy;
  dog.isPregnant = isPregnant;

  return dog;
}
```

The `breed` object sets `"Smooth Fox Terrier"` as the value for the `breed` property defined in the `Dog` object and overridden in this object. In addition, the preceding code declares a `create` function for the `SmoothFoxTerrier` construction function. The `create` function receives `name`, `age`, `favoriteToy`, and `isPregnant` as arguments, creates a new instance of `SmoothFoxTerrier`, and assigns the values received as arguments to the properties with the same name. Finally, the `create` function returns the created and initialized instance of `SmoothFoxTerrier`.

Overloading operators in JavaScript

We want to be able to compare the age of all the different `Animal` instances. JavaScript doesn't allow you to overload operators; therefore, we can create methods to achieve our goal.

We can add the following methods to `Animal.prototype`, which will be available in the prototype chain:

- `lessThan`: Less than (<)
- `lessOrEqualThan`: Less than or equal to (<=)
- `greaterThan`: Greater than (>)
- `greaterOrEqualThan`: Greater than or equal to (>=)

All the preceding methods have the same declaration. They will receive the instance that will be located at the right-hand side of the operator. We will use `other` as the only argument for these methods, and we must return a `bool` value with the result of the application of the operator, in our case, with the result of the comparison operator.

Let's consider that we have two instances of `Animal` or objects in the prototype chain named `animal1` and `animal2`. If we enter `console.log(animal1.lessThan(animal2));`, the method must return a `bool` value indicating that `this.age < other.age` is equivalent to `animal1.age < animal2.age`.

We must add the following code to add all the methods to the `Animal` prototype:

```
Animal.prototype.lessThan = function(other) {
  return this.age < other.age;
}

Animal.prototype.lessOrEqualThan = function(other) {
  return this.age <= other.age;
}

Animal.prototype.greaterThan = function(other) {
  return this.age > other.age;
}

Animal.prototype.greaterOrEqualThan = function(other) {
  return this.age >= other.age;
}
```

Understanding polymorphism in JavaScript

After we code all the constructor functions and fill up their prototypes with properties and methods, we can enter the following code on a JavaScript console. These lines call the `SmoothFoxTerrier.create` method to create an instance of `SmoothFoxTerrier` named `tom` and then call the `printBreed` and `printBreedFamily` methods:

```
var tom = SmoothFoxTerrier.create("Tom", 5, "Sneakers");
tom.printBreed();
tom.printBreedFamily();
```

The following command lines display the messages displayed on the Python console after we enter the previous code:

```
Smooth Fox Terrier
Terrier
```

We coded the `printBreed` and `printBreedFamily` methods in the prototype of the `Dog` constructor function; we didn't override these methods in any of the objects in the prototype chain. However, we have overridden the values of properties whose content these methods display: `breed` and `breedFamily`. The former property is overridden in the `SmoothFoxTerrier` prototype and the latter in the `TerrierDog` prototype.

We called the class methods from the `tom` instance; therefore, these methods took into account the values of the properties overridden in the `TerrierDog` and `SmoothFoxTerrier` objects.

If we execute the following code on the JavaScript console, all of them will display `true` as its result because `tom` is an instance of `Animal`, `Mammal`, `DomesticMammal`, `Dog`, `TerrierDog`, and `SmoothFoxTerrier`:

```
console.log(tom instanceof Animal);
console.log(tom instanceof Mammal);
console.log(tom instanceof DomesticMammal);
console.log(tom instanceof Dog);
console.log(tom instanceof TerrierDog);
console.log(tom instanceof SmoothFoxTerrier);
```

The following code creates two additional instances of `SmoothFoxTerrier`: `pluto` and `goofy`:

```
var pluto = SmoothFoxTerrier.create("Pluto", 6, "Tennis ball");
var goofy = SmoothFoxTerrier.create("Goofy", 8, "Soda bottle");
```

The following code uses the four methods that we declared in the prototype of the `Animal` object: `greaterThan` (>), `lessThan` (<), `greaterOrEqualThan` (>=), and `lessOrEqualThan` (<=). In this case, we invoke the methods on instances of `SmoothFoxTerrier` and the object inherits these methods from the `Animal` object. The methods return the results of comparing the `age` value of the different instances:

```
console.log(tom.greaterThan(pluto));
console.log(tom.lessThan(pluto));
console.log(goofy.greaterOrEqualThan(tom));
console.log(tom.lessOrEqualThan(goofy));
```

The following code calls the `bark` method for the instance named `tom` with a different number of arguments. Remember that we coded the `bark` method in the `Dog` prototype, whereas the `SmoothFoxTerrier` object inherits the method in the prototype chain:

```
tom.bark();
tom.bark(2);
tom.bark(2, pluto);
tom.bark(3, pluto, true);
```

The following code shows the results of calling the methods with all the different arguments:

```
Tom: Woof
Tom: Woof Woof
Tom to Pluto: Woof Woof
Tom to Pluto: Grr Woof Woof Woof
```

Summary

In this chapter, you learned how to take advantage of simple inheritance to specialize a base class. We designed many classes from top to bottom using properties and methods. Then, we coded these classes in Python and C#, taking advantage of the different mechanisms provided by each programming language. We coded different objects and prototypes in JavaScript.

We took advantage of operator overloading in C# and Python. We have overridden methods and properties in subclasses or object prototypes. We took advantage of polymorphism in each programming language.

Now that you learned how to take advantage of inheritance and its related concepts, we are ready to work with multiple inheritance, interfaces, and composition in Python, C#, and JavaScript, which is the topic of the next chapter.

5

Interfaces, Multiple Inheritance, and Composition

In this chapter, we will work with more complex scenarios in which we have to use instances that belong to more than one blueprint. We will use the different features included in each of the three covered programming languages to code an application that requires the combination of multiple blueprints in a single instance. We will:

- Understand how interfaces work in combination with classes
- Work with multiple inheritance of classes in Python
- Take advantage of abstract base classes in Python
- Work with interfaces and multiple inheritance in C#
- Implement interfaces in C#
- Work with composition in JavaScript

Understanding the requirement to work with multiple base classes

We have to work with two different types of characters: comic characters and game characters. A comic character has a nickname and must be able to draw speech balloons and thought balloons. The speech balloon may have another comic character as a destination.

A game character has a full name and must be able to perform the following tasks:

- Draw itself in a specific 2D position indicated by the *x* and *y* coordinates
- Move itself to a specific 2D position indicated by the *x* and *y* coordinates
- Check whether it intersects with another game character

We will work with objects that can be both a comic character and a game character. However, we will also work with objects that are just going to be either a comic character or a game character. Neither the game character nor the comic character has a generic way of performing the previously described tasks. Thus, each object that declares itself as a comic character must define all the tasks related to speech and thought balloons. Each object that declares itself as a game character must define how to draw itself, move, and check whether it intersects with another game character.

An angry dog is a comic character that has a specific way of drawing speech and thought balloons. An angry cat is both a comic character and a game character; therefore, it defines all the tasks required by both character types.

The angry cat is a very versatile character. It can use different costumes to participate in games or comics with different names. An angry cat can also be an alien, a wizard, or a knight.

An alien has a specific number of eyes and must be able to appear and disappear.

A wizard has a spell power score and can make an alien disappear.

A knight has sword power and weight values. He can unsheathe his sword. A common task for the knight is to unsheathe his swords and point it to an alien as a target.

We can create abstract classes to represent a comic character and a game character. Then, each subclass can provide its implementation of the methods. In this case, comic characters and game characters are very different. They don't perform similar tasks that might lead to confusion and problems for multiple inheritance. Thus, we can use multiple inheritance when available to create an angry cat class that inherits from both the comic and game character. In some cases, multiple inheritance is not convenient because similar superclasses might have methods with the same name. Also, it can be extremely confusing to use multiple inheritance.

In addition, we can use multiple inheritance to combine the angry cat class with the alien, wizard, and knight. This way, we will have an angry cat alien, an angry cat wizard, and an angry cat knight. We will be able to use any angry cat alien, angry cat wizard, or angry cat knight as either a comic character or a game character.

Our goals are simple, but we may face a little problem: each programming language provides different features that allow you to code your application. C# doesn't support multiple inheritance of classes, but you can use multiple inheritance with interfaces or combine interfaces with classes. Python supports multiple inheritance of classes, but it doesn't support interfaces. JavaScript doesn't work with classes or interfaces; therefore, it doesn't make sense to try to emulate multiple inheritance in this language. Instead, we will use the best features and the most natural way of each programming language to achieve our goals.

We will use multiple inheritance of classes in Python, and we will also analyze the possibility of working with abstract base classes. We will use interfaces in C# and constructor functions and composition in JavaScript.

Working with multiple inheritance in Python

We will take advantage of multiple inheritance of classes in Python. First, we will declare the base classes that we will use to create other classes that inherit from them. Then, we will create subclasses that inherit from a pair of classes. We will work with instances of these subclasses that inherit from more than one class. Finally, we will analyze the usage of abstract base classes as another way of achieving the same goal with a more strict structure.

Declaring base classes for multiple inheritance

The following lines show the code for the `ComicCharacter` class in Python:

```
class ComicCharacter:
    def __init__(self, nick_name):
        self._nick_name = nick_name

    @property
    def nick_name(self):
        return self._nick_name

    def draw_speech_balloon(self, message, destination):
        pass

    def draw_thought_balloon(self, message):
        pass
```

The preceding class declares a `nick_name` read-only property, a `draw_speech_ballon` method, and a `draw_thought_balloon` method. The `__init__` method receives `nick_name` as an argument and assigns it to the private `_nick_name` attribute that is encapsulated in the `nick_name` property. In fact, the `__init__` method and the property setter are the only two methods that include code. Our subclasses will override the `draw_speech_ballon` and `draw_thought_balloon` methods.

The following lines show the code for the `GameCharacter` class in Python:

```
class GameCharacter:
    def __init__(self, full_name, initial_score, x, y):
        self._full_name = full_name
        self.score = initial_score
        self.x = x
        self.y = y

    @property
    def full_name(self):
        return self._full_name

    def draw(self, x, y):
        pass

    def move(self, x, y):
        pass

    def is_intersecting_with(self, other_character):
        pass
```

In this case, the class declaration includes the `full-name` read-only property and three attributes: `score`, `x`, and `y`. In addition, the class declaration also includes three empty methods: `draw`, `move`, and `is_intersecting_with`. The subclasses of `GameCharacter` will override these methods.

The following lines show the code for the `Alien` class in Python:

```
class Alien:
    def __init__(self, number_of_eyes):
        self.number_of_eyes = number_of_eyes

    def appear(self):
        pass

    def disappear(self):
        pass
```

In this case, the `__init__` method receives a `number_of_eyes` argument and initializes an attribute with the same name. In addition, the class declares two empty methods: `appear` and `disappear`.

The following lines show the code for the `Wizard` class in Python:

```
class Wizard:
    def __init__(self, spell_power):
        self.spell_power = spell_power

    def disappear_alien(self, alien):
        pass
```

In this case, the `__init__` method receives a `spell_power` argument and initializes an attribute with the same name. In addition, the `Wizard` class declares an empty `disappear_alien` method.

The following lines show the code for the `Knight` class in Python:

```
class Knight:
    def __init__(self, sword_power, sword_weight):
        self.sword_power = sword_power
        self.sword_weight = sword_weight

    def unsheath_sword(self, target):
        pass
```

In this case, the `__init__` method receives `sword_power` and `sword_height` as arguments and initializes attributes with the same name. In addition, the `Knight` class declares an empty `unsheath_sword` method.

Declaring classes that override methods

Now, we will declare a class that overrides and implements all the empty methods defined in the `ComicCharacter` class. The following lines show the code for the `AngryDog` class, a subclass of `ComicCharacter`:

```
class AngryDog(ComicCharacter):
    def _speak(self, message):
        print(self.nick_name + ' -> "' + message + '"')

    def _think(self, message):
        print(self.nick_name + ' ***' + message + '***')

    def draw_speech_balloon(self, message, destination):
        if destination is None:
```

```
            composed_message = message
        else:
            composed_message = destination.nick_name + ", " + message
        self._speak(composed_message)

    def draw_thought_balloon(self, message):
        self._think(message)
```

The `AngryDog` class doesn't override the `__init__` method; therefore, it uses the method declared in its superclass. Whenever we create an instance of this class, Python will use the `__init__` method defined in the `ComicCharacter` class.

The `AngryDog` class overrides the `draw_speech_balloon` method. This method composes a message based on the value of the `destination` parameter and passes a message to the `_speak` method. This method prints this message in a specific format that includes the `nick_name` value as a prefix. If the `destination` parameter is not equal to `None`, the preceding code uses the value of the `nick_name` property.

In addition, the `AngryDog` class declares the code for the `draw_thought_balloon` method that invokes the `_think` method. This method also prints a message that includes the `nick_name` value as a prefix. So, the `AngryDog` class overrides and implements all the empty methods declared in its superclass, that is, the `ComicCharacter` class.

Now, we will declare another subclass of the `ComicCharacter` class. The following lines show the code for the `AngryCat` class:

```
class AngryCat(ComicCharacter):
    def __init__(self, nick_name, age):
        super().__init__(nick_name)
        self.age = age

    def draw_speech_balloon(self, message, destination):
        if destination is None:
            composed_message = self.nick_name + ' -> "'
            if self.age > 5:
                meow = 'Meow'
            else:
                meow = 'Meeeooow Meeeooow'
            composed_message = '{} -> "{} {}"'.format(self.nick_name,
meow, message)
        else:
            composed_message = '{} === {} ---> {}'.format(
                destination.nick_name,
                self.nick_name,
```

```
            message)
        print(composed_message)

    def draw_thought_balloon(self, message):
        print('{} thinks: {}'.format(self.nick_name, message))
```

The `AngryCat` class declares the `__init__` method that overrides the same method declared in the `ComicCharacter` superclass. This method uses `super().__init__` to invoke the `__init__` method of its superclass using `nick_name` as an argument. Then, the preceding code assigns the value of the `age` argument to the `age` attribute.

The `AngryCat` class overrides the `draw_speech_balloon` method. This method composes a message based on the value of the `destination` parameter and the value of the `age` attribute. The `draw_speech_balloon` method prints the generated message. If the `destination` parameter is not equal to `None`, the preceding code uses the value of the `nick_name` property. In addition, the `AngryCat` class declares the code for the `draw_thought_balloon` method.

The `AngryCat` class overrides and implements the empty methods declared in the `ComicCharacter` class. However, this class also declares an additional attribute named `age`.

Declaring a class with multiple base classes

Python allows you to declare a class with multiple base classes or superclasses; therefore, we can inherit attributes, properties, and methods from more than one superclass.

We want the previously coded `AngryCat` class to inherit from the `ComicCharacter` class and the `GameCharacter` class. Thus, we want to use any `AngryCat` instance as a comic character and a game character. In order to do so, we must change the class declaration and add the `GameCharacter` class to the list of superclasses for this class, change the code for the `__init__` method, and override all the empty methods declared in the added superclass.

The following line of code shows the new class declaration. This specifies that the `AngryCat` class inherits from the `ComicCharacter` class and the `GameCharacter` class:

```
class AngryCat(ComicCharacter, GameCharacter):
```

Now, we have to make changes to the `__init__` method because it worked with `super().__init__` to invoke the `__init__` method of its superclass. Now, the `AngryCat` class has two superclasses. It is necessary to call the `__init__` method for both superclasses. In addition, we have to add all the arguments required to call the `__init__` method for the added superclass: `GameCharacter`.

The following code shows the new version of the `__init__` method for the `GameCharacter` class:

```
def __init__(self, nick_name, age, full_name, initial_score, x, y):
    ComicCharacter.__init__(self, nick_name)
    GameCharacter.__init__(self, full_name, initial_score, x, y)
    self.age = age
```

The new `__init__` method receives the `nick_name` argument required to call the `__init__` method of the `ComicCharacter` superclass. Note that we use the `ComicCharacter` class name to call the `__init__` method, and we pass `self` as the first argument. This way, we initialize our instance with the `ComicChracter.__init__` method. Note that we don't use `super()` to call the `__init__` method of the base class because we have two base classes. Also, we need to specify which of them we want to use to call the `__init__` method.

The new `__init__` method also receives the arguments required to call the `__init__` method of the `GameCharacter` superclass: `full_name`, `initial_score`, `x`, and `y`. We use the `GameCharacter` class name to call the `__init__` method for the second superclass, and we pass `self` as the first argument. This way, we initialize our instance using the `GameChracter.__init__` method.

Finally, the new `__init__` method also receives an `age` argument that we use to initialize an attribute with the same name. This way, we invoked the initializers of both superclasses and added our own initialization code.

Now, it is necessary to add the code that overrides all the empty methods defined in the `GameCharacter` class. We have to add the following code to the body of the `GameCharacter` class:

```
def draw(self, x, y):
    self.x = x
    self.y = y
    print('Drawing AngryCat {} at x: {}, y: {}'.format(
        self.full_name,
        str(self.x),
        str(self.y)))

def move(self, x, y):
    self.x = x
    self.y = y
    print('Moving AngryCat {} to x: {}, y: {}'.format(
        self.full_name,
        str(self.x),
```

```
        str(self.y)))

    def is_intersecting_with(self, other_character):
        return self.x == other_character.x and self.y == other_character.y
```

The `AngryCat` class declares the preceding code to override the `draw`, `move`, and `is_intersecting_with` methods declared in the `GameCharacter` class. This class uses multiple inheritance to make `AngryCat` provide implementations for all the empty methods declared in its two superclasses: `ComicCharacter` and `GameCharacter`.

The following lines show the code for a new `AngryCatAlien` class that inherits from the `AngryCat` class and the `Alien` class:

```
class AngryCatAlien(AngryCat, Alien):
    def __init__(self, nick_name, age, full_name, initial_score, x, y,
number_of_eyes):
        AngryCat.__init__(self, nick_name, age, full_name, initial_
score, x, y)
        Alien.__init__(self, number_of_eyes)

    def appear(self):
        print("I'm {} and you can see my {} eyes.".format(
            self.full_name,
            str(self.number_of_eyes)))

    def disappear(self):
            print('{} disappears.'.format(self.full_name))
```

As a result of the preceding code, we have a new class named `AngryCatAlien`. This is a subclass of the `AngryCat` class and the `Alien` class. The `AngryCatAlien` class is also a subclass of the `ComicCharacter` class and the `GameCharacter` class via the `AngryCat` superclass.

The `__init__` method adds the `number_of_eyes` argument to the argument list defined in the `__init__` method declared in the `AngryCat` superclass. We use the first superclass name called `AngryCat` to call the `__init__` method, and we pass `self` as the first argument. This way, we initialize our instance with the `AngryCat.__init__` method.

Then, we use the second superclass class name called `Alien` to call the `__init__` method, and we pass `self` as the first argument. This way, we initialize our instance with the `Alien.__init__` method. Finally, the `AngryCat` class overrides the empty `appear` and `disappear` methods declared in the `Alien` superclass.

The following lines show the code for a new `AngryCatWizard` class that inherits from the `AngryCat` class and the `Wizard` class:

```
class AngryCatWizard(AngryCat, Wizard):
    def __init__(self, nick_name, age, full_name, initial_score, x, y,
spell_power):
        AngryCat.__init__(self, nick_name, age, full_name, initial_
score, x, y)
        Wizard.__init__(self, spell_power)

    def disappear_alien(self, alien):
        print('{} uses his {} to make the alien with {} eyes
disappear.'.format(
            self.full_name,
            self.spell_power,
            alien.number_of_eyes))
```

The `__init__` method adds the `spell_power` argument to the argument list defined in the `__init__` method declared in the `AngryCat` superclass. We use the first superclass name called `AngryCat` to call the `__init__` method, and we pass `self` as the first argument. This way, we initialize our instance with the `AngryCat.__init__` method.

Then, we use the second superclass class name called `Wizard` to call the `__init__` method, and we pass `self` as the first argument. This way, we initialize our instance with the `Wizard.__init__` method. Finally, the `AngryCat` class overrides the empty `disappear_alien` method declared in the `Wizard` superclass.

The `disappear_alien` method receives `alien` as an argument and uses its `number_of_eyes` attribute. Thus, any instance of `AngryCatAlien` would qualify as an argument for this method because it inherits the attribute from the `Alien` superclass.

The following lines show the code for a new `AngryCatKnight` class that inherits from the `AngryCat` class and the `Knight` class:

```
class AngryCatKnight(AngryCat, Knight):
    def __init__(self, nick_name, age, full_name, initial_score, x, y,
sword_power, sword_weight):
        AngryCat.__init__(self, nick_name, age, full_name, initial_
score, x, y)
        Knight.__init__(self, sword_power, sword_weight)

    def _write_lines_about_the_sword(self):
        print('{} unsheaths his sword.'.format(self.full_name))
        print('Sword Power: {} Sword Weight: {}'.format(
```

```
            str(self.sword_power),
            str(self.sword_weight)))

    def unsheath_sword(self, target):
        self._write_lines_about_the_sword()
        if target is not None:
            print('The sword targets an alien with {} eyes.'.format(
                target.number_of_eyes))
```

The `__init__` method adds the `sword_power` and `sword_weight` arguments to the argument list defined in the `__init__` method declared in the `AngryCat` superclass. We use the first superclass name called `AngryCat` to call the `__init__` method, and we pass `self` as the first argument. This way, we initialize our instance with the `AngryCat.__init__` method.

Then, we use the second superclass class name called `Knight` to call the `__init__` method, and we pass `self` as the first argument. This way, we initialize our instance with the `Knight.__init__` method. Finally, the `AngryCatKnight` class overrides the empty `unsheath_sword` method declared in the `Knight` superclass.

The `unsheath_sword` method receives an optional `target` argument as an argument and uses its `number_of_eyes` attribute when it is not equal to `None`. Thus, any instance of `AngryCatAlien` would qualify as an argument for this method because it inherits the attribute from the `Alien` superclass. If the `target` argument is not equal to `None`, the `unsheath_sword` method prints an additional message about the alien that the sword has a target, specifically, the number of eyes.

The following table summarizes all the superclasses for the classes that we have been creating. The superclasses column lists all the superclasses via the inheritance chain:

Class name	**Superclasses**
`AngryDog`	`ComicCharacter`
`AngryCat`	`ComicCharacter` and `GameCharacter`
`AngryCatAlien`	`ComicCharacter`, `GameCharacter`, `AngryCat`, and `Alien`
`AngryCatWizard`	`ComicCharacter`, `GameCharacter`, `AngryCat`, and `Wizard`
`AngryCatKnight`	`ComicCharacter`, `GameCharacter`, `AngryCat`, and `Knight`

Working with instances of classes that use multiple inheritance

Now, we will work with instances of the previously declared classes. The first two lines of the following code creates two instances of the `AngryDog` class named `angry_dog_1` and `angry_dog_2`. Then, this code calls the `draw_speech_balloon` method for `angry_dog_1` twice with a different number of arguments. The second call to this method passes `angry_dog_2` as the second argument because `angry_dog_2` is an instance of `AngryDog`, a class that inherits from the `ComicCharacter` class and includes the `nick_name` property:

```
angry_dog_1 = AngryDog("Brian")
angry_dog_2 = AngryDog("Merlin")

angry_dog_1.draw_speech_balloon("Hello, my name is " + angry_dog_1.
nick_name, None)
angry_dog_1.draw_speech_balloon("How do you do?", angry_dog_2)
angry_dog_2.draw_thought_balloon("Who are you? I think.")
```

The following code creates an instance of the `AngryCat` class named `angry_cat_1`. Its `nick_name` is `Garfield`. The next line calls the `draw_speech_balloon` method for the new instance to introduce Garfield in the comic. Then, `angry_dog_1` calls the `draw_speech_balloon` method and passes `angry_cat_1` as the `destination` argument because `angry_cat_1` is an instance of `AngryCat`, a class that inherits from the `ComicCharacter` class and includes the `nick_name` property. Thus, we can also use instances of `AngryCat` whenever we need an argument that provides either a `nick_name` property or attribute:

```
angry_cat_1 = AngryCat("Garfield", 10, "Mr. Garfield", 0, 10, 20)
angry_cat_1.draw_speech_balloon("Hello, my name is " + angry_cat_1.
nick_name, None)
angry_dog_1.draw_speech_balloon("Hello " + angry_cat_1.nick_name,
angry_cat_1)
```

The following code creates an instance of the `AngryCatAlien` class named `alien_1`. Its `nick_name` is `Alien`. The next line checks whether the call to the `is_intersecting_with` method with the `angry_cat_1` parameter returns `true`. The `is_intersecting_with` method requires an instance that provides the `x` and `y` attributes as the argument. We can use `angry_cat_1` as the argument because one of its superclasses is `ComicCharacter`; therefore, it inherits the attributes of `x` and `y`. The `is_intersecting_with` method will return `true` because the `x` and `y` attributes of both instances have the same value. The line in the `if` block calls the `move` method for `alien_1`. Then, the following code calls the `appear` method:

```
alien_1 = AngryCatAlien("Alien", 120, "Mr. Alien", 0, 10, 20, 3)
```

```
if alien_1.is_intersecting_with(angry_cat_1):
    alien_1.move(angry_cat_1.x + 20, angry_cat_1.y + 20)
alien_1.appear()
```

The following code creates an instance of the `AngryCatWizard` class named `wizard_1`. Its `nick_name` is `Gandalf`. The lines thereafter call the `draw` method and then the `disappear_alien` method with `alien_1` as a parameter. The `draw` method requires an instance that provides the `number_of_eyes` attribute as an argument. We can use `alien_1` as the argument because one of its superclasses is `Alien`; therefore, it inherits the `number_of_eyes` attribute. Then, a call to the `appear` method for `alien1` makes the alien with three eyes appear again:

```
wizard_1 = AngryCatWizard("Gandalf", 75, "Mr. Gandalf", 10000, 30, 40,
100);
wizard_1.draw(wizard_1.x, wizard_1.y)
wizard_1.disappear_alien(alien_1)
alien_1.appear()
```

The following code creates an instance of the `AngryCatKnight` class named `knight_1`. Its `nick_name` is `Camelot`. The next few lines call the `draw` method and then the `UnsheathSword` method with `alien_1` as a parameter. The `draw` method requires an instance that provides the `number_of_eyes` attribute as the argument. We can use `alien_1` as the argument because one of its superclasses is `Alien`; therefore, it inherits the `number_of_eyes` attribute:

```
knight_1 = AngryCatKnight("Camelot", 35, "Sir Camelot", 5000, 50, 50,
100, 30)
knight_1.draw(knight_1.x, knight_1.y)
knight_1.unsheath_sword(alien_1)
```

Finally, the following code calls the `draw_thought_balloon` and `draw_speech_balloon` methods for `alien_1`. We can do this because `alien1` is an instance of `AngryCatAlien`; this class inherits all the methods from one of its superclasses: the `AngryCat` class. These methods were declared as empty methods in the `ComicCharacter` class, that is, one of the superclasses of `AngryCat`. The call to the `draw_speech_balloon` method passes `knight_1` as the `destination` argument because `knight_1` is an instance of `AngryCatKnight`. Thus, we can also use instances of `AngryCatKnight` whenever we need an argument that provides either a `nick_name` property or attribute:

```
alien_1.draw_thought_balloon("I must be friendly or I'm dead...")
alien_1.draw_speech_balloon("Pleased to meet you, Sir.", knight_1)
```

After you execute all the preceding code snippets, you will see the following lines on the Python console (see *Figure 1*):

```
Brian -> "Hello, my name is Brian"
Brian -> "Merlin, How do you do?"
Merlin ***Who are you? I think.***
Garfield -> "Meow Hello, my name is Garfield"
Brian -> "Garfield, Hello Garfield"
Moving AngryCat Mr. Alien to x: 30, y: 40
I'm Mr. Alien and you can see my 3 eyes.
Drawing AngryCat Mr. Gandalf at x: 30, y: 40
Mr. Gandalf uses his 100 to make the alien with 3 eyes disappear.
I'm Mr. Alien and you can see my 3 eyes.
Drawing AngryCat Sir Camelot at x: 50, y: 50
Sir Camelot unsheaths his sword.
Sword Power: 100 Sword Weight:30
The sword targets an alien with 3 eyes.
Alien thinks: I must be friendly or I'm dead...
Camelot === Alien ---> "Pleased to meet you, Sir."
```

```
Python Console
>>> angry_dog_1 = AngryDog("Brian")
angry_dog_2 = AngryDog("Merlin")
>>> angry_dog_1.draw_speech_balloon("Hello, my name is " + angry_dog_1.nick_name, None)
angry_dog_1.draw_speech_balloon("How do you do?", angry_dog_2)
angry_dog_2.draw_thought_balloon("Who are you? I think.")
Brian -> "Hello, my name is Brian"
Brian -> "Merlin, How do you do?"
Merlin ***Who are you? I think.***
>>> angry_cat_1 = AngryCat("Garfield", 10, "Mr. Garfield", 0, 10, 20)
angry_cat_1.draw_speech_balloon("Hello, my name is " + angry_cat_1.nick_name, None)
angry_dog_1.draw_speech_balloon("Hello " + angry_cat_1.nick_name, angry_cat_1)
Garfield -> "Meow Hello, my name is Garfield"
Brian -> "Garfield, Hello Garfield"
>>> alien_1 = AngryCatAlien("Alien", 120, "Mr. Alien", 0, 10, 20, 3)
if alien_1.is_intersecting_with(angry_cat_1):
    alien_1.move(angry_cat_1.x + 20, angry_cat_1.y + 20)
alien_1.appear()
Moving AngryCat Mr. Alien to x: 30, y: 40
I'm Mr. Alien and you can see my 3 eyes.
>>> wizard_1 = AngryCatWizard("Gandalf", 75, "Mr. Gandalf", 10000, 30, 40, 100);
wizard_1.draw(wizard_1.x, wizard_1.y)
wizard_1.disappear_alien(alien_1)
alien_1.appear()
Drawing AngryCat Mr. Gandalf at x: 30, y: 40
Mr. Gandalf uses his 100 to make the alien with 3 eyes disappear.
I'm Mr. Alien and you can see my 3 eyes.
>>> knight_1 = AngryCatKnight("Camelot", 35, "Sir Camelot", 5000, 50, 50, 100, 30)
knight_1.draw(knight_1.x, knight_1.y)
knight_1.unsheath_sword(alien_1)
Drawing AngryCat Sir Camelot at x: 50, y: 50
Sir Camelot unsheaths his sword.
Sword Power: 100 Sword Weight: 30
The sword targets an alien with 3 eyes.
>>> alien_1.draw_thought_balloon("I must be friendly or I'm dead...")
alien_1.draw_speech_balloon("Pleased to meet you, Sir.", knight_1)
Alien thinks: I must be friendly or I'm dead...
Camelot === Alien ---> "Pleased to meet you, Sir."
```

Figure 1

We can use the isinstance function with alien_1. All the following calls to this function will return True because alien_1 is an instance of the AngryCatAlien class and inherits from all its superclasses: AngryCat, Knight, ComicCharacter, and GameCharacter:

```
isinstance(alien_1, AngryCat)
isinstance(alien_1, ComicCharacter)
isinstance(alien_1, GameCharacter)
isinstance(alien_1, Alien)
```

Working with abstract base classes

If we want to be stricter and make sure that our classes provide specific methods, the abc module (**abstract base classes**) allows you to declare abstract base classes in Python. For example, we can use all the features included in this module to declare the ComicCharacter class as an abstract base class in which both draw_speech_balloon and draw_thought_balloon are abstract methods.

The following lines show the code for a new version of the ComicCharacter class, which is declared as an abstract base class:

```
import abc
from abc import ABCMeta
from abc import abstractmethod


class ComicCharacter(metaclass=ABCMeta):
    def __init__(self, nick_name):
        self._nick_name = nick_name

    @abstractmethod
    def draw_speech_balloon(self, message, destination):
        return NotImplemented

    @property
    def nick_name(self):
        return self._nick_name

    @abstractmethod
    def draw_thought_balloon(self, message):
        return NotImplemented
```

The class header specifies `metaclass=ABCMeta`; this is the location in which we specify the superclass. This way, the `abc` module registers a class as an abstract base class and allows you to use specific decorators. Note the usage of the `@absctractmethod` decorator in the `draw_speech_balloon` and `draw_thought_balloon` methods to declare them as abstract methods.

As a result of the declaration of the `ComicCharacter` class with two abstract methods, Python will raise an error whenever we try to create an instance of `ComicCharacter`. For example, we enter the following line in the Python console:

```
scooby = ComicCharacter("Scooby")
```

Python will display the `TypeError: Can't instantiate abstract class ComicCharacter with abstract methods draw_speech_balloon, draw_thought_balloon` error message. This way, we can make sure that we just enable the creation of instances of all the classes that should be instantiated. Without any additional changes to the subclasses of `ComicCharacter`, we can make sure that nobody can create instances of the `ComicCharacter` abstract base class.

Interfaces and multiple inheritance in C#

You can think of an *interface* as a special case of an abstract class. An interface defines properties and methods that a class must implement in order to be considered a member of a group identified with the interface name.

For example, in C#, the language that supports interfaces, we can create the `IAlien` interface that specifies the following elements:

- The `NumberOfEyes` property
- The parameterless method named `Appear`
- The parameterless method named `Disappear`

Once we define an interface, we can use them to specify the required type for an argument. This way, instead of using classes as types, we can use interfaces as types and an instance of any class that implements the specific interface as the argument. For example, if we use `IAlien` as the required type for an argument, we can pass an instance of any class that implements `IAlien` as the argument.

However, you must take into account some limitations of all the interfaces compared with classes. Interfaces cannot declare constructors, destructors, constants, or fields. You cannot specify accessibility modifiers in any members of interfaces. You can declare properties, methods, events, and indexers as members of any interface.

Declaring interfaces

Now, it is time to code all the interfaces in C#. The following lines show the code for the `IComicCharacter` interface in C#. The `public` modifier, followed by the `interface` keyword and the `IComicCharacter` interface name composes the interface declaration. As happens with class declarations, the interface body is enclosed in curly brackets ({}). By convention, interface names start with an uppercase `I` letter:

```
public interface IComicCharacter
{
  string NickName { get; set; }
  void DrawSpeechBalloon(string message);
  void DrawSpeechBalloon(IComicCharacter destination, string message);
  void DrawThoughtBalloon(string message);
}
```

The preceding interface declares the `NickName` string property, the `DrawSpeechBaloon` method overloaded twice, and the `DrawThoughtBalloon` method. The interface includes only the method declaration because all the classes that implement the `IComicCharacter` interface will be responsible for providing the implementation of the two overloads of the `DrawSpeechBalloon` method and the `DrawThoughtBalloon` method. Note that there is no declaration for any constructor.

The following lines show the code for the `IGameCharacter` interface in C#:

```
public interface IGameCharacter
{
  string FullName { get; set; }
  uint Score { get; set; }
  uint X { get; set; }
  uint Y { get; set; }
  void Draw(uint x, uint y);
  void Move(uint x, uint y);
  bool IsIntersectingWith(IGameCharacter otherCharacter);
}
```

In this case, the interface declaration includes four properties: `FullName`, `Score`, `X`, and `Y`. In addition, it also includes three methods: `Draw`, `Move`, and `IsIntersectingWith`. Note that we don't include access modifiers in either the four properties or the three methods.

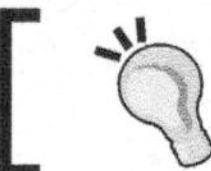

> We cannot add access modifiers to different members of an interface.

The following lines show the code for the `IAlien` interface in C#:

```
public interface IAlien
{
  int NumberOfEyes { get; set; }
  void Appear();
  void Disappear();
}
```

In this case, the interface declaration includes the `NumberOfEyes` property and the `Appear` method and the `Disappear` method. Note that we don't include the code for either the getter or setter methods of the `NumberOfEyes` property. As happens with these methods, all the classes that implement the `IAlien` interface will be responsible for providing the implementation of the getter and setter methods for the `NumberOfEyes` property.

The following lines show the code for the `IWizard` interface in C#:

```
public interface IWizard
{
    int SpellPower { get; set; }
    void DisappearAlien(IAlien alien);
}
```

In this case, the interface declaration includes the `SpellPower` property and the `DisappearAlien` method. As happened in other method declarations included in previously declared interfaces, we will use an interface name as the type of an argument in a method declaration. In this case, the `alien` argument for the `DisappearAlien` method is `IAlien`. Thus, we will be able to call the `DisappearAlien` method with any class that implements the `IAlien` interface.

The following lines show the code for the `IKnight` interface in C#:

```
public interface IKnight
{
  int SwordPower { get; set; }
  int SwordWeight { get; set; }
  void UnsheathSword();
  void UnsheathSword(IAlien target);
}
```

In this case, the interface declaration includes two properties: `SwordPower` and `SwordWeight` and the `UnsheathSword` method, which is overloaded twice.

Declaring classes that implement interfaces

Now, we will declare a class that implements the `IComicCharacter` interface. The following lines show the code for the `AngryDog` class. Instead of specifying a superclass, the class declaration includes the name of the previously declared `IComicCharacter` interface after the `AngryDog` class name and the colon (`:`). We can read the class declaration as, "the `AngryDog` class implements the `IComicCharacter` interface":

```
public class AngryDog : IComicCharacter
{
  public string NickName { get; set; }

  public AngryDog(string nickName)
  {
    this.NickName = nickName;
  }

  protected void Speak(string message)
  {
    Console.WriteLine("{0} -> \"{1}\"", this.NickName, message);
  }

  protected void Think(string message)
  {
    Console.WriteLine("{0} -> ***{1}***", this.NickName, message);
  }

  public void DrawSpeechBalloon(string message)
  {
    Speak(message);
  }

  public void DrawSpeechBalloon(IComicCharacter destination, string
message)
  {
    Speak(String.Format("{0}, {1}", destination.NickName, message));
  }

  public void DrawThoughtBalloon(string message)
  {
    Think(message);
  }
}
```

The `AngryDog` class declares a constructor that assigns the value of the required `nickName` argument to the `NickName` property. This class uses auto-implemented properties to declare the `NickName` property and define both the getter and setter methods.

The `AngryDog` class declares the code for the two versions of the `DrawSpeechBalloon` method. Both methods call the protected `Speak` method. This method prints a message on a console in a specific format that includes the `NickName` value as the prefix. In addition, the class declares the code for the `DrawThoughtBalloon` method that invokes the protected `Think` method. This method also prints a message on the console, which includes the `NickName` value as the prefix.

The `AngryDog` class implements the property and all the methods declared in the `IComicCharacter` interface. However, this class also declares two protected members, specifically two protected methods. As long as we implement all the members declared in the interface or interfaces listed in the class declaration, we can add any desired additional member to this class.

Now, we will declare another class that implements the same interface that the `AngryDog` class implemented, that is, the `IComicCharacter` interface. The following lines show the code for the `AngryCat` class:

```
public class AngryCat : IComicCharacter
{
  public string NickName { get; set; }
  public int Age { get; set; }

  public AngryCat(string nickName, int age)
  {
    this.NickName = nickName;
    this.Age = age;
  }

  public void DrawSpeechBalloon(string message)
  {
    if (this.Age > 5)
    {
      Console.WriteLine("{0} -> \"Meow {1}\"", this.NickName,
message);
    }
    else
    {
      Console.WriteLine("{0} -> \"Meeeooow Meeeooow {1}\"", this.
NickName, message);
    }
```

```
    }

    public void DrawSpeechBalloon(IComicCharacter destination, string
  message)
    {
      Console.WriteLine("{0} === {1} ---> \"{2}\"", destination.
  NickName, this.NickName, message);
    }

    public void DrawThoughtBalloon(string message)
    {
      Console.WriteLine("{0} thinks: {1}", this.NickName, message);
    }
  }
```

The `AngryCat` class declares a constructor that assigns the value of the required `nickName` and `age` arguments to the properties of `NickName` and `Age`. This class uses auto-implemented properties to declare the properties of `NickName` and `Age` and their getter and setter methods.

The `AngryCat` class declares the code for the two versions of the `DrawSpeechBalloon` method. The version that requires only a message argument uses the value of the `Age` property to generate a different message when the `Age` value is greater than `5`. In addition, this class declares the code for the `DrawThoughtBalloon` method.

The `AngryCat` class implements the property and all the methods declared in the `IComicCharacter` interface. However, this class also declares an additional property: `Age`, which isn't required by the `IComicCharacter` interface.

If we comment the line that declares the `NickName` property in the `AngryCat` class, the class won't be implementing all the required members of the `IComicCharacter` interface:

```
//public string NickName { get; set; }
```

If we try to compile the code after commenting the previous line, the IDE will display the `Error 1 ConsoleApplication1.AngryCat' does not implement interface member 'ConsoleApplication1.IComicCharacter.NickName'` error. Thus, the compiler enforces you to implement all the members of an interface. If we uncomment the line that declares the `NickName` property, we will be able to compile the project again, as shown in the following code:

```
public string NickName { get; set; }
```

Interfaces allow you to make sure that all the classes that implement them define all the members specified in the interface. If they don't, the code won't compile.

Working with multiple inheritance

C# doesn't allow you to declare a class with multiple base classes or superclasses; therefore, there is no support for multiple inheritance of classes. A subclass can inherit from just one class. However, a class can implement one or more interfaces. In addition, we can declare classes that inherit from a superclass and implement one or more interfaces.

We want the `AngryCat` class to implement the `IComicCharacter` and `IGameCharacter` interfaces. Thus, we want to use any `AngryCat` instance as the comic character and the game character. In order to do so, we must change the class declaration, add the `IGameCharacter` interface to the list of interfaces implemented by the `AngryCat` class, and declare all the members included in this interface in the `AngryCat` class.

The following lines show the new class declaration that specifies that the `AngryCat` class implements the `IComicCharacter` interface and the `IGameCharacter` interface:

```
public class AngryCat : IComicCharacter, IGameCharacter
```

If we try to compile a project after changing the class declaration, it won't compile because we didn't implement all the members required by the `IGameCharacter` interface. The IDE will display the following seven errors:

- **Error 1**: `'ConsoleApplication1.AngryCat' does not implement interface member 'ConsoleApplication1.IGameCharacter.IsIntersectingWith(ConsoleApplication1.IGameCharacter)'`
- **Error 2**: `'ConsoleApplication1.AngryCat' does not implement interface member 'ConsoleApplication1.IGameCharacter.Move(uint, uint)'`
- **Error 3**: `'ConsoleApplication1.AngryCat' does not implement interface member 'ConsoleApplication1.IGameCharacter.Draw(uint, uint)'`
- **Error 4**: `'ConsoleApplication1.AngryCat' does not implement interface member 'ConsoleApplication1.IGameCharacter.Y'`
- **Error 5**: `'ConsoleApplication1.AngryCat' does not implement interface member 'ConsoleApplication1.IGameCharacter.X'`

- **Error 6**: `'ConsoleApplication1.AngryCat' does not implement interface member 'ConsoleApplication1.IGameCharacter.Score'`
- **Error 7**: `'ConsoleApplication1.AngryCat' does not implement interface member 'ConsoleApplication1.IGameCharacter.FullName'`

We have to add the following code to the body of the `AngryCat` class in order to implement all the properties specified in the `IGameCharacter` interface with auto-implemented properties:

```
public uint Score { get; set; }
public string FullName { get; set; }
public uint X { get; set; }
public uint Y { get; set; }
```

We have to add the following code to the body of the `AngryCat` class to implement all the methods specified in the `IGameCharacter` interface:

```
public void Draw(uint x, uint y)
{
  X = x;
  Y = y;
  Console.WriteLine("Drawing AngryCat {0} at x: {1}, y: {2}", this.
FullName, x, y);
}

public void Move(uint x, uint y)
{
  X = x;
  Y = y;
  Console.WriteLine("Moving AngryCat {0} to x: {1}, y: {2}", this.
FullName, x, y);
}

public bool IsIntersectingWith(IGameCharacter otherCharacter)
{
  return (this.X == otherCharacter.X) && (this.Y == otherCharacter.Y);
}
```

Now, the `AngryCat` class declares the code for all the three methods: `Draw`, `Move`, and `IsIntersectingWith`. These are required to comply with the `IGameCharacter` interface. Finally, it is necessary to replace the previous constructor with a new one that requires additional arguments and sets the initial values of the recently added properties. The following lines show the code for the new constructor:

```
public AngryCat(string nickName, int age, string fullName, uint
initialScore, uint x, uint y)
```

```
{
    this.NickName = nickName;
    this.Age = age;
    this.FullName = fullName;
    this.Score = initialScore;
    this.X = x;
    this.Y = y;
}
```

The new constructor assigns the value of all the additionally required arguments: `fullName`, `score`, `x`, and `y` to the `FullName`, `InitialScore`, `X`, and `Y` properties. Thus, we will need to specify more arguments whenever we want to create an instance of the `AngryCat` class.

The following lines show the code for a new `AngryCatAlien` class that inherits from the `AngryCat` class and implements the `IAlien` interface. Note that the class declaration includes the `AngryCat` superclass and the implemented `IAlien` interface separated by a comma after the colon (`:`):

```
public class AngryCatAlien : AngryCat, IAlien
{
  public int NumberOfEyes { get; set; }

  public AngryCatAlien(string nickName, int age, string fullName, uint
initialScore, uint x, uint y, int numberOfEyes)
    : base(nickName, age, fullName, initialScore, x, y)
  {
    this.NumberOfEyes = numberOfEyes;
  }

  public void Appear()
  {
    Console.WriteLine("I'm {0} and you can see my {1} eyes.", this.
FullName, this.NumberOfEyes);
  }

  public void Disappear()
  {
    Console.WriteLine("{0} disappears.", this.FullName);
  }
}
```

As a result of the previous code, we have a new class named `AngryCatAlien` that implements the following interfaces:

- `IComicCharacter`: This interface is implemented by the `AngryCat` superclass and inherited by `AngryCatAlien`
- `IGameCharacter`: This interface is implemented by the `AngryCat` superclass and inherited by `AngryCatAlien`
- `IAlien`: This interface is implemented by `AngryCatAlien`

The new constructor adds the `numberOfEyes` argument to the argument list defined in the base constructor, that is, the constructor defined in the `AngryCat` superclass. In this case, the constructor calls the base constructor. Then, it initializes the `NumberOfEyes` property with the value received in the `numberOfEyes` argument. The `AngryCat` class implements the `Appear` and `Disappear` methods required by the `IAlien` interface.

The following lines show the code for the new `AngryCatWizard` class that inherits from the `AngryCat` class and implements the `IWizard` interface. Note that the class declaration includes the `AngryCat` superclass and the implemented `IWizard` interface separated by a comma after the colon (`:`):

```
public class AngryCatWizard : AngryCat, IWizard
{
  public int SpellPower { get; set; }

  public AngryCatWizard(string nickName, int age, string fullName,
uint initialScore, uint x, uint y, int spellPower)
  : base(nickName, age, fullName, initialScore, x, y)
  {
    this.SpellPower = spellPower;
  }

  public void DisappearAlien(IAlien alien)
  {
    Console.WriteLine(
    "{0} uses his {1} spell power to make the alien with {2} eyes
disappear.",
    this.FullName,
    this.SpellPower,
    alien.NumberOfEyes);
  }
}
```

As happened with the `AngryCatAlien` class, the new `AngryCatWizard` class implements three interfaces. Two of these interfaces are implemented by the `AngryCat` superclass and inherited by `AngryCatWizard: IComicCharacter` and `IGameCharacter`. The `AngryCatWizard` class adds the implementation of the `IWizard` interface.

The constructor adds a `spellPower` argument to the argument list defined in the base constructor, that is, the constructor defined in the `AngryCat` superclass. The constructor calls the base constructor and then initializes the `SpellPower` property with the value received in the `spellPower` argument. The `AngryCatWizard` class implements the `DisappearAlien` method required by the `IWizard` interface.

The `DisappearAlien` method receives the `IAlien` interface as the argument. Thus, any instance of `AngryCatAlien` would qualify as the argument for this method, that is, any instance of any class that implements the `IAlien` interface.

The following lines show the code for the new `AngryCatKnight` class that inherits from the `AngryCat` class and implements the `IKnight` interface. Note that the class declaration includes the `AngryCat` superclass and the implemented `IKnight` interface separated by a comma after the colon (`:`):

```
public class AngryCatKnight : AngryCat, IKnight
{
  public int SwordPower { get; set; }
  public int SwordWeight { get; set; }

  public AngryCatKnight(
  string nickName, int age, string fullName,
  uint initialScore, uint x, uint y,
  int swordPower, int swordWeight)
  : base(nickName, age, fullName, initialScore, x, y)
  {
    this.SwordPower = swordPower;
    this.SwordWeight = swordWeight;
  }

  private void WriteLinesAboutTheSword()
  {
    Console.WriteLine(
    "{0} unsheaths his sword.",
    this.FullName);
    Console.WriteLine(
    "Sword power: {0}. Sword Weight: {1}.",
    this.SwordPower,
    this.SwordWeight);
```

```
    }

    public void UnsheathSword()
    {
      this.WriteLinesAboutTheSword();
    }

    public void UnsheathSword(IAlien target)
    {
      this.WriteLinesAboutTheSword();
      Console.WriteLine(
      "The sword targets an alien with {0} eyes.",
      target.NumberOfEyes);
    }
  }
```

As happened with the two previously coded classes that inherited from the `AngryCat` class and implemented an interface, the new `AngryCatKnight` class implements three interfaces. Two of these interfaces are implemented by the `AngryCat` superclass and inherited by `AngryCatKnight: IComicCharacter` and `IGameCharacter`. The `AngryCatKnight` class adds the implementation of the `IKnight` interface.

The constructor adds the `swordPower` and `swordWeight` arguments to the argument list defined in the base constructor, that is, the constructor defined in the `AngryCat` superclass. This constructor calls the base constructor and then initializes the `SwordPower` and `SwordWeight` properties with the values received in the `swordPower` and `swordHeight` arguments.

The `AngryCat` class implements the two versions of the `UnsheathSword` method required by the `IKnight` interface. Both methods call the private `WriteLinesAboutTheSword` method and the overloaded version that receives the `IAlien` interface as the argument. It prints an additional message about the alien that the sword has a target: the number of eyes.

The following table summarizes all the interfaces implemented by each of the classes that we have been creating:

Class name	**Implemented interfaces**
`AngryDog`	`IComicCharacter`
`AngryCat`	`IComicCharacter` and `IGameCharacter`
`AngryCatAlien`	`IComicCharacter`, `IGameCharacter`, and `IAlien`
`AngryCatWizard`	`IComicCharacter`, `IGameCharacter`, and `IWizard`
`AngryCatKnight`	`IComicCharacter`, `IGameCharacter`, and `IKnight`

Working with methods that receive interfaces as arguments

The following lines show the code for the `Main` method of a console application that uses all the previously declared classes:

```
public static void Main(string[] args)
{
  var angryDog1 = new AngryDog("Brian");
  var angryDog2 = new AngryDog("Merlin");

  angryDog1.DrawSpeechBalloon(String.Format("Hello, my name is {0}",
angryDog1.NickName));
  angryDog1.DrawSpeechBalloon(angryDog2, "How do you do?");
  angryDog2.DrawThoughtBalloon("Who are you? I think.");

  var angryCat1 = new AngryCat("Garfield", 10, "Mr. Garfield", 0, 10,
20);
  angryCat1.DrawSpeechBalloon(String.Format("Hello, my name is {0}",
angryCat1.NickName));
  angryDog1.DrawSpeechBalloon(angryCat1, String.Format("Hello {0}",
angryCat1.NickName));

  var alien1 = new AngryCatAlien("Alien", 120, "Mr. Alien", 0, 10, 20,
3);
  if (alien1.IsIntersectingWith(angryCat1))
  {
    alien1.Move(angryCat1.X + 20, angryCat1.Y + 20);
  }
  alien1.Appear();

  var wizard1 = new AngryCatWizard("Gandalf", 75, "Mr. Gandalf",
10000, 30, 40, 100);
  wizard1.Draw(wizard1.X, wizard1.Y);
  wizard1.DisappearAlien(alien1);

  alien1.Appear();
  var knight1 = new AngryCatKnight("Camelot", 35, "Sir Camelot", 5000,
50, 50, 100, 30);
  knight1.Draw(knight1.X, knight1.Y);
  knight1.UnsheathSword(alien1);

  alien1.DrawThoughtBalloon("I must be friendly or I'm dead...");
  alien1.DrawSpeechBalloon(knight1, "Pleased to meet you, Sir.");
  Console.ReadLine();
}
```

After you execute the previous console application, you will see the following output on the console output:

```
Brian -> "Hello, my name is Brian"
Brian -> "Merlin, How do you do?"
Merlin -> ***Who are you? I think.***
Garfield -> "Meow Hello, my name is Garfield"
Brian -> "Garfield, Hello Garfield"
Moving AngryCat Mr. Alien to x: 30, y: 40
I'm Mr. Alien and you can see my 3 eyes.
Drawing AngryCat Mr. Gandalf at x: 30, y: 40
Mr. Gandalf uses his 100 spell power to make the alien with 3 eyes
disappear.
I'm Mr. Alien and you can see my 3 eyes.
Drawing AngryCat Sir Camelot at x: 50, y: 50
Sir Camelot unsheaths his sword.
Sword power: 100. Sword Weight: 30.
The sword targets an alien with 3 eyes.
Alien thinks: I must be friendly or I'm dead...
Camelot === Alien ---> "Pleased to meet you, Sir."
```

The first two lines create two instances of the `AngryDog` class: `angryDog1` and `angryDog2`. Then, the code calls the two versions of the `DrawSpeechBalloon` method for `angryDog1`. The second call to this method passes `angryDog2` as the `IComicCharacter` argument because `angryDog2` is an instance of `AngryDog`, a class that implements the `IComicCharacter` interface:

```
var angryDog1 = new AngryDog("Brian");
var angryDog2 = new AngryDog("Merlin");
angryDog1.DrawSpeechBalloon(String.Format("Hello, my name is {0}",
angryDog1.NickName));
angryDog1.DrawSpeechBalloon(angryDog2, "How do you do?");
angryDog2.DrawThoughtBalloon("Who are you? I think.");
```

Bear in mind that when we work with interfaces, we use them to specify the argument types instead of using class names. Multiple classes can implement a single interface; therefore, instances of different classes can qualify as an argument of a specific interface.

The first line in the following code creates an instance of the `AngryCat` class called `angryCat1`. Its `NickName` is `Garfield`. The next line calls the `DrawSpeechBalloon` method for the new instance to introduce `Garfield` as a comic character. Then, `angryDog1` calls the `DrawSpeechBalloon` method and passes `angryCat1` as the `IComicCharacter` argument because `angryCat1` is an instance of `AngryCat`, a class that implements the `IComicCharacter` interface. Thus, we can also use instances of `AngryCat` whenever we need the `IComicCharacter` argument:

```
var angryCat1 = new AngryCat("Garfield", 10, "Mr. Garfield", 0, 10,
20);
angryCat1.DrawSpeechBalloon(String.Format("Hello, my name is {0}",
angryCat1.NickName));
angryDog1.DrawSpeechBalloon(angryCat1, String.Format("Hello {0}",
angryCat1.NickName));
```

The first line in the following code creates an instance of the `AngryCatAlien` class named `alien1`. Its `NickName` is `Alien`. The next line checks whether the call to the `IsIntersectingWith` method with `angryCat1` as a parameter returns `true`. The `IsIntersectingWith` method requires the `IComicCharacter` argument; therefore, we can use `angryCat1`. This method will return `true` because the `X` and `Y` properties of both instances have the same value. The line in the `if` block calls the `Move` method for `alien1`. Then, the code calls the `Appear` method:

```
var alien1 = new AngryCatAlien("Alien", 120, "Mr. Alien", 0, 10, 20,
3);
if (alien1.IsIntersectingWith(angryCat1))
{
    alien1.Move(angryCat1.X + 20, angryCat1.Y + 20);
}
alien1.Appear();
```

The first line in the following code creates an instance of the `AngryCatWizard` class named `wizard1`. Its `NickName` is `Gandalf`. The next line calls the `Draw` method and then the `DisappearAlien` method with `alien1` as the parameter. The `DisappearAlien` method requires the `IAlien` argument; therefore, we can use `alien1`, the previously created instance of `AngryCatAlien` that implements the `IAlien` interface. Then, a call to the `Appear` method for `alien1` makes the alien with three eyes appear again:

```
var wizard1 = new AngryCatWizard("Gandalf", 75, "Mr. Gandalf", 10000,
30, 40, 100);
wizard1.Draw(wizard1.X, wizard1.Y);
wizard1.DisappearAlien(alien1);
alien1.Appear();
```

The first line in the following code creates an instance of the AngryCatKnight class named knight1. Its NickName is Camelot. The next few lines call the Draw method and then the UnsheathSword method with alien1 as the parameter. The method requires the IAlien argument; therefore, we can use alien1, the previously created instance of AngryCatAlien that implements the IAlien interface:

```
var knight1 = new AngryCatKnight("Camelot", 35, "Sir Camelot", 5000,
50, 50, 100, 30);
knight1.Draw(knight1.X, knight1.Y);
knight1.UnsheathSword(alien1);
```

Finally, the code calls the DrawThoughtBalloon and DrawSpeechBalloon methods for alien1. We can do this because alien1 is an instance of AngryCatAlien; this class inherits the implementation of the IComicCharacter interface from its AngryCat superclass. The call to the DrawSpeechBalloon method passes knight1 as the IComicCharacter argument because knight1 is an instance of AngryCatKnight, a class that also inherits the implementation of the IComicCharacter interface from its AngryCat superclass. Thus, we can also use instances of AngryCatKnight whenever we need the IComicCharacter argument.

Working with composition in JavaScript

As previously explained, JavaScript doesn't provide support for interfaces or multiple inheritance. JavaScript allows you to add properties and methods on the fly; therefore, we might create a function that takes advantage of this possibility to emulate multiple inheritance and generate an object that combines two existing objects, a technique known as mix-in.

However, instead of creating functions to create a mix-in, we will create constructor functions and use compositions to access objects within objects. We want to create an application by taking advantage of the feature provided by JavaScript.

Declaring base constructor functions for composition

The following lines show the code for the ComicCharacter constructor function in JavaScript:

```
function ComicCharacter(nickName) {
  this.nickName = nickName;
}
```

The constructor function receives the `nickName` argument and uses this value to initialize the `nickName` field.

The following lines show the code for the `GameCharacter` constructor function in JavaScript:

```
function GameCharacter(fullName, initialScore, x, y) {
  this.fullName = fullName;
  this.initialScore = initialScore;
  this.x = x;
  this.y = y;
}
```

The constructor function receives four arguments: `fullName`, `score`, `x`, and `y` and uses these values to initialize fields with the same name.

The following lines show the code for the `Alien` constructor function in JavaScript:

```
function Alien(numberOfEyes) {
  this.numberOfEyes = numberOfEyes;
}
```

The constructor function receives the `numberOfEyes` argument and uses this value to initialize the `numberOfEyes` field.

The following lines show the code for the `Wizard` constructor function in JavaScript:

```
function Wizard(spellPower) {
  this.spellPower = spellPower;
}
```

The constructor function receives the `spellPower` argument and uses this value to initialize the `spellPower` field.

The following lines show the code for the `Knight` constructor function in JavaScript:

```
function Knight(swordPower, swordHeight) {
  this.swordPower = swordPower;
  this.swordHeight = swordHeight;
}
```

The constructor function receives two arguments: `swordPower` and `swordHeight`. The function uses these values to initialize fields with the same name.

We declared five constructor functions that receive arguments and initialize fields with the same name used for all the arguments. We will use these constructor functions to create instances that we will save within fields of other objects.

Declaring constructor functions that use composition

Now, we will declare a constructor function that saves the `ComicCharacter` instance in the `comicCharacter` field. The following lines show the code for the `AngryDog` constructor function:

```
function AngryDog(nickName) {
  this.comicCharacter = new ComicCharacter(nickName);

  Object.defineProperty(this, "nickName", {
    get: function() {
      return this.comicCharacter.nickName;
    }
  });

  this.drawSpeechBalloon = function(message, destination) {
    var composedMessage = "";
    if (destination) {
      composedMessage = destination.nickName + ", " + message;
    } else {
      composedMessage = message;
    }
    console.log(this.nickName + ' -> "' + composedMessage + '"');
  }

  this.drawThoughtBalloon = function(message) {
    console.log(this.nickName + ' ***' + message + '***')
  }
}
```

The `AngryDog` constructor function receives `nickName` as its argument. The function uses this argument to call the `ComicCharacter` constructor function in order to create an instance and save it in the `comicCharacter` field.

The preceding code defines a `nickName` read-only property whose getter function returns the value of the `nickName` field of the previously created `ComicCharacter` object, which is accessed through `this.comicCharacter.nickName`. This way, whenever we create the `AngryDog` object and retrieve the value of its nickname property, the instance will use the saved `ComicCharacter` object to return the value of its `nickName` field.

The `AngryDog` constructor function declares the `drawSpeechBalloon` method. This method composes a message based on the value of the `message` and `destination` parameters and prints a message in a specific format that includes the `nickName` value as its prefix. If the `destination` parameter is specified, the preceding code uses the value of the `nickName` field or property.

In addition, the constructor function declares the code for the `drawThoughtBalloon` method. This method also prints a message with the `nickName` value as its prefix. So, the `AngryDog` constructor function defines two methods that use the `ComicCharacter` object to access its `nickName` field through the `nickName` property.

Now, we will declare another constructor function that saves the `ComicCharacter` instance in the `comicCharacter` field. The following lines show the code for the `AngryCat` constructor function:

```
function AngryCat(nickName, age) {
  this.comicCharacter = new ComicCharacter(nickName);
  this.age = age;

  Object.defineProperty(this, "nickName", {
    get: function() {
      return this.comicCharacter.nickName;
    }
  });

  this.drawSpeechBalloon = function(message, destination) {
    var composedMessage = "";
    if (destination) {
      composedMessage = destination.nickName + ' === ' +
      this.nickName + ' ---> "' + message + '"';
    } else {
      composedMessage = this.nickName + ' -> "';
      if (this.age > 5) {
        composedMessage += "Meow";
      } else {
        composedMessage += "Meeeooow Meeeooow";
      }
      composedMessage += ' ' + message + '"';
    }
    console.log(composedMessage);
  }

  this.drawThoughtBalloon = function(message) {
    console.log(this.comicCharacter.nickName + ' ***' + message +
'***');
  }
}
```

The `AngryCat` constructor function receives two arguments: `nickName` and `age`. This function uses the `nickname` argument to call the `ComicCharacter` constructor function in order to create an instance and save it in the `comicCharacter` field. The code initializes the `age` field with the value received in the `age` argument.

As happened in the `AngryCat` constructor function, the preceding code also defines the `nickName` read-only property whose getter function returns the value of the `nickName` field of the previously created `ComicCharacter` object, which is accessed through `this.comicCharacter.nickName`. This way, whenever we create an `AngryCat` object and retrieve the value of its nickname property, the instance will use the saved `ComicCharacter` object to return the value of its `nickName` field.

The `AngryDog` constructor function declares the `drawSpeechBalloon` method that composes a message based on the value of the `age` attribute and the values of the `message` and `destination` parameters. The `drawSpeechBalloon` method prints a message in a specific format that includes the `nickName` value as its prefix. If the `destination` parameter is specified, the code uses the value of the `nickName` field or property.

In addition, the constructor function declares the code for the `drawThoughtBalloon` method. This method also prints a message including the `nickName` value as its prefix. So, as happened with `AngryDog`, the `AngryCat` constructor function defines two methods that use the `ComicCharacter` object to access its `nickName` field through the `nickName` property.

Working with an object composed of many objects

We want the previously coded `AngryCat` constructor function to be able to work as both the comic and game character. In order to do so, we will add some arguments to the constructor function and save the `GameCharacter` instance in the `gameCharacter` field (among other changes). Here is the code for the new `AngryCat` constructor function:

```
function AngryCat(nickName, age, fullName, initialScore, x, y) {
  this.comicCharacter = new ComicCharacter(nickName);
  this.gameCharacter = new GameCharacter(fullName, initialScore, x,
y);
  this.age = age;
```

We added the necessary arguments: `fullName`, `initialScore`, `x`, and `y` to create the `GameCharacter` object. This way, we have access to the `GameCharacter` object through `this.gameCharacter`. The following code adds the same read-only `nickName` property that we defined in the previous version of the constructor function and four additional properties:

```
Object.defineProperty(this, "nickName", {
  get: function() {
    return this.comicCharacter.nickName;
  }
});

Object.defineProperty(this, "fullName", {
  get: function() {
    return this.gameCharacter.fullName;
  }
});

Object.defineProperty(this, "score", {
  get: function() {
    return this.gameCharacter.score;
  },
  set: function(val) {
    this.gameCharacter.score = val;
  }
});

Object.defineProperty(this, "x", {
  get: function() {
    return this.gameCharacter.x;
  },
  set: function(val) {
    this.gameCharacter.x = val;
  }
});

Object.defineProperty(this, "y", {
  get: function() {
    return this.gameCharacter.y;
  },
  set: function(val) {
    this.gameCharacter.y = val;
  }
});
```

The preceding code defines the `fullName` read-only property whose getter function returns the value of the `fullName` field of the previously created `GameCharacter` object, which is accessed through `this.gameCharacter.fullName`. This way, whenever we create the `AngryCat` object and retrieve the value of its `fullName` property, the instance will use the saved `GameCharacter` object to return the value of its `fullName` field. The other three new properties (`score`, `x`, and `y`) use the same technique with the difference that they also define setter methods that assign a new value to the field with the same name defined in the `GameCharacter` object.

In this case, the `GameCharacter` object uses fields and doesn't define properties with a specific code—such as validations—in the setter method. However, imagine a more complex scenario in which the `GameCharacter` object requires many validations and defines properties instead of fields. We would be reusing these validations by delegating the getter and setter methods to the `GameCharacter` object just by reading and writing to its properties.

The following code defines the methods that we defined in the previous version of the constructor function:

```
this.drawSpeechBalloon = function(message, destination) {
  var composedMessage = "";
  if (destination) {
    composedMessage = destination.nickName + ' === ' +
    this.nickName + ' ---> "' + message + '"';
  } else {
    composedMessage = this.nickName + ' -> "';
    if (this.age > 5) {
      composedMessage += "Meow";
    } else {
      composedMessage += "Meeeooow Meeeooow";
    }
    composedMessage += ' ' + message + '"';
  }
  console.log(composedMessage);
}

this.drawThoughtBalloon = function(message) {
  console.log(this.nickName + ' ***' + message + '***');
}
```

The following code declares three methods: `draw`, `move`, and `isIntersectingWith`. These methods access the previously defined properties of `fullName`, `x`, and `y`:

```
this.draw = function(x, y) {
  this.x = x;
  this.y = y;
  console.log("Drawing AngryCat " + this.fullName +
  " at x: " + this.x +
  ", y: " + this.y);
}

this.move = function(x, y) {
  this.x = x;
  this.y = y;
  console.log("Drawing AngryCat " + this.fullName +
  " at x: " + this.x +
  ", y: " + this.y);
}

this.isIntersectingWith = function(otherCharacter) {
  return ((this.x == otherCharacter.x) &&
  (this.y == otherCharacter.y));
}
```

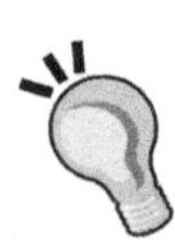

JavaScript allows you to add attributes, properties, and methods to any object at any time. We take advantage of this feature to extend the object created with the `AngryCat` constructor function to `AngryCat` + `Alien`, `AngryCat` + `Wizard`, and `AngryCat` + `Knight`. We will create and save an instance of the `Alien`, `Wizard`, or `Knight` objects and add the necessary methods and properties to extend our `AngryCat` object on the fly.

The following code declares the `createAlien` method that receives the `numberOfEyes` argument. The method calls the `Alien` constructor function with the `numberOfEyes` value received in the argument and saves the `Alien` instance in the `alien` field. The next few lines add the `numberOfEyes` property. This works as a bridge to the `this.alien.numberOfEyes` attribute. The following code also adds two methods: `appear` and `disappear`:

```
this.createAlien = function(numberOfEyes) {
  this.alien = new Alien(numberOfEyes);

  Object.defineProperty(this, "numberOfEyes", {
    get: function() {
      return this.alien.numberOfEyes;
```

```
      },
      set: function(val) {
        this.alien.numberOfEyes = val;
      }
    });

    this.appear = function() {
      console.log("I'm " + this.fullName +
      " and you can see my " + this.numberOfEyes +
      " eyes.");
    }

    this.disappear = function() {
      console.log(this.fullName + " disappears.");
    }
  }
```

The following code declares the `createWizard` method that receives the `spellPower` argument. The method calls the `Wizard` constructor function with the `spellPower` value received in the argument and saves the `Wizard` instance in the `wizard` field. The next few lines add the `spellPower` property. This works as a bridge to the `this.wizard.spellPower` attribute. The following code also adds the `disappearAlien` method that receives the `alien` argument and uses its `numberOfEyes` field:

```
  this.createWizard = function(spellPower) {
    this.wizard = new Wizard(spellPower);

    Object.defineProperty(this, "spellPower", {
      get: function() {
        return this.wizard.spellPower;
      },
      set: function(val) {
        this.wizard.spellPower = val;
      }
    });

    this.disappearAlien = function(alien) {
      console.log(this.fullName + " uses his " +
      this.spellPower + " to make the alien with " +
      alien.numberOfEyes + " eyes disappear.");
    }
  }
```

Finally, the following code declares the `createKnight` method. This method receives two arguments: `swordPower` and `swordHeight` and calls the `Knight` constructor function with the `swordPower` and `swordHeight` values received in all the arguments and saves the `Knight` instance in the `knight` field. The next few lines add the `swordPower` and `swordHeight` properties that work as a bridge to the `this.wizard.swordPower` and `this.wizard.swordHeight` attributes. The following code also adds the `unsheathSword` method. This method receives the `target` argument and uses its `numberOfEyes` field and calls another new method: `writeLinesAboutTheSword`. Note that with the following lines, we finish the code for the `AngryCat` constructor function:

```
this.createKnight = function(swordPower, swordHeight) {
  this.knight = new Knight(swordPower, swordHeight);

  Object.defineProperty(this, "swordPower", {
    get: function() {
      return this.knight.swordPower;
    },
    set: function(val) {
      this.knight.swordPower = val;
    }
  });

  Object.defineProperty(this, "swordHeight", {
    get: function() {
      return this.knight.swordHeight;
    },
    set: function(val) {
      this.knight.swordHeight = val;
    }
  });

  this.writeLinesAboutTheSword = function() {
    console.log(this.fullName + " unsheaths his sword.");
    console.log("Sword Power: " + this.swordPower +
    ". Sword Weight: " + this.swordWeight);
  };

  this.unsheathSword = function(target) {
    this.writeLinesAboutTheSword();
    if (target) {
```

```
            console.log("The sword targets an alien with " +
            target.numberOfEyes + " eyes.");
          }
        }
      }
    }
```

Now, we will code three new constructor functions: `AngryCatAlien`, `AngryCatWizard`, and `AngryCatKnight`. These constructor functions allows you to easily create instances of `AngryCat` + `Alien`, `AngryCat` + `Wizard`, and `AngryCat` + `Knight`.

The following lines show the code for the `AngryCatAlien` constructor function, which receives all the necessary arguments to call the `AngryCat` constructor function. Then, it calls the `createAlien` method for the created object. Finally, the following code returns the object after the call to `createAlien` that added properties and methods:

```
var AngryCatAlien = function(nickName, age, fullName, initialScore, x,
y, numberOfEyes) {
  var alien = new AngryCat(nickName, age, fullName, initialScore, x,
y);
  alien.createAlien(numberOfEyes);
  return alien;
}
```

The following lines show the code for the `AngryCatWizard` constructor function, which receives all the necessary arguments to call the `AngryCat` constructor function. Then, it calls the `createWizard` method for the created object. Finally, the following code returns the object after the call to `createWizard` that added properties and methods:

```
var AngryCatWizard = function(nickName, age, fullName, initialScore,
x, y, spellPower) {
  var wizard = new AngryCat(nickName, age, fullName, initialScore, x,
y);
  wizard.createWizard(spellPower);
  return wizard;
}
```

The following lines show the code for the `AngryCatKnight` constructor function. This function receives all the necessary arguments to call the `AngryCat` constructor function. Then, it calls the `createKnight` method for the created object. Finally, the following code returns the object after the call to `createKnight` that added properties and methods:

```
var AngryCatKnight = function(nickName, age, fullName, initialScore,
x, y, swordPower, swordHeight) {
  var knight = new AngryCat(nickName, age, fullName, initialScore, x,
y);
  knight.createKnight(swordPower, swordHeight);
  return knight;
}
```

The following table summarizes the objects that are included in other objects after we create instances with all the different constructor functions:

Constructor function	Includes instances of
`AngryDog`	`ComicCharacter`
`AngryCat`	`ComicCharacter` and `GameCharacter`
`AngryCatAlien`	`AngryCat`, `ComicCharacter`, `GameCharacter`, and `Alien`
`AngryCatWizard`	`AngryCat`, `ComicCharacter`, `GameCharacter`, and `Wizard`
`AngryCatKnight`	`AngryCat`, `ComicCharacter`, `GameCharacter`, and `Knight`

Working with instances composed of many objects

Now, we will work with instances created using all the previously declared constructor functions. In the following code, the first two lines create two `AngryDog` objects named `angryDog1` and `angryDog2`. Then, the code calls the `drawSpeechBalloon` method for `angryDog1` twice with a different number of arguments. The second call to this method passes `angryDog2` as the second argument because `angryDog2` is an `AngryDog` object and includes the `nickName` property:

```
var angryDog1 = new AngryDog("Brian");
var angryDog2 = new AngryDog("Merlin");

angryDog1.drawSpeechBalloon("Hello, my name is " + angryDog1.
nickName);
angryDog1.drawSpeechBalloon("How do you do?", angryDog2);
angryDog2.drawThoughtBalloon("Who are you? I think.");
```

The following code creates the AngryCat object named angryCat1. Its nickName is Garfield. The next line calls the drawSpeechBalloon method for the new instance to introduce Garfield in the comic character. Then, angryDog1 calls the drawSpeechBalloon method and passes angryCat1 as the destination argument because angryCat1 is the AngryCat object and includes the nickName property. Thus, we can also use AngryCat objects whenever we need the argument that provides the nickName property or field:

```
var angryCat1 = new AngryCat("Garfield", 10, "Mr. Garfield", 0, 10,
20);
angryCat1.drawSpeechBalloon("Hello, my name is " + angryCat1.
nickName);
angryDog1.drawSpeechBalloon("Hello " + angryCat1.NickName, angryCat1);
```

The following code creates the AngryCatAlien object named alien1. Its nickName is Alien. The next few lines check whether the call to the isIntersectingWith method with angryCat1 as its parameter returns true. The method requires an instance that provides the x and y fields or properties as the argument. We can use angryCat1 as the argument because one of its included objects is ComicCharacter; therefore, it provides the x and y attributes. This method will return true because the x and y properties of both instances have the same value. The line within the if block calls the move method for alien1. Then, the following code also calls the appear method:

```
var alien1 = AngryCatAlien("Alien", 120, "Mr. Alien", 0, 10, 20, 3);
if (alien1.isIntersectingWith(angryCat1)) {
  alien1.move(angryCat1.x + 20, angryCat1.y + 20);
}
alien1.appear();
```

The first line in the following code creates the AngryCatWizard object named wizard1. Its nickName is Gandalf. The next lines call the draw method and then the disappearAlien method with alien1 as the parameter. The method requires an instance that provides the numberOfEyes field or property as the argument. We can use alien1 as the argument because one of its included objects is Alien; therefore, it includes the numberOfEyes field or property. Then, a call to the appear method for alien1 makes the alien with three eyes appear again:

```
var wizard1 = new AngryCatWizard("Gandalf", 75, "Mr. Gandalf", 10000,
30, 40, 100);
wizard1.draw(wizard1.x, wizard1.y);
wizard1.disappearAlien(alien1);
alien1.appear();
```

The first line in the following code creates the `AngryCatKnight` object named `knight1`. Its `nickName` is `Camelot`. The next lines call the `draw` method and then the `unsheathSword` method with `alien1` as the parameter. The method requires an instance that provides the `numberOfEyes` field or property as the argument. We can use `alien1` as the argument because one of its included objects is `Alien`; therefore, it includes the `numberOfEyes` attribute:

```
var knight1 = new AngryCatKnight("Camelot", 35, "Sir Camelot", 5000,
50, 50, 100, 30);
knight1.draw(knight1.x, knight1.y);
knight1.unsheathSword(alien1);
```

Finally, the following code calls the `drawThoughtBalloon` and `drawSpeechBalloon` methods for `alien1`. We can do this because `alien1` is the `AngryCatAlien` object and includes the methods defined in the `AngryCat` constructor function. The call to the `drawSpeechBalloon` method passes `knight1` as the `destination` argument because `knight1` is the `AngryCatKnight` object. Thus, we can also use instances of `AngryCatKnight` whenever we need an argument that provides the `nickName` property or field:

```
alien1.drawThoughtBalloon("I must be friendly or I'm dead...");
alien1.drawSpeechBalloon("Pleased to meet you, Sir.", knight1);
```

After you execute all the preceding code snippets, you will see the following output on the JavaScript console (see *Figure 2*):

```
Brian -> "Hello, my name is Brian"
Brian -> "Merlin, How do you do?"
Merlin ***Who are you? I think.***
Garfield -> "Meow Hello, my name is Garfield"
Brian -> "Garfield, Hello undefined"
Drawing AngryCat Mr. Alien at x: 30, y: 40
I'm Mr. Alien and you can see my 3 eyes.
Drawing AngryCat Mr. Gandalf at x: 30, y: 40
Mr. Gandalf uses his 100 to make the alien with 3 eyes disappear.
I'm Mr. Alien and you can see my 3 eyes.
Drawing AngryCat Sir Camelot at x: 50, y: 50
Sir Camelot unsheaths his sword.
Sword Power: 100. Sword Weight: undefined
```

```
The sword targets an alien with 3 eyes.
Alien ***I must be friendly or I'm dead...***
Camelot === Alien ---> "Pleased to meet you, Sir."
```

```
> var angryDog1 = new AngryDog("Brian");
  var angryDog2 = new AngryDog("Merlin");
< undefined
> angryDog1.drawSpeechBalloon("Hello, my name is " + angryDog1.nickName);
  angryDog1.drawSpeechBalloon("How do you do?", angryDog2);
  angryDog2.drawThoughtBalloon("Who are you? I think.");
  Brian -> "Hello, my name is Brian"                                    VM173:42
  Brian -> "Merlin, How do you do?"                                     VM173:42
  Merlin ***Who are you? I think.***                                    VM173:46
< undefined
> var angryCat1 = new AngryCat("Garfield", 10, "Mr. Garfield", 0, 10, 20);
  angryCat1.drawSpeechBalloon("Hello, my name is " + angryCat1.nickName);
  angryDog1.drawSpeechBalloon("Hello " + angryCat1.NickName, angryCat1);
  Garfield -> "Meow Hello, my name is Garfield"                        VM173:147
  Brian -> "Garfield, Hello undefined"                                  VM173:42
< undefined
> var alien1 = AngryCatAlien("Alien", 120, "Mr. Alien", 0, 10, 20, 3);
  if (alien1.isIntersectingWith(angryCat1)) {
      alien1.move(angryCat1.x + 20, angryCat1.y + 20);
  }
  alien1.appear();
  Drawing AngryCat Mr. Alien at x: 30, y: 40                           VM173:165
  I'm Mr. Alien and you can see my 3 eyes.                             VM173:188
< undefined
> var wizard1 = new AngryCatWizard("Gandalf", 75, "Mr. Gandalf", 10000, 30, 40, 100);
  wizard1.draw(wizard1.x, wizard1.y);
  wizard1.disappearAlien(alien1);
  alien1.appear();
  Drawing AngryCat Mr. Gandalf at x: 30, y: 40                         VM173:157
  Mr. Gandalf uses his 100 to make the alien with 3 eyes disappear.    VM173:211
  I'm Mr. Alien and you can see my 3 eyes.                             VM173:188
< undefined
> var knight1 = new AngryCatKnight("Camelot", 35, "Sir Camelot", 5000, 50, 50, 100, 30);
  knight1.draw(knight1.x, knight1.y);
  knight1.unsheathSword(alien1);
  Drawing AngryCat Sir Camelot at x: 50, y: 50                         VM173:157
  Sir Camelot unsheaths his sword.                                     VM173:239
  Sword Power: 100. Sword Weight: undefined                            VM173:240
  The sword targets an alien with 3 eyes.                              VM173:247
< undefined
> alien1.drawThoughtBalloon("I must be friendly or I'm dead...");
  alien1.drawSpeechBalloon("Pleased to meet you, Sir.", knight1);
  Alien ***I must be friendly or I'm dead...***                        VM173:151
  Camelot === Alien ---> "Pleased to meet you, Sir."                   VM173:147
< undefined
```

Figure 2

Summary

In this chapter, you learned how to declare and combine multiple blueprints to generate a single instance. We worked with multiple inheritance of classes in Python. You also learned how to transform a base class to an abstract base class. We declared interfaces in C#. Then, we implemented them with different classes. We also combined interfaces with classes to take advantage of multiple inheritance in C#.

We took advantage of the flexibility of JavaScript that allowed us to add properties and methods to an existing object. We combined constructor functions with composition to generate all the necessary blueprints for our application without creating complex functions that emulate multiple inheritance in a language that wasn't designed with this feature in mind.

Now that we have learned about interfaces, multiple inheritance and composition, we are ready to work with duck typing and generics, which is the topic of the next chapter.

6
Duck Typing and Generics

In this chapter, we will write code that we will maximize code reuse by writing code capable of working with objects of different types. We will take advantage of the different mechanisms to maximize code reuse in each of the three covered programming languages: Python, JavaScript, and C#. We will cover the following topics :

- Understanding parametric polymorphism and generics
- Understanding duck typing
- Working with duck typing in Python
- Working with generics in C#
- Declaring classes that work with one and two constrained generic types in C#
- Working with duck typing in JavaScript

Understanding parametric polymorphism and duck typing

Let's imagine that we want to organize a party of specific animals. We don't want to mix cats with dogs because the party would end up with dogs chasing cats. We want a party, and we don't want intruders. However, at the same time, we want to take advantage of all the procedures we create to organize the party and replicate them with frogs in another party, a party of frogs. We want to reuse these procedures and use them for either dogs or frogs. However, in the future, we will probably want to use them with parrots, lions, tigers, and horses.

In C#, we can declare an interface to specify all the requirements for an animal and write generic code that works with any class that implements the interface. Parametric polymorphism allows you to write generic and reusable code that can work with values without depending on the type while keeping the full static type safety. We can take advantage of parametric polymorphism through generics, also known as generic programming. Once we declare an interface that specifies the requirements for an animal, we can create a class that can work with any instance that implements this interface. This way, we can reuse the code that can generate a party of dogs and create a party of frogs, a party of parrots, or a party of any other animal.

Python's default philosophy is a bit different. Python uses duck typing. Here, the presence of certain attributes or properties and methods make an object suitable to its usage as a specific animal. If we require animals to have a name property and provide sing and dance methods, we can consider any object as an animal as long as it provides the required name property, the sing method, and the dance method. Any instance that provides the required property and methods can be used as an animal.

Let's think about a situation where we see a bird. The bird quacks, swims, and walks like a duck; we can call this bird a duck. Very similar examples related to a bird and a duck generated the duck typing name. We don't need additional information to work with this bird as a duck.

We can add code to constrain types in Python. However, we don't want to write code against Python's most common practices; therefore, we will take advantage of duck typing in Python. We will also take advantage of duck typing in JavaScript. In fact, you might notice that we have been working with duck typing in the examples used in the previous chapters. It is important to note that you can also work with duck typing in C#. However, it requires some workarounds.

Working with duck typing in Python

We will use the `Animal` base class to generalize the requirements for animals. First, we will specialize the base class in two subclasses: `Dog` and `Frog`. Then, we will create a `Party` class that will be able to work with instances of any `Animal` subclass through duck typing. We will work with a party of dogs and a party of frogs.

Then, we will create a `HorseDeeJay` class and generate a subclass of the `Party` class named `PartyWithDeeJay`. The new subclass will work with instances of any `Animal` subclass and any instance that provides the properties and methods declared in the `HorseDeeJay` class through duck typing. We will work with the party of dogs with a DJ.

Declaring a base class that defines the generic behavior

We will create many classes that require the following `import` statement:

```
import random
```

Now, we will declare a base class named `Animal`:

```
class Animal:
    dance_characters = ""
    spelled_sound_1 = ""
    spelled_sound_2 = ""
    spelled_sound_3 = ""

    def __init__(self, name):
        self._name = name

    @property
    def name(self):
        return self._name

    def dance(self):
        print('{} dances {}'.format(self._name, type(self).dance_
characters))


    def say(self, message):
        print('{} says: {}'.format(self._name, message))

    def say_goodbye(self, destination):
        print('{} says goodbye to {}: {} {} {} '.format(
            self._name,
            destination.name,
            type(self).spelled_sound_1,
            type(self).spelled_sound_2,
            type(self).spelled_sound_1))

    def say_welcome(self, destination):
        print('{} welcomes {}: {}'.format(
            self._name,
            destination.name,
```

```
            type(self).spelled_sound_2))


    def sing(self):
        spelled_sing_sound = type(self).spelled_sound_1 + \
            " "
        print('{} sings: {}. {}. {}. '.format(
            self._name,
            spelled_sing_sound * 3,
            spelled_sing_sound * 2,
            spelled_sing_sound))
```

The `Animal` class declares the following four class attributes, all of them initialized with an empty string. The subclasses of `Animal` will override these class attributes with the appropriate strings according to the animal:

- `dance_characters`
- `spelled_sound_1`
- `spelled_sound_2`
- `spelled_sound_3`

Then, the `Animal` class declares an `__init__` method that assigns the value of the required `name` argument to the `_name` protected attribute. This class declares the `name` read-only property that encapsulates the `_name` protected attribute.

The `dance` method uses the value retrieved from the `dance_characters` class attribute to print a message. This message indicates that the animal is dancing. Note the usage of `type(self)` to access the class attribute in a generic way instead of using the actual class name. The `say` method prints the message received as an argument.

Both the `say_welcome` and `say_goodbye` methods receive a `destination` argument that they will use to print the name of the destination of the message. Therefore, whenever we call a method, the destination argument must be an object that has either a name attribute or property in order to be considered as an animal. Any instance of any subclass of `Animal` qualifies as the destination argument for both methods.

The `say_welcome` method uses a combination of strings retrieved from the `spelled_sound_1` and `spelled_sound_3` class attributes to say welcome to another animal. The `say_goodbye` method uses the string retrieved from the `spelled_sound_2` class attribute to say goodbye to another animal.

Declaring subclasses for duck typing

Now, we will create a subclass of `Animal`, a `Dog` class that overrides the string class attributes defined in the `Animal` class to provide all the values that are appropriate for a dog:

```
class Dog(Animal):
    dance_characters = "/-\ \-\ /-/"
    spelled_sound_1 = "Woof"
    spelled_sound_2 = "Wooooof"
    spelled_sound_3 = "Grr"
```

With just a few additional lines of code, we will create another subclass of `Animal`, a `Frog` class that also overrides the string class attributes defined in the `Animal` class to provide all the values that are appropriate for a frog:

```
class Frog(Animal):
    dance_characters = "/|\ \|/ ^ ^ "
    spelled_sound_1 = "Ribbit"
    spelled_sound_2 = "Croak"
    spelled_sound_3 = "Croooaaak"
```

Declaring a class that works with duck typing

The following code declares the `Party` class that takes advantage of duck typing to work with instances of any class that provides either a `name` attribute or property. It implements the `dance`, `say`, `say_goodbye`, `say_welcome`, and `sing` methods. The `__init__` method receives `leader` that the code assigns to the `_leader` protected attribute. In addition, the following code creates a list with `leader` as one of its members and saves it in the `_members` protected attribute. This way, the `leader` argument specifies the first party leader and also the first member of the party, that is, the first element added to the `_members` list:

```
class Party:
    def __init__(self, leader):
        self._leader = leader
        self._members = [leader]
```

The following code declares the `add_member` method that receives the `member` argument. The code adds the member received as an argument to the `_members` list and calls the `_leader.say_welcome` method with `member` as the argument to make the party leader welcome the new member:

```
    def add_member(self, member):
        self._members.append(member)
        self._leader.say_welcome(member)
```

The following code declares the `remove_member` method that receives the `member` argument. It checks whether the member to be removed is the party leader. The `remove_member` method raises a `ValueError` exception if the member is the party leader. If the member isn't the party leader, the code removes this member from the `_members` list and calls the `say_goodbye` method for the removed member. This way, the member who leaves the party says goodbye to the party leader:

```
    def remove_member(self, member):
        if member == self._leader:
            raise ValueError(
                "You cannot remove the leader from the party")
        self._members.remove(member)
        member.say_goodbye(self._leader)
```

The following code declares the `dance` method that calls the method with the same name for each member of the `_members` list:

```
    def dance(self):
        for member in self._members:
            member.dance()
```

The following code declares the `sing` method that calls the method with the same name for each member of the `_members` list:

```
    def sing(self):
        for member in self._members:
            member.sing()
```

Finally, the following code declares the `vote_leader` method. This code makes sure that there are at least two members in the `_members` list when we call this method; if we have just one member, the method raises the `ValueError` exception. If we have at least two members, the code generates a new random leader (who is different from the existing leader) for the party. The code calls the `say` method for the actual leader to explain to other party members that another leader has been voted for. Finally, the code calls the `dance` method for the new leader and sets the new value for the `_leader` protected attribute:

```
    def vote_leader(self):
        if len(self._members) == 1:
            raise ValueError("You need at least two members to vote a
new Leader.")
        new_leader = self._leader
        while new_leader == self._leader:
            random_leader = random.randrange(len(self._members))
            new_leader = self._members[random_leader]
```

```
            self._leader.say('{} has been voted as our new party
leader.'.format(new_leader.name))
        new_leader.dance()
        self._leader = new_leader
```

Using a generic class for multiple types

We have two classes that inherit from the `Animal` class: `Dog` and `Frog`. Both classes have all the required attributes and methods that allow you to work with their instances as arguments of the methods of the previously coded `Party` class. We can start working with instances of the `Dog` class to create a party of dogs.

The following code creates four instances of the `Dog` class: `jake`, `duke`, `lady`, and `dakota`:

```
jake = Dog("Jake")
duke = Dog("Duke")
lady = Dog("Lady")
dakota = Dog("Dakota")
```

The following line of code creates a `Party` instance named `dogsParty` and passes `jake` as the argument. This way, we create the party of frogs in which Jake is the party leader:

```
dogs_party = Party(jake)
```

The following code adds the previously created three instances of `Dog` to the dogs' party by calling the `add_member` method:

```
dogs_party.add_member(duke)
dogs_party.add_member(lady)
dogs_party.add_member(dakota)
```

The following code calls the `dance` method to make all the dogs dance, removes a member who isn't the party leader, votes for a new leader, and finally calls the `sing` method to make all the dogs sing:

```
dogs_party.dance()
dogs_party.remove_member(duke)
dogs_party.vote_leader()
dogs_party.sing()
```

The following lines display the output generated on the Python console after running the preceding code:

```
Jake welcomes Duke: Wooooof
Jake welcomes Lady: Wooooof
```

```
Jake welcomes Dakota: Wooooof
Jake dances /-\ \-\ /-/
Duke dances /-\ \-\ /-/
Lady dances /-\ \-\ /-/
Dakota dances /-\ \-\ /-/
Duke says goodbye to Jake: Woof Wooooof Grr
Jake says: Dakota has been voted as our new party leader.
Dakota dances /-\ \-\ /-/
Jake sings: Woof Woof Woof . Woof Woof . Woof .
Lady sings: Woof Woof Woof . Woof Woof . Woof .
Dakota sings: Woof Woof Woof . Woof Woof . Woof .
```

What about the party of frogs? The following code creates four instances of the `Frog` class: `frog1`, `frog2`, `frog3`, and `frog4`:

```
frog1 = Frog("Frog #1")
frog2 = Frog("Frog #2")
frog3 = Frog("Frog #3")
frog4 = Frog("Frog #4")
```

The following code creates a `Party` instance named `frogsParty` and passes `frog1` as the argument. This way, we create the party of dogs in which `Frog #1` is the party leader:

```
frogs_party = Party(frog1)
```

The following code adds the previously created three instances of `Frog` to the frogs' party by calling the `add_member` method:

```
frogs_party.add_member(frog2)
frogs_party.add_member(frog3)
frogs_party.add_member(frog4)
```

The following code calls the `dance` method to make all the frogs dance, removes a member who isn't the party leader, votes for a new leader, and finally calls the `sing` method to make all the frogs sing:

```
frogs_party.dance()
frogs_party.remove_member(frog3)
frogs_party.vote_leader()
frogs_party.sing()
```

The following lines display the output generated in the Python console after running the preceding code:

```
Frog #1 welcomes Frog #2: Croak
Frog #1 welcomes Frog #3: Croak
Frog #1 welcomes Frog #4: Croak
Frog #1 dances /|\ \|/ ^ ^
Frog #2 dances /|\ \|/ ^ ^
Frog #3 dances /|\ \|/ ^ ^
Frog #4 dances /|\ \|/ ^ ^
Frog #3 says goodbye to Frog #1: Ribbit Croak Croooaaak
Frog #1 says: Frog #2 has been voted as our new party leader.
Frog #2 dances /|\ \|/ ^ ^
Frog #1 sings: Ribbit Ribbit Ribbit . Ribbit Ribbit . Ribbit .
Frog #2 sings: Ribbit Ribbit Ribbit . Ribbit Ribbit . Ribbit .
Frog #4 sings: Ribbit Ribbit Ribbit . Ribbit Ribbit . Ribbit .
```

Working with duck typing in mind

Now, we will create a new class that declares properties and methods that we will call from the subclass of the previously created `Party` class. As long as we use instances that provide the required properties and methods, we can use the instances of any class with the new subclass of `Party`. Here is the code for the `HorseDeeJay` class:

```
class HorseDeeJay:
    def __init__(self, name):
        self._name = name

    @property
    def name(self):
        return self._name

    def play_music_to_dance(self):
            print("My name is {}. Let's Dance.".format(self.name))

    def play_music_to_sing(self):
        print("Time to sing!")
```

The `HorseDeeJay` class declares the `__init__` method that assigns the value of the required `name` argument to the `_name` protected field. The class declares the `Name` read-only property that encapsulates the related field.

The `play_music_to_dance` method prints a message that displays the horse DJ name and invites all its party members to dance. The `play_music_to_sing` method prints a message that invites all its party members to sing.

The following code declares the subclass of the previously created `Party` class. This class can work with the instance of the `HorseDeeJay` class for the `dee_jay` argument required by the `__init__` method. Note that the `__init__` method receives two arguments: `leader` and `deejay`. Both these arguments specify the first party leader, the first member of the party, and the DJ who will make all party members dance and sing. Note that the method calls the `__init__` method defined in the `Party` superclass with `leader` as an argument:

```
class PartyWithDeeJay(Party):
    def __init__(self, leader, dee_jay):
        super().__init__(leader)
        self._dee_jay = dee_jay
```

The following code declares the `dee_jay` read-only property that encapsulates the previously created `_dee_jay` attribute:

```
    @property
    def dee_jay(self):
        return self._dee_jay
```

The following code declares the `dance` method that overrides the method with the same declaration included in the superclass. The code calls the `_dee_jay.play_music_to_dance` method. Then, it calls the `super().dance` method, that is, the `dance` method defined in the `Party` superclass:

```
    def dance(self):
        self._dee_jay.play_music_to_dance()
        super().dance()
```

Finally, the following code declares the `sing` method that overrides the method with the same declaration included in the superclass. The code calls the `_dee_jay.play_music_to_sing` method and then calls the `super().sing` method, that is, the `sing` method defined in the `Party` superclass:

```
    def sing(self):
        self._dee_jay.play_music_to_sing()
        super().sing()
```

Here is the code that we can run on a Python console to create a `HorseDeeJay` instance named `silver`. Then, the code creates a `PartyWithDeeJay` instance named `silverParty` and passes `jake` and `silver` as arguments. This way, we can create a party with a dog leader and a horse DJ, where Jake is the party leader and Silver is the DJ:

```
silver = HorseDeeJay("Silver")
silverParty = PartyWithDeeJay(jake, silver)
```

The following code adds the previously created three instances of `Dog` to the party by calling the `add_member` method:

```
silverParty.add_member(duke)
silverParty.add_member(lady)
silverParty.add_member(dakota)
```

The following code calls the `dance` method to make the DJ invite all the dogs to dance and then make them dance. Then, the code removes a member who isn't the party leader, votes for a new leader, and finally calls the `sing` method to make the DJ invite all the dogs to sing and then make them sing:

```
silverParty.dance()
silverParty.remove_member(duke)
silverParty.vote_leader()
silverParty.sing()
```

The following lines display the console output after we run the added code:

```
My name is Silver. Let's Dance.
Jake dances /-\ \-\ /-/
Duke dances /-\ \-\ /-/
Lady dances /-\ \-\ /-/
Dakota dances /-\ \-\ /-/
Duke says goodbye to Jake: Woof Wooooof Grr
Jake says: Dakota has been voted as our new party leader.
Dakota dances /-\ \-\ /-/
Time to sing!
Jake sings: Woof Woof Woof . Woof Woof . Woof .
Lady sings: Woof Woof Woof . Woof Woof . Woof .
Dakota sings: Woof Woof Woof . Woof Woof . Woof .
```

Working with generics in C#

We will create an `IAnimal` interface to specify the requirements that a type must meet in order to be considered an animal. We will create the `Animal` abstract base class that implements this interface. Then, we will specialize this class in two subclasses: `Dog` and `Frog`. Later, we will create the `Party` class that will be able to work with instances of any class that implements the `IAnimal` interface through generics. We will work with the party of dogs and frogs.

Now, we will create an **`IDeeJay`** interface and implement it in a `HorseDeeJay` class. We will also create a subclass of the `Party` class named `PartyWithDeeJay` that will use generics to work with instances of any type that implement the `IAnimal` interface and instances of any type that implements the `IDeeJay` interface. Then, we will work with the party of dogs with a DJ.

Declaring an interface to be used as a constraint

Now, it is time to code one of the interfaces that will be used as a constraint later when we define the class that takes advantage of generics. The following lines show the code for the `IAnimal` interface in C#. The `public` modifier, followed by the `interface` keyword and the `IAnimal` interface name composes the interface declaration. Don't forget that we cannot declare constructors within interfaces:

```
public interface IAnimal
{
  string Name { get; set; }

  void Dance();
  void Say(string message);
  void SayGoodbye(IAnimal destination);
  void SayWelcome(IAnimal destination);
  void Sing();
}
```

The `IAnimal` interface declares a `Name` string property and five methods: `Dance`, `Say`, `SayGoodbye`, `SayWelcome`, and `Sing`. The interface includes only the method declaration because the classes that implement the `IAnimal` interface will be responsible for providing the implementation of the getter method and the setter method for the `Name` property and the other five methods.

Declaring an abstract base class that implements two interfaces

Now, we will declare an abstract class named `Animal` that implements both the previously defined `IAnimal` interface and the `IEquatable<IAnimal>` interface. The `IEquatable<T>` interface defines a generalized `Equals` method that we must implement in our class to determine equality of instances. As we are implementing the `IAnimal` interface, we have to replace `T` with `IAnimal` and implement `IEquatable<IAnimal>`. This way, we will be able to determine equality of instances of classes that implement the `IAnimal` interface. We can read the class declaration as "the `Animal` class implements both the `IAnimal` and `IEquatable<Animal>` interfaces":

```
public abstract class Animal: IAnimal, IEquatable<IAnimal>
{
  protected string _name;

  public string Name
  {
    get { return this._name; }
    set { throw new InvalidOperationException("Name is a read-only
property."); }
  }

  public virtual string DanceCharacters { get { return string.Empty; }
}
  public virtual string SpelledSound1 { get { return string.Empty; } }
  public virtual string SpelledSound2 { get { return string.Empty; } }
  public virtual string SpelledSound3 { get { return string.Empty; } }

  public Animal(string name)
  {
    this._name = name;
  }

  public void Dance()
  {
    Console.WriteLine(
    String.Format(
    "{0} dances {1}",
    this.Name,
    DanceCharacters));
  }

  public bool Equals(IAnimal otherAnimal)
```

```
    {
      return (this == otherAnimal);
    }

    public void Say(string message)
    {
      Console.WriteLine(
      String.Format(
      "{0} says: {1}",
      this.Name, message));
    }

    public void SayGoodbye(IAnimal destination)
    {
      Console.WriteLine(
      String.Format(
      "{0} says goodbye to {1}: {2} {3} {4}",
      this.Name,
      destination.Name,
      SpelledSound1,
      SpelledSound3,
      SpelledSound1));
    }

    public void SayWelcome(IAnimal destination)
    {
      Console.WriteLine(
      String.Format(
      "{0} welcomes {1}: {2}",
      this.Name,
      destination.Name,
      SpelledSound2));
    }

    public void Sing()
    {
      var spelledSingSound = SpelledSound1 + " ";
      var sb = new StringBuilder();
      sb.Append(String.Format("{0} sings: ", this.Name));
      sb.Append(String.Concat(Enumerable.Repeat(spelledSingSound, 3)));
      sb.Append(". ");
      sb.Append(String.Concat(Enumerable.Repeat(spelledSingSound, 2)));
      sb.Append(". ");
      sb.Append(spelledSingSound);
```

```
        sb.Append(". ");
        Console.WriteLine(sb.ToString());
    }
}
```

The Animal class declares a constructor that assigns the value of the required name argument to the _name protected field. This class declares the Name read-only property that encapsulates the _name private field. The interface requires a Name property; therefore, it is necessary to create both setter and getter public methods. We cannot use auto-implemented properties with a private setter because the setter method must be public. Thus, we defined the public setter method that throws an InvalidOperationException to avoid users of subclasses of this abstract class to change the value of the Name property.

Then, the abstract class declared the following four virtual string properties. All of them define a getter method that returns an empty string that the subclasses will override with the appropriate strings according to the animal:

- DanceCharacters
- SpelledSound1
- SpelledSound2
- SpelledSound2

The Dance method uses the value retrieved from the DanceCharacters property to print a message. This message indicates that the animal is dancing. The Say method prints the message received as the argument. Both the SayWelcome and SayGoodbye methods receive IAnimal as the argument that they use to print the name of the destination of the message. SayWelcome uses a combination of strings retrieved from SpelledSound1 and SpelledSound3 to say welcome to another animal. SayGoodbye uses the string retrieved from SpelledSound2 to say goodbye to another animal.

The Equals method receives another IAnimal as the argument and uses the == operator between the current instance and the received instance to check whether the instances are the same or not. In a more complex scenario, you might want to code this method to compare the values of certain properties to determine equality. In our case, we want to keep the code as simple as possible to focus on generics. We needed to implement the Equals method to conform to the IEquatable<IAnimal> interface.

Declaring subclasses of an abstract base class

We have the abstract `Animal` class that implements `IAnimal` and `IEquatable<IAnimal>`. Now, we will create a subclass of `Animal`, a `Dog` class that overrides the virtual string properties defined in the `Animal` class to provide the appropriate values for a dog, and declare a constructor that just calls the base constructor:

```
public class Dog: Animal
{
  public override string SpelledSound1
  {
    get { return "Woof"; }
  }
  public override string SpelledSound2
  {
    get { return "Wooooof"; }
  }

  public override string SpelledSound3
  {
    get { return "Grr"; }
  }

  public override string DanceCharacters
  {
    get { return @"/-\ \-\ /-/"; }
  }

  public Dog(string name): base(name)
  {
  }
}
```

With just a few additional lines of code, we will create another subclass of `Animal`, a `Frog` class that also overrides all the virtual string properties defined in the `Animal` class to provide the appropriate values for a frog, and declare a constructor that just calls the base constructor:

```
public class Frog: Animal
{
  public override string SpelledSound1
  {
```

```
    get { return "Ribbit"; }
  }

  public override string SpelledSound2
  {
    get { return "Croak"; }
  }

  public override string SpelledSound3
  {
    get { return "Croooaaak"; }
  }

  public override string DanceCharacters
  {
    get { return @"/|\ \|/ ^ ^ "; }
  }

  public Frog(string name)
  : base(name)
  {
  }
}
```

Declaring a class that works with a constrained generic type

The following line declares a `Party` class that takes advantage of generics to work with many types. The class name is followed by a less than sign (<), `T` that identifies the generic type parameter, and a greater than sign (>). The `where` keyword, followed by `T` that identifies the type and a colon (`:`) indicates that the `T` generic type parameter has to be a type that implements the specified interface, that is, the `IAnimal` interface:

```
public class Party<T> where T: IAnimal
```

The following line starts the class body and declares a private `List` (`System.Generics.Collection.List`) of the type specified by `T`. `List`, which uses generics to specify the type of all the elements that will be added to the list:

```
{
  private List<T> _members;
```

The following line declares a public `Leader` property whose type is `T`:

```
public T Leader { get; private set; }
```

The following code declares the constructor that receives the `leader` argument whose type is `T`. This argument specifies the first party leader and the first member of the party as well, that is, the first element added to the `_members` list:

```
public Party(T leader)
{
  this.Leader = leader;
  this._members = new List<T>();
  this._members.Add(leader);
}
```

The following code declares the `AddMember` method that receives the `member` argument whose type is `T`. The code adds the member received as an argument to the `_members List<T>` and calls the `Leader.SayWelcome` method with `member` as the argument to make the party leader welcome the new member:

```
public void AddMember(T member)
{
  this._members.Add(member);
  Leader.SayWelcome(member);
}
```

The following code declares the `RemoveMember` method that receives the `member` argument whose type is `T`. The code checks whether the member to be removed is the party leader. The method throws an exception if the member is the party leader. The code returns the `bool` result, calls the remove method of the `_members List<T>` with the member received as an argument, and calls the `SayGoodbye` method for the successfully removed member. This way, the member that leaves the party says goodbye to the party leader:

```
public bool RemoveMember(T member)
{
  if (member.Equals(this.Leader))
  {
    throw new InvalidOperationException("You cannot remove the leader
from the party.");
  }
  var result = this._members.Remove(member);
  if (result)
```

```
    {
      member.SayGoodbye(this.Leader);
    }
    return result;
  }
```

The following code declares the `Dance` method that calls the method with the same name for each member of the `_members` list. We will use the `virtual` keyword because we will override this method in a future subclass:

```
public virtual void Dance()
{
  foreach (var member in _members)
  {
    member.Dance();
  }
}
```

The following code declares the `Sing` method that calls the method with the same name for each member of the `_members` list. We will use the `virtual` keyword because we will override this method in a future subclass:

```
public virtual void Sing()
{
  foreach (var member in _members)
  {
    member.Sing();
  }
}
```

Finally, the following code declares the `VoteLeader` method. This code makes sure that there are at least two members in the `_members` list when we call this method; if we have just one member, the method throws an `InvalidOperationException`. If we have at least two members, the code generates a new random leader (who is different from the existing leader) for the party. The code calls the `Say` method for the actual leader to explain it to all the other party members that another leader has been voted for. Finally, the code calls the `Dance` method for the new leader and sets the new value for the `Leader` property:

```
public void VoteLeader()
{
  if (this._members.Count == 1)
  {
    throw new InvalidOperationException("You need at least two members
to vote a new Leader.");
```

```
    }

    var newLeader = this.Leader;
    while (newLeader.Equals(this.Leader))
    {
      var randomLeader =
      new Random().Next(this._members.Count);
      newLeader = this._members[randomLeader];
    }

    this.Leader.Say(
    String.Format(
    "{0} has been voted as our new party leader.",
    newLeader.Name));
    newLeader.Dance();
    this.Leader = newLeader;
  }
  }
```

Using a generic class for multiple types

We can create instances of the `Party<T>` class by replacing the `T` generic type parameter with any type name that conforms to all the constraints specified in the declaration of the `Party<T>` class. So far, we have two concrete classes: `Dog` and `Frog` that implement the `IAnimal` interface. Thus, we can use `Dog` to create an instance of `Party<Dog>`.

The following code shows the first few lines of the console application that creates four instances of the `Dog` class: `jake`, `duke`, `lady`, and `dakota`. Then, the `Main` method creates the `Party<Dog>` instance named `dogsParty` and passes `jake` as the argument. This way, we create the party of dogs in which Jake is the party leader:

```
class Program
{
  static void Main(string[] args)
  {
    var jake = new Dog("Jake");
    var duke = new Dog("Duke");
    var lady = new Dog("Lady");
    var dakota = new Dog("Dakota");
    var dogsParty = new Party<Dog>(jake);
```

The dogsParty instance will only accept the Dog instance for all the arguments in which the class definition used the generic type parameter named T. The following code adds the previously created three instances of Dog to the dogs' party by calling the AddMember method:

```
dogsParty.AddMember(duke);
dogsParty.AddMember(lady);
dogsParty.AddMember(dakota);
```

The following code calls the Dance method to make all the dogs dance, removes a member who isn't the party leader, votes for a new leader, and finally calls the Sing method to make all the dogs sing:

```
dogsParty.Dance();
dogsParty.RemoveMember(duke);
dogsParty.VoteLeader();
dogsParty.Sing();
```

We can use Frog to create an instance of Party<Frog>. The following code creates four instances of the Frog class: frog1, frog2, frog3, and frog4. Then, the code creates a Party<Frog> instance named frogsParty and passes frog1 as the argument. This way, we create the party of frogs in which Frog #1 is the party leader:

```
var frog1 = new Frog("Frog #1");
var frog2 = new Frog("Frog #2");
var frog3 = new Frog("Frog #3");
var frog4 = new Frog("Frog #4");
var frogsParty = new Party<Frog>(frog1);
```

The frogsParty instance will only accept the Frog instance for all the arguments in which the class definition used the generic type parameter named T. The following code adds the previously created three instances of Frog to the frogs' party by calling the AddMember method:

```
frogsParty.AddMember(frog2);
frogsParty.AddMember(frog3);
frogsParty.AddMember(frog4);
```

The following code calls the Dance method to make all the frogs dance, removes a member who isn't the party leader, votes for a new leader, and finally calls the Sing method to make all the frogs sing:

```
frogsParty.Dance();
frogsParty.RemoveMember(frog3);
frogsParty.VoteLeader();
```

```
        frogsParty.Sing();
        Console.ReadLine();
    }
}
```

The following lines show the console output after we run the preceding code snippets:

```
Jake welcomes Dakota: Wooooof
Jake dances /-\ \-\ /-/
Duke dances /-\ \-\ /-/
Lady dances /-\ \-\ /-/
Dakota dances /-\ \-\ /-/
Duke says goodbye to Jake: Woof Grr Woof
Jake says: Lady has been voted as our new party leader.
Lady dances /-\ \-\ /-/
Jake sings: Woof Woof Woof . Woof Woof . Woof .
Lady sings: Woof Woof Woof . Woof Woof . Woof .
Dakota sings: Woof Woof Woof . Woof Woof . Woof .
Frog #1 welcomes Frog #2: Croak
Frog #1 welcomes Frog #3: Croak
Frog #1 welcomes Frog #4: Croak
Frog #1 dances /|\ \|/ ^ ^
Frog #2 dances /|\ \|/ ^ ^
Frog #3 dances /|\ \|/ ^ ^
Frog #4 dances /|\ \|/ ^ ^
Frog #3 says goodbye to Frog #1: Ribbit Croooaaak Ribbit
Frog #1 says: Frog #2 has been voted as our new party leader.
Frog #2 dances /|\ \|/ ^ ^
Frog #1 sings: Ribbit Ribbit Ribbit . Ribbit Ribbit . Ribbit .
Frog #2 sings: Ribbit Ribbit Ribbit . Ribbit Ribbit . Ribbit .
Frog #4 sings: Ribbit Ribbit Ribbit . Ribbit Ribbit . Ribbit .
```

Declaring a class that works with two constrained generic types

Now, it is time to code another interface that will be used as a constraint later when we define another class that takes advantage of generics with two constrained generic types. The following lines show the code for the `IDeeJay` interface in C#. The `public` modifier, followed by the `interface` keyword and the `IDeeJay` interface name composes the interface declaration:

```
public interface IDeeJay
{
  string Name { get; set; }

  void PlayMusicToDance();
  void PlayMusicToSing();
}
```

The `IDeeJay` interface declares the `Name` string property and two methods: `PlayMusicToDance` and `PlayMusicToSing`. This interface includes only the method declaration because the classes that implement the `IDeeJay` interface will be responsible for providing the implementation of the getter and setter methods for the `Name` property and the other two methods.

Now, we will declare a class named `HorseDeeJay` that implements the previously defined `IDeeJay` interface. We can read the class declaration as, "the `HorseDeeJay` class implements the `IDeeJay` interface":

```
public class HorseDeeJay: IDeeJay
{
  protected string _name;

  public string Name
  {
    get { return this._name; }
    set { throw new InvalidOperationException("Name is a read-only
property."); }
  }

  public HorseDeeJay(string name)
  {
    this._name = name;
  }

  public void PlayMusicToDance()
```

```
    {
      Console.WriteLine(
      String.Format(
      "My name is {0}. Let's Dance.",
      this.Name));
    }

    public void PlayMusicToSing()
    {
      Console.WriteLine("Time to sing!");
    }
  }
```

The `HorseDeeJay` class declares a constructor that assigns the value of the required `name` argument to the `_name` protected field. The class declares the `Name` read-only property that encapsulates a related field. As happened with the `IAnimal` interface, the `HorseDeeJay` interface requires the `Name` property; therefore, it is necessary to create both setter and getter public methods. We cannot use auto-implemented properties with a private setter method because the setter method must be public. Thus, we defined the public setter method that throws an `InvalidOperationException` to avoid users of subclasses of this abstract class to change the value of the `Name` property.

The `PlayMusicToDance` method prints a message that displays the horse DJ name and invites all the party members to dance. The `PlayMusicToSing` method prints a message that invites all the party members to sing.

The following code declares the subclass of the previously created `Party<T>` class that takes advantage of generics to work with two constrained types. The class name is followed by a less than sign (<), `T` that identifies the generic type parameter, a comma (`,`), `K` that identifies the second generic type parameter, and a greater than sign (>). The first `where` keyword, followed by `T` that identifies the first type and a colon (`:`) indicates that the `T` generic type parameter has to be a type that implements the specified interface, that is, the `IAnimal` interface. The second `where` keyword, followed by `K` that identifies the second type and a colon (`:`) indicates that the `K` generic type parameter has to be a type that implements the specified interface, that is, the `IDeeJay` interface. This way, the `Party<T>` class specifies constraints for the `T` and `K` generic type parameters. Don't forget that we are talking about a subclass of `Party<T>`:

```
public class PartyWithDeeJay<T, K>: Party<T> where T: IAnimal
where K: IDeeJay
```

The following line starts the class body and declares the public `DeeJay` auto-implemented property of the type specified by `K`:

```
{
  public K DeeJay { get; private set; }
```

The following code declares a constructor that receives two arguments: `leader` and `deejay`, whose types are `T` and `K`. These arguments specify the first party leader, the first member of the party, and the DJ that will make all the party members dance and sing. Note that the constructor calls the base constructor, that is, the `Party<T>` constructor with `leader` as the argument:

```
  public PartyWithDeeJay(T leader, K deeJay): base(leader)
  {
    this.DeeJay = deeJay;
  }
```

The following code declares the `Dance` method that overrides the method with the same declaration included in the superclass. The code calls the `DeeJay.PlayMusicToDance` method and then calls the `base.Dance` method, that is, the `Dance` method defined in the `Party<T>` superclass:

```
  public override void Dance()
  {
    this.DeeJay.PlayMusicToDance();
    base.Dance();
  }
```

Finally, the following code declares the `Sing` method that overrides the method with the same declaration included in the superclass. The code calls the `DeeJay.PlayMusicToSing` method and then calls the `base.Sing` method, that is, the `Sing` method defined in the `Party<T>` superclass:

```
  public override void Sing()
  {
    this.DeeJay.PlayMusicToSing();
    base.Sing();
  }
}
```

Using a generic class with two generic type parameters

We can create instances of the `PartyWithDeeJay<T, K>` class by replacing both the `T` and `K` generic type parameters with any type names that conform to the constraints specified in the declaration of the `PartyWithDeeJay<T, K>` class. We have two concrete classes that implement the `IAnimal` interface: `Dog` and `Frog` and one class that implements the `IDeeJay` interface: `HorseDeeJay`. Thus, we can use `Dog` and `HorseDeeJay` to create an instance of `PartyWithDeeJay<Dog, HorseDeeJay>`.

The following is the code that we can add to our previously created console application to create the `HorseDeeJay` instance named `silver`. Then, the code creates the `PartyWithDeeJay<Dog, HorseDeeJay>` instance named `silverParty` and passes `jake` and `silver` as arguments. This way, we can create a party with a dog leader and a horse DJ, where Jake is the party leader and Silver is the DJ:

```
var silver = new HorseDeeJay("Silver");
var silverParty = new PartyWithDeeJay<Dog, HorseDeeJay>(jake, silver);
```

The `silverParty` instance will only accept the `Dog` instance for all the arguments in which the class definition uses the generic type parameter named `T`. The following code adds the previously created three instances of `Dog` to the party by calling the `AddMember` method:

```
silverParty.AddMember(duke);
silverParty.AddMember(lady);
silverParty.AddMember(dakota);
```

The following code calls the `Dance` method to make the DJ invite all the dogs to dance and then make them dance. Then, the code removes a member who isn't the party leader, votes for a new leader, and finally calls the `Sing` method to make the DJ invite all the dogs to sing and then make them sing:

```
silverParty.Dance();
silverParty.RemoveMember(duke);
silverParty.VoteLeader();
silverParty.Sing();
```

The following lines display the console output after we run the added code:

```
My name is Silver. Let's Dance.
Jake dances /-\ \-\ /-/
Duke dances /-\ \-\ /-/
Lady dances /-\ \-\ /-/
Dakota dances /-\ \-\ /-/
```

```
Duke says goodbye to Jake: Woof Grr Woof
Jake says: Lady has been voted as our new party leader.
Lady dances /-\ \-\ /-/
Time to sing!
Jake sings: Woof Woof Woof . Woof Woof . Woof .
Lady sings: Woof Woof Woof . Woof Woof . Woof .
Dakota sings: Woof Woof Woof . Woof Woof . Woof .
```

Working with duck typing in JavaScript

We will create an `Animal` constructor function and customize its prototype to generalize all the requirements for animals. We will create two constructor functions: `Dog` and `Frog` that will use `Animal` as its prototype. Then, we will create a `Party` constructor function that will be able to work with instances of any object that includes `Animal` in its prototype chain through duck typing. We will work with the party of dogs and the party of frogs.

Then, we will create a `HorseDeeJay` constructor function and generate a new version of the `Party` constructor function that will work with any object that includes `Animal` in its prototype and any object that provides the properties and methods declared in the `HorseDeeJay` prototype through duck typing. We will work with the party of dogs with a DJ.

Declaring a constructor function that defines the generic behavior

Now, we will declare the `Animal` constructor function. Then, we will add properties and methods to its prototype:

```
Animal = function() { };
Animal.prototype.name = "";
Animal.prototype.danceCharacters = "";
Animal.prototype.spelledSound1 = "";
Animal.prototype.spelledSound2 = "";
Animal.prototype.spelledSound3 = "";

Animal.prototype.dance = function() {
  console.log(this.name + " dances " + this.danceCharacters);
}

Animal.prototype.say = function(message) {
```

```
    console.log(this.name + " says: " + message);
  }

  Animal.prototype.sayGoodbye = function(destination) {
    console.log(this.name + " says goodbye to "
    + destination.name + ": "
    + this.spelledSound1 + " "
    + this.spelledSound2 + " "
    + this.spelledSound3 + " ");
  }

  Animal.prototype.sayWelcome = function(destination) {
    console.log(this.name + " welcomes "
    + destination.name + ": "
    + this.spelledSound2);
  }

  Animal.prototype.sing = function() {
    var spelledSingSound = this.spelledSound1 + " ";
    var message = this.name + " sings: " + Array(4).
  join(spelledSingSound) + ". " + Array(3).join(spelledSingSound) + ". "
  + spelledSingSound + ". ";

    console.log(message);
  }
```

The preceding code declared the following five properties for the prototype (all of them initialized with an empty string). The constructor functions that will use `Animal` as its prototype will override these properties with the appropriate strings according to the animal. These constructor functions will receive the value to be set to `name` as the argument:

- `name`
- `danceCharacters`
- `spelledSound1`
- `spelledSound2`
- `spelledSound3`

The `dance` method uses the value retrieved from the `danceCharacters` property to print a message. This message indicates that the animal is dancing. The `say` method prints the message received as an argument.

Both the `sayWelcome` and `sayGoodbye` methods receive the `destination` argument that they use to print the name of the destination of the message. Thus, whenever we call this method, the destination argument must be the object that has the `name` property to be considered an animal. Any instance of any constructor function that has `Animal` as its prototype qualifies as the destination argument for both methods.

The `sayWelcome` method uses a combination of strings retrieved from the `spelledSound1` and `spelledSound3` properties to say welcome to another animal. The `sayGoodbye` method uses the string retrieved from the `spelledSound2` property to say goodbye to another animal.

Working with the prototype chain and duck typing

Now, we will create a constructor function that will use `Animal` as its prototype. The `Dog` constructor function overrides the string properties defined in the `Animal` prototype to provide all the appropriate values for a dog. The constructor function receives `name` as the argument and assigns its value to the property with the same name:

```
Dog = function(name) {
    this.name = name;
};
Dog.prototype = new Animal();
Dog.prototype.constructor = Dog;
Dog.prototype.danceCharacters = "/-\\ \\-\\ /-/";
Dog.prototype.spelledSound1 = "Woof";
Dog.prototype.spelledSound2 = "Wooooof";
Dog.prototype.spelledSound3 = "Grr";
```

With just a few additional lines of code, we will create another constructor function that uses `Animal` as its prototype. The `Frog` constructor function also overrides the string class attributes defined in the `Animal` constructor function to provide all the appropriate values for a frog:

```
Frog = function(name) {
  this.name = name;
};
Frog.prototype = new Animal();
Frog.prototype.constructor = Frog;
Frog.prototype.danceCharacters = "/|\\ \\|/ ^ ^ ";
Frog.prototype.spelledSound1 = "Ribbit";
Frog.prototype.spelledSound2 = "Croak";
Frog.prototype.spelledSound3 = "Crooooaaak";
```

Declaring methods that work with duck typing

The following code declares the `Party` constructor function that takes advantage of duck typing to work with instances of any class that provides the `name` property and implements the `dance`, `say`, `sayGoodbye`, `sayWelcome`, and `sing` methods. This constructor function receives a `leader` argument that the code assigns to the `leader` property. In addition, the code creates a `leader` array as one of its members and saves it in the `members` property. This way, the `leader` argument specifies the first party leader and also the first member of the party, that is, the first element added to the `members` array:

```
Party = function(leader) {
  this.leader = leader;
  this.members = [leader];
}
```

The following code declares the `addMember` method that receives the `member` argument. The code adds the member received as an argument to the `members` array and calls the `leader.sayWelcome` method with `member` as the argument to make the party leader welcome the new member:

```
Party.prototype.addMember = function(member) {
  this.members.push(member);
  this.leader.sayWelcome(member);
}
```

The following code declares the `removeMember` method that receives the `member` argument. The code checks whether the member to be removed is the party leader. The method throws an exception if the member is the party leader. If the member isn't the party leader, the code removes the member from the `members` array and calls the `sayGoodbye` method for the removed member. This way, the member who leaves the party says goodbye to the party leader:

```
Party.prototype.removeMember = function(member) {
  if (member == this.leader) {
    throw "You cannot remove the leader from the party";
  }
  var index = this.members.indexOf(member);
  if (index > -1) {
    this.members.splice(index, 1);
    member.sayGoodbye(this.leader);
    return true;
  }
  else {
    return false;
  }
}
```

The following code declares the `dance` method that calls the method with the same name for each member of the `members` array:

```
Party.prototype.dance = function() {
  this.members.forEach(function (member) { member.dance(); });
}
```

The following code declares the `sing` method that calls the method with the same name for each member of the `members` array:

```
Party.prototype.sing = function() {
  this.members.forEach(function (member) { member.sing(); });
}
```

Finally, the following code declares the `voteLeader` method. The code makes sure that there are at least two members in the `members` array when we call this method; if we have just one member, the method throws an exception. If we have at least two members, the code generates a new pseudo-random leader (who is different from the existing leader) for the party. The code calls the `say` method for the actual leader to make it explain to the other party members that another leader has been voted for. Finally, the code calls the `dance` method for the new leader and sets the new value for the `leader` property:

```
Party.prototype.voteLeader = function() {
  if (this.members.length == 1) {
    throw "You need at least two members to vote a new Leader.";
  }
  var newLeader = this.leader;
  while (newLeader == this.leader) {
    var randomLeader = Math.floor(Math.random() * (this.members.length
- 1)) + 1;
    newLeader = this.members[randomLeader];
  }
  this.leader.say(newLeader.name + " has been voted as our new party
leader.");
  newLeader.dance();
  this.leader = newLeader;
}
```

Using generic methods for multiple objects

We have two constructor functions: `Dog` and `Frog` that use the `Animal` constructor function as their prototype. Both these constructor functions define all the properties and methods required that allows you to work with their instances as arguments of the methods of the previously coded `Party` prototype methods. We can start working with `Dog` objects to create the party of dogs.

The following code creates four `Dog` objects: `jake`, `duke`, `lady` and `dakota`:

```
var jake = new Dog("Jake");
var duke = new Dog("Duke");
var lady = new Dog("Lady");
var dakota = new Dog("Dakota");
```

The following line creates a `Party` object named `dogsParty` and passes `jake` as the argument. This way, we create the party of dogs in which Jake is the party leader:

```
var dogsParty = new Party(jake);
```

The following code adds the previously created three `Dog` objects to the dogs' party by calling the `addMember` method:

```
dogsParty.addMember(duke);
dogsParty.addMember(lady);
dogsParty.addMember(dakota);
```

The following code calls the `dance` method to make all the dogs dance, removes a member who isn't the party leader, votes for a new leader, and finally calls the `sing` method to make all the dogs sing:

```
dogsParty.dance();
dogsParty.removeMember(duke);
dogsParty.voteLeader();
dogsParty.sing();
```

The following lines display the output generated on the JavaScript console after running the preceding code snippets:

```
Jake welcomes Duke: Wooooof
Jake welcomes Lady: Wooooof
Jake welcomes Dakota: Wooooof
Jake dances /-\ \-\ /-/
Duke dances /-\ \-\ /-/
Lady dances /-\ \-\ /-/
Dakota dances /-\ \-\ /-/
```

```
Duke says goodbye to Jake: Woof Wooooof Grr
Jake says: Dakota has been voted as our new party leader.
Dakota dances /-\ \-\ /-/
Jake sings: Woof Woof Woof . Woof Woof . Woof .
Lady sings: Woof Woof Woof . Woof Woof . Woof .
Dakota sings: Woof Woof Woof . Woof Woof . Woof .
```

Now, what about the party of frogs? The following code creates four `Frog` objects: `frog1`, `frog2`, `frog3`, and `frog4`:

```
var frog1 = new Frog("Frog #1");
var frog2 = new Frog("Frog #2");
var frog3 = new Frog("Frog #3");
var frog4 = new Frog("Frog #4");
```

The following line creates a `Party` object named `frogsParty` and passes `frog1` as the argument. This way, we create the party of dogs in which `Frog #1` is the party leader:

```
var frogsParty = new Party(frog1);
```

The following code adds the previously created three `Frog` objects to the frogs' party by calling the `addMember` method:

```
frogsParty.addMember(frog2);
frogsParty.addMember(frog3);
frogsParty.addMember(frog4);
```

The following code calls the `dance` method to make all the frogs dance, removes a member who isn't the party leader, votes for a new leader, and finally calls the `sing` method to make all the frogs sing:

```
frogsParty.dance();
frogsParty.removeMember(frog3);
frogsParty.voteLeader();
frogsParty.sing();
```

The following lines display the output generated on the JavaScript console after running the previous code:

```
Frog #1 welcomes Frog #2: Croak
Frog #1 welcomes Frog #3: Croak
Frog #1 welcomes Frog #4: Croak
Frog #1 dances /|\ \|/ ^ ^
Frog #2 dances /|\ \|/ ^ ^
```

```
Frog #3 dances /|\ \|/ ^ ^
Frog #4 dances /|\ \|/ ^ ^
Frog #3 says goodbye to Frog #1: Ribbit Croak Croooaaak
Frog #1 says: Frog #2 has been voted as our new party leader.
Frog #2 dances /|\ \|/ ^ ^
Frog #1 sings: Ribbit Ribbit Ribbit . Ribbit Ribbit . Ribbit .
Frog #2 sings: Ribbit Ribbit Ribbit . Ribbit Ribbit . Ribbit .
Frog #4 sings: Ribbit Ribbit Ribbit . Ribbit Ribbit . Ribbit .
```

Working with duck typing in mind

Now, we will create a new constructor function that declares properties and methods that we will call from an object that includes `Party` in its prototype chain. As long as we use objects that provide all the required properties and methods, we can use all the objects created by using any constructor function with the new object. The following lines show the code for the `HorseDeeJay` constructor function:

```
HorseDeeJay = function(name) {
  this.name = name;
};
HorseDeeJay.prototype.playMusicToDance = function() {
  console.log("My name is " + this.name + ". Let's Dance.");
}
HorseDeeJay.prototype.playMusicToSing = function() {
  console.log("Time to sing!");
}
```

The `HorseDeeJay` constructor function class assigns the value of the `name` argument to the `name` property. The `playMusicToDance` method prints a message that displays the horse DJ name and invites all the party members to dance. The `playMusicToSing` method prints a message that invites all the party members to sing.

Now, we will make a few changes to the previously created `Party` constructor function and its prototype to allow it to work with a `HorseDeeJay` object. The following code shows the new version of the constructor function that receives two arguments: `leader` and `deejay`. These arguments specify the first party leader, the first member of the party, and the DJ that will make all the party members dance and sing:

```
Party = function(leader, deeJay) {
  this.leader = leader;
  this.deeJay = deeJay;
  this.members = [leader];
}
```

The following code declares the new version of the `dance` method. The code calls the `deeJay.playMusicToDance` method and then calls the `dance` method for each member of the party:

```
Party.prototype.dance = function() {
  this.deeJay.playMusicToDance();
  this.members.forEach(function (member) { member.dance(); });
}
```

Finally, the following code declares the new version of the `sing` method. The code calls the `deeJay.playMusicToSing` method and then calls the `sing` method for each member of the party:

```
Party.prototype.sing = function() {
  this.deeJay.playMusicToSing();
  this.members.forEach(function (member) { member.sing(); });
}
```

The other methods defined for the `Party` prototype are the same that we defined in the previous version. The following code shows the lines that we can run on the JavaScript console to create a `HorseDeeJay` object named `silver`. Then, the code creates a `PartyWithDeeJay` object named `silverParty` and passes `jake` and `silver` as arguments. This way, we create a party with a dog leader and a horse DJ in which Jake is the party leader and Silver is the DJ:

```
var silver = new HorseDeeJay("Silver");
var silverParty = new Party(jake, silver);
```

The following code adds the previously created three `Dog` objects to the party by calling the `addMember` method:

```
silverParty.addMember(duke);
silverParty.addMember(lady);
silverParty.addMember(dakota);
```

The following code calls the `dance` method to make the DJ invite all the dogs to dance and then make them dance. Then, the code removes a member who isn't the party leader, votes for a new leader, and finally calls the `sing` method to make the DJ invite all the dogs to sing and then make them sing:

```
silverParty.dance();
silverParty.removeMember(duke);
silverParty.voteLeader();
silverParty.sing();
```

The following lines display the JavaScript console output after we run the added code:

```
My name is Silver. Let's Dance.
Jake dances /-\ \-\ /-/
Duke dances /-\ \-\ /-/
Lady dances /-\ \-\ /-/
Dakota dances /-\ \-\ /-/
Duke says goodbye to Jake: Woof Wooooof Grr
Jake says: Dakota has been voted as our new party leader.
Dakota dances /-\ \-\ /-/
Time to sing!
Jake sings: Woof Woof Woof . Woof Woof . Woof .
Lady sings: Woof Woof Woof . Woof Woof . Woof .
Dakota sings: Woof Woof Woof . Woof Woof . Woof .
```

Summary

In this chapter, you learned how to maximize code reuse by writing code capable of working with objects of different types. We took advantage of duck typing in Python and JavaScript. We worked with interfaces and generics in C#. We created classes capable of working with one and two constrained generic types.

Now that you learned how to work with duck typing and generics, we are ready to organize complex object-oriented code in Python, JavaScript, and C#, which is the topic of the next chapter.

7
Organization of Object-Oriented Code

In this chapter, we will write code for a complex application that requires dozens of classes, interfaces, and constructor functions according to the programing language that we use. We will take advantage of the different available features to organize a large number of pieces of code in each of the three covered programming languages: Python, JavaScript, and C#. We will:

- Understand the importance of organizing object-oriented code
- Think about the best ways to organize object-oriented code
- Work with source files organized in folders and module hierarchies in Python
- Work with folders, namespaces, and namespace hierarchies in C#
- Combine objects, nested objects, and constructor functions in JavaScript

Thinking about the best ways to organize code

When you have just a few classes or constructor functions and their prototypes, hundreds of lines of object-oriented code are easy to organize and maintain. However, as the number of object-oriented blueprints start to increase, it is necessary to follow some rules to organize the code and make it easy to maintain.

A very well written object-oriented code can generate a maintenance headache if it isn't organized in an effective way. We don't have to forget that a well written object-oriented code promotes code reuse.

As you learned in the previous six chapters, each programming language provides different elements and resources to generate object-oriented code. In addition, each programming language provides its own mechanisms that allow you to organize and group different object-oriented elements. Thus, it is necessary to define rules for each of the three programming languages: Python, C# and, JavaScript.

Imagine that we have to create and furnish house floor plans with a drawing software that allows you to load objects from files. We have a huge amount of objects to compose our floor plan, such as entry doors, interior doors, square rooms, interior walls, windows, spiral stairs, straight stairs, and kitchen islands. If we use a single folder in our file system to save all the object files, it will take us a huge amount of time to select the desired object each time we have to add an object to our floor plan.

We can organize our objects in the following five folders:

- `Build`
- `Furnish`
- `Decorate`
- `Landscape`
- `Outdoor`

Now, whenever we need bathroom furniture, we will explore the `Furnish` folder. Whenever we need outdoor structures, we will explore the `Outdoor` folder. However, there are still too many objects in each of these folders. For example, the `Build` folder includes the following types of objects:

- `Rooms`
- `Walls`
- `Areas`
- `Doors`
- `Windows`
- `Stairs`
- `Fireplaces`

We can create subfolders within each main category folder to provide a better organization of our object files. The `Build` category will have one subfolder for each of the types of objects indicated in the previous list.

The `Furnish` category will have the following subfolders:

- `Living room`
- `Dining room`
- `Kitchen`
- `Bathroom`
- `Bedroom`
- `Office`
- `Laundry and utility`
- `Other rooms`

The `Decorate` category will have the following subfolders:

- `Paint and walls`
- `Flooring`
- `Countertops`
- `Art and decor`
- `Electronics`
- `Lighting and fans`

The `Landscape` category will have the following subfolders:

- `Areas definition`
- `Materials`
- `Trees and plants`

Finally, the `Outdoor` category will have the following subfolders:

- `Living`
- `Accessories`
- `Structures`

This way, the `Build/Rooms` subfolder will include the following four objects:

- `Square room`
- `L-shaped room`
- `Small room`
- `Closet`

However, the `Furnish/Bedroom` subfolder includes too many objects that we can organize in seven types. So, we will create the following six subfolders:

- `Beds`
- `Kids' beds`
- `Night tables`
- `Dressers`
- `Mirrors`
- `Nursery`

Whenever we need bedroom mirrors, we will go to the `Furnish/Bedroom/Mirrors` subfolder. Whenever we need beds, we will go to the `Furnish/Bedroom/Beds` subfolder. Our objects are organized in a hierarchical directory tree.

Now, let's go back to object-oriented code. Instead of objects, we will have to organize classes, interfaces, constructor functions, and prototypes according to the programming language used. For example, if we have a class that defines the blueprint for a square room, we can organize it in such a way that we can find it in a `build.rooms` container. This way, we will find all the classes related to `Build/Rooms` in the `build.rooms` container. If we need to add another class related to `Build/Rooms`, we would add it in the `build.rooms` container.

Organizing object-oriented code in Python

Python makes it easy to logically organize object-oriented code with modules. We will work with a hierarchy of folders to organize the code of an application that allows you to create and furnish house floor plans. Then, we will use code from different folders and the source files of Python.

Working with source files organized in folders

We will create the following six folders to organize the code in our house floor plan layout application. Then, we will add subfolders and the source files of Python to each of the previously created folders:

- `Build`
- `Decorate`
- `Furnish`
- `General`

- `Landscape`
- `Outdoor`

We will include all the base classes in the `general` folder. The following lines show the code for the `general/floor_plan_element.py` Python source file that declares a `FloorPlanElement` base class. We will use this class as the superclass for all the classes that specialize the floor plan element:

```
class FloorPlanElement:
    category = "Undefined"
    description = "Undefined"

    def __init__(self, x, y, width, height, parent):
        self.x = x
        self.y = y
        self.width = width
        self.height = height
        self.parent = parent

    def move_to(self, x, y):
        self.x = x
        self.y = y

    def print_category(self):
        print(type(self).category)

    def print_description(self):
        print(type(self).description)

    def draw(self):
        self.print_category()
        self.print_description()
        print("X: " + str(self.x) +
              ", Y: " + str(self.y) +
              ". Width: " + str(self.width) +
              ", Height: " + str(self.height) + ".")
```

The `FloorPlanElement` class declares two class attributes that the subclasses will override: `category` and `description`. The class declares an `__init__` method that receives five arguments: `x`, `y`, `width`, `height`, and `parent`. The `__init__` method initializes attributes with the same name using all the values received as arguments. This way, each `FloorPlanElement` instance will have a 2D location specified by `x` and `y`, `width` and `height`, and a `parent` element.

In addition, the FloorPlanElement class declares the following instance methods:

- move_to: This method moves the floor plan element to the new location specified by the x and y arguments
- print_category: This method prints the value of the category class attribute
- print_description: This method prints the value of the description class attribute
- draw: This method prints the category, description, 2D location, and width and height of the floor plan element

The FloorPlanElement class is located in the general/floor_plan_element.py file. All the classes that specialize floor plan elements will inherit from the FloorPlanElement class. These classes will be located in other Python source files that will have to let Python know that they want to use the FloorPlanElement class that is located in another module, that is, in another Python source file.

Importing modules

We will create the following Python source files in the previously created Build folder. We won't add code to all the files in order to keep our example simple. However, we will imagine that we have a more complex project:

- areas.py
- doors.py
- fireplaces.py
- rooms.py
- stairs.py
- walls.py
- windows.py

Here is the code for the build/rooms.py Python source file that declares five classes: Room, SquareRoom, LShapedRoom, SmallRoom, and Closet:

```
from general.floor_plan_element import FloorPlanElement


class Room(FloorPlanElement):
    category = "Room"


class SquareRoom(Room):
```

```
        description = "Square room"

        def __init__(self, x, y, width, parent):
            super().__init__(x, y, width, width, parent)


    class LShapedRoom(Room):
        description = "L-Shaped room"


    class SmallRoom(Room):
        description = "Small room"


    class Closet(Room):
        description = "Closet"
```

The first line in the preceding code uses the `from` statement to import a specific class from a module into the current namespace. To be specific, the code imports the `FloorPlanElement` class from the `general.floor_plan_element` module, that is, from the `general/floor_plan_element.py` file, as shown in the following line:

```
from general.floor_plan_element import FloorPlanElement
```

This way, the next few lines declare the `Room` class as a subclass of the `FloorPlanElement` class as if the class were defined in the same Python source file. This class overrides the value of the category class attribute with the `"Room"` value. The `SquareRoom` class represents a square room; therefore, it isn't necessary to specify the width and height to create an instance of this type of room. The `__init__` method uses the `width` value to specify the values for both width and height in the call to the `__init__` method defined in the superclass, that is, the `FloorPlanElement` class. Each subclass of the `Room` class overrides the `description` class attribute with an appropriate value.

In this case, the `from` statement combined with the `import` statement imported just one class definition into the current namespace. We can use the following import statement to import all the items from the `general.floor_plan_element` module, that is, from the `general/floor_plan_element.py` file. However, we must be careful when we specify `*` after the import statement because we should import only the elements that we need from the other module:

```
from general.floor_plan_element import *
```

Another option is to execute an import statement in order to import the required module. However, we would need to make changes to the `Room` class declaration and add the modules path as a prefix to `FloorPlanElement`, that is, we have to replace `FloorPlanElement` with `general.floor_plan_element.FloorPlanElement`, as shown in the following code:

```
import general.floor_plan_element


class Room(general.floor_plan_element.FloorPlanElement):
    category = "Room"
```

Here is the code for the `build/doors.py` Python source file that declares two classes: `Door` and `EntryDoor`:

```
from general.floor_plan_element import FloorPlanElement


class Door(FloorPlanElement):
    category = "Door"


class EntryDoor(Door):
    description = "Entry Door"
```

The first line in the preceding code uses the `from` statement to import the `FloorPlanElement` class from the `general.floor_plan_element` module, that is, from the `general/floor_plan_element.py` file. The next few lines declare the `Door` class as a subclass of the `FloorPlanElement` class as if the class were defined in the same Python source file. The `FloorPlanElement` class overrides the value of the category class attribute with the `"Door"` value. The `EntryDoor` class represents an entry door and just overrides the `description` class attribute with an appropriate value.

We will create the following Python source files in the previously created `Decorate` folder:

- `art_and_decor.py`
- `countertops.py`
- `electronics.py`
- `flooring.py`
- `lighting_and_fans.py`
- `paint_and_walls.py`

We will create the following Python source files in the previously created `Furnish` folder:

- `bathroom.py`
- `dining_room.py`
- `kitchen.py`
- `laundry_and_utility.py`
- `living_room.py`
- `office.py`
- `other_rooms.py`

We will create a `Bedroom` subfolder within the `Furnish` folder. Then, we will create the following Python source files within the `Furnish/Bedroom` subfolder:

- `beds.py`
- `dressers.py`
- `kids_beds.py`
- `mirrors.py`
- `night_tables.py`
- `nursery.py`

The following lines show the code for the `Furnish/Bedroom/beds.py` Python source file that declares two classes: `Bed` and `FabricBed`:

```
from general.floor_plan_element import FloorPlanElement


class Bed(FloorPlanElement):
    category = "Bed"
    description = "Generic bed"


class FabricBed(Bed):
    description = "Fabric bed"
```

The first line in the preceding code uses the `from` statement to import the `FloorPlanElement` class from the `general.floor_plan_element` module, that is, from the `general/floor_plan_element.py` file. The next few lines declare the `Bed` class as a subclass of the `FloorPlanElement` class as if the class were defined in the same Python source file. The `FloorPlanElement` class overrides the value of the `category` class attribute with the `"Bed"` value and `description` with `"Generic Bed"`. The `FabricBed` class represents a fabric bed and just overrides the `description` class attribute with an appropriate value.

We will create the following Python source files in the previously created `Landscape` folder:

- `areas_definition.py`
- `materials.py`
- `trees_and_plants.py`

Finally, we will create the following Python source files in the previously created `Outdoor` folder:

- `accessories.py`
- `living.py`
- `structures.py`

Working with module hierarchies

Now, we will create the `__main__.py` Python source file in the project's root folder, that is, the same folder that includes the following subfolders: `Build`, `Decorate`, `Furnish`, `General`, `Landscape`, and `Outdoor`. The following is the code that imports many of the previously defined modules and works with instances of all the imported classes:

```
from build.rooms import *
from build.doors import *
from furnish.bedroom.beds import *

if __name__ == "__main__":
    room1 = SquareRoom(0, 0, 200, None)
    door1 = EntryDoor(100, 1, 50, 5, room1)
    bedroom1 = SquareRoom(100, 200, 180, None)
    bed1 = FabricBed(130, 230, 120, 110, bedroom1)
    room1.draw()
    door1.draw()
    bedroom1.draw()
    bed1.draw()
```

The first line in the preceding code uses the `from` statement to import all the classes from the following modules into the current namespace:

- `build.rooms`: `build/rooms.py`
- `build.doors`: `build/doors.py`
- `furnish.bedroom.beds`: `furnish/bedrooms/beds.py`

This way, we can access the `SquareRoom`, `EntryDoor` and `FabricBed` classes as if they were defined in the `__main__.py` Python source file. The following is the output generated with the preceding code:

```
Room
Square room
X: 0, Y: 0. Width: 200, Height: 200.
Door
Entry Door
X: 100, Y: 1. Width: 50, Height: 5.
Room
Square room
X: 100, Y: 200. Width: 180, Height: 180.
Bed
Fabric bed
X: 130, Y: 230. Width: 120, Height: 110.
```

In this case, we just need these three classes; therefore, we can use the following `from` statements to import just the classes we need:

```
from build.rooms import SquareRoom
from build.doors import EntryDoor
from furnish.bedroom.beds import FabricBed
```

Another option is to use the `import` keyword and add the necessary modules hierarchy separated by dots (`.`) to each class defined in modules. The following lines show the version of the code that uses the `import` keyword and adds the necessary prefixes to each class:

```
import build.doors
import build.rooms
import furnish.bedroom.beds

if __name__ == "__main__":
    room1 = build.SquareRoom(0, 0, 200, None)
    door1 = build.EntryDoor(100, 1, 50, 5, room1)
```

```
    bedroom1 = build.SquareRoom(100, 200, 180, None)
    bed1 = furnish.bedroom.beds.FabricBed(130, 230, 120, 110,
bedroom1)
    room1.draw()
    door1.draw()
    bedroom1.draw()
    bed1.draw()
```

Now, let's imagine that we have to code an application that has to draw the floor plans for 30 extremely complex houses that will be displayed in a 4K display. We will have to work with most of the elements defined in all the different modules. We would like to have all the classes defined in the Python source files included in the `Build` folder with just one line. It is possible to do so by adding the `__init__.py` Python source file to the `Build` folder and including the following code to import all the classes defined in each of the Python source files included in this folder:

```
from .areas import *
from .doors import *
from .fireplaces import *
from .rooms import SquareRoom, LShapedRoom, SmallRoom, Closet
from .stairs import *
from .walls import *
from .windows import *
```

This way, if we use the `import` keyword with the `build` module, we will be able to access all the classes defined in each of the Python source files included in the `build` module by adding the `build.` prefix to each class name. In fact, we won't be able to access all the classes because we excluded the `Room` class in the `from .rooms import` statement and specified only four classes to import from this module. After we add the `__init__.py` Python source file to the `Build` folder, we can change the `__main__.py` Python source code with the following code:

```
import build
from furnish.bedroom.beds import FabricBed

if __name__ == "__main__":
    room1 = build.SquareRoom(0, 0, 200, None)
    door1 = build.EntryDoor(100, 1, 50, 5, room1)
    bedroom1 = build.SquareRoom(100, 200, 180, None)
    bed1 = FabricBed(130, 230, 120, 110, bedroom1)
    room1.draw()
    door1.draw()
    bedroom1.draw()
    bed1.draw()
```

If we don't want to use prefixes and just want to import all the classes defined in the build module, we can use the following `from ... import` statement:

```
from build import *
```

We can add the appropriate code in the `__init__.py` Python source file for each folder and then use the appropriate **`import`** or **`from ... import`** statements based on our needs.

Organizing object-oriented code in C#

C# allows you to use namespaces to declare a scope that contains a set of related elements. Thus, we can use namespaces to organize interfaces and classes. We will work with nested namespaces to organize the code of an application. This allows you to create and furnish house floor plans. Then, we will use interfaces and classes from different namespaces in diverse pieces of code.

Working with folders

We will create a Windows console application named `Chapter7`. Visual Studio will automatically add a `Program.cs` C# source file in the solution's root folder. We will create the following six folders to organize the code in our house floor plan layout application. Then, we will add subfolders and C# source files in each of the previously created folders. Visual Studio will use these folders and subfolders to automatically generate the namespaces for each new C# source file:

- `Build`
- `Decorate`
- `Furnish`
- `General`
- `Landscape`
- `Outdoor`

We will use the C# source file for each interface or class. We will add the `IFloorPlanElement` interface to a file named `IFloorPlanElement.cs` in the `General` folder. The following is the code for the `General\IFloorPlanElement.cs` C# source file that declares the `IFloorPlanElement` interface:

```
namespace Chapter7.General
{
  public interface IFloorPlanElement
  {
```

```
        string Category { get; set; }
        string Description { get; set; }
        double X { get; set; }
        double Y { get; set; }
        double Width { get; set; }
        double Height { get; set; }
        IFloorPlanElement Parent { get; set; }

        void MoveTo(double x, double y);
        void PrintCategory();
        void PrintDescription();
        void Draw();
    }
}
```

If we use Visual Studio to create a new interface in the `General` folder, the IDE will automatically include a line with the `namespace` keyword, followed by the `Chapter7.General` name. The declaration of the interface will be enclosed in brackets after the line that declares the namespace. The IDE uses the folder name in which we will add the interface to automatically generate a default namespace name. In this case, the generated name is the initial namespace, that is, the `Chapter7` solution name, followed by a dot (`.`) and the folder that contains the new C# source file, that is, `General`.

The `IFloorPlanElement` interface declares the following required members:

- Two string properties: `Category` and `Description`
- Four double properties: `X`, `Y`, `Width`, and `Height`
- The `IFloorPlanElement` property: `Parent`
- The `MoveTo` method that receives two arguments: `x` and `y`
- The `PrintCategory` method
- The `PrintDescription` method
- The `Draw` method

Now, we will add the `FloorPlanElement` abstract class that implements the previously created `IFloorPlanElement` interface to a file named `FloorPlanElement.cs` in the `General` folder. The following is the code for the `General\FloorPlanElement.cs` C# source file that declares the `FloorPlanElement` class:

```
namespace Chapter7.General
{
  using System;

  public abstract class FloorPlanElement: IFloorPlanElement
  {
    public virtual string Category
    {
      get { return "Undefined"; }
      set { throw new InvalidOperationException(); }
    }

    public virtual string Description
    {
      get { return "Undefined"; }
      set { throw new InvalidOperationException(); }
    }

    public double X { get; set; }
    public double Y { get; set; }
    public double Width { get; set; }
    public double Height { get; set; }

    private IFloorPlanElement _parent;
    public IFloorPlanElement Parent
    {
      get { return _parent; }
      set { throw new InvalidOperationException(); }
    }

    public FloorPlanElement(double x, double y, double width, double
height, IFloorPlanElement parent)
    {
      this.X = x;
      this.Y = y;
      this.Width = width;
      this.Height = height;
      this._parent = parent;
```

```
        }

        public void MoveTo(double x, double y)
        {
          this.X = x;
          this.Y = y;
        }

        public void PrintCategory()
        {
          Console.WriteLine(this.Category);
        }

        public void PrintDescription()
        {
          Console.WriteLine(this.Description);
        }

        public void Draw()
        {
          this.PrintCategory();
          this.PrintDescription();
          Console.WriteLine(
          "X: {0}, Y: {1}. Width: {2}, Height: {3}.",
          this.X,
          this.Y,
          this.Width,
          this.Height);
        }
      }
    }
```

Note that the abstract class is declared in the same namespace that we used for the `IFloorPlanElement` interface; therefore, both the class and the interface are in the same scope. We can reference the interface name in the class declaration without any namespace prefix because both the class and the interface are declared in the same namespace.

The abstract class declares a constructor that receives five arguments: `x`, `y`, `width`, `height`, and `parent`. The preceding code initializes all the properties with the values received as arguments. This way, each `FloorPlanElement` instance will have a 2D location specified by the `X` and `Y` properties, a `Width` and a `Height` value, and a `Parent` element that will be of any class that implements the `IFloorPlanElement` interface.

The FloorPlanElement abstract class declares two virtual read-only properties that the subclasses will override: Category and Description. In addition, the abstract class declares all the other properties required by the IFloorPlanElement interface: X, Y, Width, Height, and Parent. Note that Parent is a read-only property that encapsulates the private _parent field.

The abstract class declares the following instance methods:

- MoveTo: This method moves the floor plan element to the new location specified by the x and y arguments
- PrintCategory: This method prints the value of the Category class attribute to the console output
- PrintDescription: This method prints the value of the Description class attribute to the console output
- Draw: This method prints the category, description, 2D location, width, and height of the floor plan element to the console output

The FloorPlanElement abstract class is located in the General\FloorPlanElement.cs file. All the classes that specialize floor plan elements will inherit from the FloorPlanElement class; therefore they will implement the IFloorPlanElement interface. These classes will be located in other C# source files that will have to use the using statement to let C# know that they want to use the FloorPlanElement class that is located in another namespace, that is, in the Chapter7.General namespace.

Using namespaces

We will create the following folders in the previously created Build folder. We won't add C# source files to all the folders in order to keep our example simple. However, we will imagine that we have a more complex project:

- Areas
- Doors
- Fireplaces
- Rooms
- Stairs
- Walls
- Windows

Now, we will add the `Room` abstract class, which inherits from the previously created `FloorPlanElement` abstract class, to a file named `Room.cs` within the `Build\Rooms` subfolder. The following lines show the code for the `Build\Rooms\Room.cs` C# source file that declares the `Room` class. The class just overrides the getter and setter methods for the `Category` property. The getter method returns the `"Room"` value. In addition, the class declares a constructor that just calls the base constructor:

```
namespace Chapter7.Build.Rooms
{
  using System;
  using General;

  public abstract class Room : FloorPlanElement
  {
    public override string Category
    {
      get { return "Room"; }
      set { throw new InvalidOperationException(); }
    }

    public Room(double x, double y, double width, double height,
IFloorPlanElement parent) : base(x, y, width, height, parent)
    {
    }
  }
}
```

If we use Visual Studio to create a new interface in the `Build\Rooms` folder, the IDE will automatically include a line with the `namespace` keyword, followed by the `Chapter7.Build.Rooms` name. The declaration of the interface will be enclosed in brackets after the line that declares the namespace. The IDE uses the folder names in which we will add the interface to automatically generate a default namespace name. In this case, the generated name is the initial namespace, that is, the solution name, the folder, and the subfolder, all of them separated by a dot (`.`), that is, `Chapter7.Build.Rooms`.

The new class inherits from the `FloorPlanElement` class that was declared in another namespace, that is, in the `Chapter7.General` namespace. We had to specify the class name from which the new abstract class inherits; therefore, we added the `using` statement, followed by `General`. This way, we don't need to specify the full qualifier for the `FloorPlanElement` class; we can reference it by just using its class name.

Bear in mind that the real namespace name is Chapter7.General. However, we are under the scope of the Chapter7 namespace because we include the using line in the namespace declaration so that we don't need to include Chapter7. as a prefix. This way, we can just specify General. If we don't include the using statement, followed by the General namespace, we should use a full qualifier to reference the FloorPlanElement class, as shown in the following line that declares the Room abstract class:

```
public abstract class Room : General.FloorPlanElement
```

In addition, it will be necessary to add a full qualifier to reference the IFloorPlanElement interface in the constructor declaration:

```
public Room(double x, double y, double width, double height, General.
IFloorPlanElement parent) : base(x, y, width, height, parent)
```

If we decide to include the using statement before and outside the namespace declaration, we should use the following line:

```
using Chapter7.General;
```

Now, we will add a SquareRoom class, which inherits from the previously created Room abstract class, to a file named SquareRoom.cs within the Build\Rooms subfolder. The following is the code for the Build\Rooms\SquareRoom.cs C# source file that declares the SquareRoom class. The class just overrides the getter and setter methods for the Description property. The getter method returns the "Square room" value. The SquareRoom class represents a square room; therefore, it isn't necessary to specify both the width and height to create an instance of this type of room. The constructor uses the width value to specify the values for both width and height in the call to the base constructor:

```
namespace Chapter7.Build.Rooms
{
  using System;
  using General;

  class SquareRoom : Room
  {
    public override string Description
    {
      get { return "Square room"; }
      set { throw new InvalidOperationException(); }
    }

    public SquareRoom(double x, double y, double width,
IFloorPlanElement parent) : base(x, y, width, width, parent)
```

```
      {
      }
    }
  }
```

As occurred in the `Room` abstract class file, we added the `using` statement, followed by `General`. This way, we don't need to specify the full qualifier for the `IFloorPlanElement` interface. The `Room` class is declared in the same namespace in which we declare this new class; therefore, the `Room` class is under scope.

Now, we will add the `LShapedRoom` class, which also inherits from the `Room` abstract class, to a file named `LShapedRoom.cs` within the `Build\Rooms` subfolder. The following code shows the `Build\Rooms\LShapedRoom.cs` C# source file that declares the `SquareRoom` class. The class just overrides the getter and setter methods for the `Description` property. The getter method returns the `"L-Shaped room"` value. In addition, the class declares a constructor that just calls the base constructor:

```
namespace Chapter7.Build.Rooms
{
  using System;
  using General;

  public class LShapedRoom: Room
  {
    public override string Description
    {
      get { return "L-Shaped room"; }
      set { throw new InvalidOperationException(); }
    }

    public LShapedRoom(double x, double y, double width, double
height, IFloorPlanElement parent) : base(x, y, width, height, parent)
    {
    }
  }
}
```

Now, we will add the `SmallRoom` class that also inherits from the `Room` abstract class to a file named `SmallRoom.cs` within the `Build\Rooms` subfolder. The following code shows the `Build\Rooms\SmallRoom.cs` C# source file that declares the `SmallRoom` class. The class just overrides the getter and setter methods for the `Description` property. The getter method returns the `"Small room"` value. In addition, the class declares a constructor that just calls the base constructor:

```
namespace Chapter7.Build.Rooms
{
```

```
  using System;
  using General;

  public class SmallRoom : Room
  {
    public override string Description
    {
      get { return "Small room"; }
      set { throw new InvalidOperationException(); }
    }

    public SmallRoom(double x, double y, double width, double height,
IFloorPlanElement parent)
      : base(x, y, width, height, parent)
    {
    }
  }
}
```

Now, we will add the `Closet` class (which also inherits from the `Room` abstract class) to a file named `Closet.cs` within the `Build\Rooms` subfolder. The following is the code for the `Build\Rooms\Closet.cs` C# source file that declares the `Closet` class. The class just overrides the getter and setter methods for the `Description` property. The getter method returns the `"Closet"` value. In addition, the class declares a constructor that just calls the base constructor:

```
namespace Chapter7.Build.Rooms
{
  using System;
  using General;

  public class Closet : Room
  {
    public override string Description
    {
      get { return "Closet"; }
      set { throw new InvalidOperationException(); }
    }

    public Closet(double x, double y, double width, double height,
IFloorPlanElement parent)
      : base(x, y, width, height, parent)
    {
    }
  }
}
```

We will add the Door abstract class, which inherits from the previously created FloorPlanElement abstract class, to a file named Door.cs within the Build\Doors subfolder. The following is the code for the Build\Doors\Door.cs C# source file that declares a Door class. This class just overrides the getter and setter methods for the Category property. The getter method returns the "Door" value. In addition, the Door class declares a constructor that just calls the base constructor:

```
namespace Chapter7.Build.Doors
{
  using System;
  using General;

  public abstract class Door : FloorPlanElement
  {
    public override string Category
    {
      get { return "Door"; }
      set { throw new InvalidOperationException(); }
    }

    public Door(double x, double y, double width, double height,
IFloorPlanElement parent)
      : base(x, y, width, height, parent)
    {
    }
  }
}
```

The Door class is included in the Chapter7.Build.Doors namespace. The new class inherits from the FloorPlanElement class that was declared in another namespace, that is, in the Chapter7.General namespace.

Now, we will add the EntryDoor class, which inherits from the Door abstract class, to a file named EntryDoor.cs within the Build\Doors subfolder. The following is the code for the Build\Doors\EntryDoor.cs C# source file that declares the EntryDoor class. This class just overrides the getter and setter methods for the Description property. The getter method returns the "Entry Door" value. In addition, the class declares a constructor that just calls the base constructor:

```
namespace Chapter7.Build.Doors
{
  using System;
  using General;

  public class EntryDoor : Door
```

```
    {
      public override string Description
      {
        get { return "Entry Door"; }
        set { throw new InvalidOperationException(); }
      }

      public EntryDoor(double x, double y, double width, double height,
  IFloorPlanElement parent)
        : base(x, y, width, height, parent)
      {
      }
    }
  }
```

We will create the following subfolders in the previously created `Decorate` folder. Each of these subfolders will generate a namespace in the `Chapter7.Decorate` namespace and will include the following classes:

- `ArtAndDecor`
- `Countertops`
- `Electronics`
- `Flooring`
- `LightingAndFans`
- `PaintAndWalls`

We will create the following subfolders in the previously created `Furnish` folder. Each of these subfolders will generate a namespace in the `Chapter7.Furnish` namespace and will include classes. The `Bedroom` subfolder will include the additional subfolders:

- `Bathroom`
- `Bedroom`
- `DiningRoom`
- `Kitchen`
- `LaundryAndUtility`
- `LivingRoom`
- `Office`
- `OtherRooms`

We will create the following subfolders within the previously created `Furnish\Bedroom` subfolder:

- `Beds`
- `Dressers`
- `KidsBeds`
- `Mirrors`
- `NightTables`
- `Nursery`

We will add the `Bed` class, which inherits from the previously created `FloorPlanElement` abstract class, to a file named `Bed.cs` within the `Furnish\Bedroom\Beds` subfolder. The following is the code for the `Furnish\Bedroom\Beds\Bed.cs` C# source file that declares the `Bed` class. The class just overrides the getter and setter methods for the properties of `Category` and `Description`. The getter method for the `Category` property returns the `"Bed"` value and the getter method for `Description` returns `"Generic Bed"`. In addition, the class declares a constructor that just calls the base constructor:

```
namespace Chapter7.Furnish.Bedroom.Beds
{
  using System;
  using General;

  public class Bed : FloorPlanElement
  {
    public override string Category
    {
      get { return "Bed"; }
      set { throw new InvalidOperationException(); }
    }

    public override string Description
    {
      get { return "Generic Bed"; }
      set { throw new InvalidOperationException(); }
    }

    public Bed(double x, double y, double width, double height,
IFloorPlanElement parent)
```

```
        : base(x, y, width, height, parent)
      {
      }
    }
}
```

The `Bed` class is included in the `Chapter7.Furnish.Bedroom.Beds` namespace. The new class inherits from the `FloorPlanElement` class. This class was declared in another namespace, that is, in the `Chapter7.General` namespace.

Now, we will add the `FabricBed` class to a file named `FabricBed.cs` within the `Furnish\Bedroom\Beds` subfolder. The `FabricBed` class inherits from the `Bed` class. The following is the code for the `Furnish\Bedroom\Beds\FabricBed.cs` C# source file that declares the `FabricBed` class. The class just overrides the getter and setter methods for the `Description` property. The getter method returns the `"Fabric Bed"` value. In addition, the class declares a constructor that just calls the base constructor:

```
namespace Chapter7.Furnish.Bedroom.Beds
{
  using System;
  using General;

  public class FabricBed : Bed
  {
    public override string Description
    {
      get { return "Fabric Bed"; }
      set { throw new InvalidOperationException(); }
    }

    public FabricBed(double x, double y, double width, double height,
IFloorPlanElement parent)
        : base(x, y, width, height, parent)
    {
    }
  }
}
```

We will create the following subfolders in the previously created `Landscape` folder. Each of these subfolders will generate a namespace in the `Chapter7.Landscape` namespace and will include the following classes:

- `AreasDefinition`
- `Materials`
- `TreesAndPlants`

Finally, we will create the following subfolders in the previously created `Outdoor` folder. Each of these subfolders will generate a namespace in the `Chapter7.Outdoor` namespace and will include the following classes:

- `Accessories`
- `Living`
- `Structures`

Working with namespace hierarchies in C#

Now, we will change the code for the `Program.cs` C# source file in the project's root folder, that is, the same folder that includes the `Build`, `Decorate`, `Furnish`, `General`, `Landscape`, and `Outdoor` subfolders. The following code uses many `using` directives to list all the namespaces to be used frequently. Then, the `Main` method works with instances of the classes defined in many different namespaces:

```
namespace Chapter7
{
  using System;
  using Build.Rooms;
  using Build.Doors;
  using Furnish.Bedroom.Beds;

  class Program
  {
    static void Main(string[] args)
    {
      var room1 = new SquareRoom(0, 0, 200, null);
      var door1 = new EntryDoor(100, 1, 50, 5, room1);
      var bedroom1 = new SquareRoom(100, 200, 180, null);
      var bed1 = new FabricBed(130, 230, 120, 110, bedroom1);
      room1.Draw();
      door1.Draw();
      bedroom1.Draw();
      bed1.Draw();
```

```
            Console.ReadLine();
        }
    }
}
```

The first line in the preceding code declares that we are working in the `Chapter7` namespace and using many `using` directives to make it simpler to access the classes declared in the specified namespaces:

- `Build.Rooms`: `Chapter7.Build.Rooms`
- `Build.Doors`: `Chapter7.Build.Doors`
- `Furnish.Bedroom.Beds`: `Chapter7.Bedroom.Beds`

This way, we can access the `SquareRoom`, `EntryDoor`, and `FabricBed` classes without any prefixes as if they were defined in the `Chapter7` namespace. The following lines show the output generated with the preceding code:

```
Room
Square room
X: 0, Y: 0. Width: 200, Height: 200.
Door
Entry Door
X: 100, Y: 1. Width: 50, Height: 5.
Room
Square room
X: 100, Y: 200. Width: 180, Height: 180.
Bed
Fabric Bed
X: 130, Y: 230. Width: 120, Height: 110.
```

In this case, we just need these three classes. Remember that we have included the `using` directives in the `Chapter7` namespace declaration. If we want to move the `using` directives before and outside the namespace declaration, we should use the following code that adds `Chapter7.` as a prefix to each namespace:

```
using Chapter7.Build.Rooms;
using Chapter7.Build.Doors;
using Chapter7.Furnish.Bedroom.Beds;
```

Another option is to remove the `using` directives and use full qualifiers for each of the required classes, that is, include the complete namespace name and a dot (`.`) as a prefix for each class. The following is the version of the code that removes the `using` directives and works with full qualifiers for each class:

```
namespace Chapter7
{
  using System;

  class Program
  {
    static void Main(string[] args)
    {
      var room1 = new Build.Rooms.SquareRoom(0, 0, 200, null);
      var door1 = new Build.Doors.EntryDoor(100, 1, 50, 5, room1);
      var bedroom1 = new Build.Rooms.SquareRoom(100, 200, 180, null);
      var bed1 = new Furnish.Bedroom.Beds.FabricBed(130, 230, 120,
110, bedroom1);
      room1.Draw();
      door1.Draw();
      bedroom1.Draw();
      bed1.Draw();

      Console.ReadLine();
    }
  }
}
```

Now, let's imagine that we have to code an application that has to draw the floor plans for 30 extremely complex houses that will be displayed in a 4K display. We will have to work with most of the elements defined in the different namespaces. We would like to have all the classes defined in the diverse namespaces accessed without prefixes. We would require the following `using` directives in the `Chapter7` namespace declaration:

```
using Build.Areas;
using Build.Doors;
using Build.Fireplaces;
using Build.Rooms;
using Build.Stairs;
using Build.Walls;
using Build.Windows;
using Decorate.ArtAndDecor;
using Decorate.Countertops;
using Decorate.Electronics;
```

```
using Decorate.Flooring;
using Decorate.LightingAndFans;
using Decorate.PaintAndWalls;
using Furnish.Bathroom;
using Furnish.Bedroom.Beds;
using Furnish.Bedroom.Dressers;
using Furnish.Bedroom.KidsBeds;
using Furnish.Bedroom.Mirrors;
using Furnish.Bedroom.NightTables;
using Furnish.Bedroom.Nursery;
using Furnish.DiningRoom;
using Furnish.Kitchen;
using Furnish.LaundryAndUtility;
using Furnish.LivingRoom;
using Furnish.Office;
using Furnish.OtherRooms;
using Landscape.AreasDefinition;
using Landscape.Materials;
using Landscape.TreesAndPlants;
using Outdoor.Accesories;
using Outdoor.Living;
using Outdoor.Structures;
```

Organizing object-oriented code in JavaScript

JavaScript was born as a scripting language that has grown up to become a language that creates entire apps. The usage of plain JavaScript without additional libraries doesn't provide a standardized mechanism to organize code in namespaces or modules.

We can easily organize our constructor functions with plain JavaScript, but in some cases, we can benefit from the usage of specialized libraries, such as `Require.js` (`http://www.requirejs.org/`), that provide a better mechanism to organize complex code in modules and solve the problem of dependencies and different ways of loading modules as well. In this case, we will organize our code using plain JavaScript without additional libraries.

Working with objects to organize code

We will create a base global object named `APP` to use it to define all the elements of our house floor plan layout application. Then, we will add the following properties to the base object to create a hierarchy of objects linked to this base object:

- `Build`
- `Decorate`
- `Furnish`
- `General`
- `Landscape`
- `Outdoor`

We will add the base constructor function in the `APP.General` object. The following code creates the `APP` object if it doesn't exist. It also defines the `General` property if it doesn't exist. Then, the code defines the `FloorPlanElement` constructor function and its prototype. We will use this constructor functions as the base of the prototype chain for other objects that will specialize the floor plan element:

```
var APP = APP || {};
APP.General = APP.General || {};
APP.General.FloorPlanElement = function() { };
APP.General.FloorPlanElement.prototype.category = "Undefined";
APP.General.FloorPlanElement.prototype.description = "Undefined";
APP.General.FloorPlanElement.prototype.x = 0;
APP.General.FloorPlanElement.prototype.y = 0;
APP.General.FloorPlanElement.prototype.width = 0;
APP.General.FloorPlanElement.prototype.height = 0;
APP.General.FloorPlanElement.prototype.parent = null;

APP.General.FloorPlanElement.prototype.initialize = function(x, y,
width, height, parent) {
  this.x = x;
  this.y = y;
  this.width = width;
  this.height = height;
  this.parent = parent;
}

APP.General.FloorPlanElement.prototype.moveTo = function(x, y) {
  this.x = x;
```

```
  this.y = y;
}

APP.General.FloorPlanElement.prototype.printCategory = function() {
  console.log(this.category);
}

APP.General.FloorPlanElement.prototype.printDescription = function() {
  console.log(this.description);
}

APP.General.FloorPlanElement.prototype.draw = function() {
  this.printCategory();
  this.printDescription();
  console.log("X: " + this.x +
    ", Y: " + this.y +
    ". Width: " + this.width +
    ", Height: " + this.height + ".");
}
```

The `FloorPlanElement` prototype declares two properties that the subclasses will override: `category` and `description`. The prototype declares an `initialize` method that receives five arguments: `x`, `y`, `width`, `height`, and `parent`. The `initialize` method initializes the current instance properties with the same name with all the values received as arguments. This way, each constructor function in the prototype chain that ends up in the `FloorPlanElement` prototype will have a 2D location specified by `x` and `y`, `width` and `height` values, and a `parent` element. Each constructor function in the prototype chain will call the `initialize` method to initialize the instance.

In addition, the `FloorPlanElement` prototype declares the following methods:

- `moveTo`: This method moves the floor plan element to the new location specified by the `x` and `y` arguments
- `printCategory`: This method prints the value of the `category` property
- `printDescription`: This method prints the value of the `description` property
- `draw`: This method prints the category, description, 2D location, and width and height of the floor plan element

In this case, we will include all the constructor functions in the same JavaScript file. However, the same code can be moved to different JavaScript source files because whenever we declare a new group of related constructor functions, we will include the first few lines of the preceding code that creates the `APP` object if it doesn't exist and defines the property we use to generate the hierarchy of related constructor functions if it doesn't exist. However, if we separate code in different JavaScript source files, we have to make sure that we load them in the necessary order to avoid dependency problems. We won't add code to check for the existence of specific constructor functions, but we can easily define flags for this goal.

Declaring constructor functions within objects

The following code declares five constructor functions: `Room`, `SquareRoom`, `LShapedRoom`, `SmallRoom`, and `Closet`. The code defines these constructor functions as properties of the `APP.Build.Rooms` object:

```
var APP = APP || {};
APP.Build = APP.Build || {};
APP.Build.Rooms = APP.Build.Rooms || {};
APP.Build.Rooms.Room = function() { };
APP.Build.Rooms.Room.prototype = new APP.General.FloorPlanElement();
APP.Build.Rooms.Room.prototype.constructor = APP.Build.Rooms.Room;
APP.Build.Rooms.Room.prototype.category = "Room";

APP.Build.Rooms.SquareRoom = function(x, y, width, parent) {

  this.initialize(x, y, width, width, parent);
};
APP.Build.Rooms.SquareRoom.prototype = new APP.Build.Rooms.Room();
APP.Build.Rooms.SquareRoom.prototype.constructor = APP.Build.Rooms.
SquareRoom;
APP.Build.Rooms.SquareRoom.prototype.description = "Square room";

APP.Build.Rooms.LShapedRoom = function(x, y, width, height, parent) {
  this.initialize(x, y, width, height, parent);
};
APP.Build.Rooms.LShapedRoom.prototype = new APP.Build.Rooms.Room();
APP.Build.Rooms.LShapedRoom.prototype.constructor = APP.Build.Rooms.
LShapedRoom;
APP.Build.Rooms.LShapedRoom.prototype.description = "L-Shaped room";

APP.Build.Rooms.SmallRoom = function(x, y, width, height, parent) {
```

```
  this.initialize(x, y, width, height, parent);
};
APP.Build.Rooms.SmallRoom.prototype = new APP.Build.Rooms.Room();
APP.Build.Rooms.SmallRoom.prototype.constructor = APP.Build.Rooms.
SmallRoom;
APP.Build.Rooms.SmallRoom.prototype.description = "Small room";

APP.Build.Rooms.Closet = function(x, y, width, height, parent) {
  this.initialize(x, y, width, height, parent);
};
APP.Build.Rooms.Closet.prototype = new APP.Build.Rooms.Room();
APP.Build.Rooms.Closet.prototype.constructor = APP.Build.Rooms.Closet;
APP.Build.Rooms.Closet.prototype.description = "Closet";
```

The `APP.Build.Rooms.Room` constructor function specifies the previously defined `APP.General.FloorPlanElement` object as its prototype. The `APP.Build.Rooms.Room` prototype overrides the value of the `category` property with the `"Room"` value. The `App.Build.Rooms.SquareRoom` constructor function generates an object that represents the square room; therefore, it isn't necessary to specify both the width and height to create an instance of this type of room. The constructor function uses the `width` value to specify the values for both `width` and `height` in the call to the `initialize` method defined in the `APP.General.FloorPlanElement` prototype. Each constructor function that defines `APP.Build.Rooms.Room` as its prototype overrides the `description` property with an appropriate value.

The following code declares two constructor functions: `Door` and `EntryDoor`. The following code defines these constructor functions as properties of the `APP.Build.Doors` object:

```
var APP = APP || {};
APP.Build = APP.Build || {};
APP.Build.Doors = APP.Build.Doors || {};
APP.Build.Doors.Door = function() { };
APP.Build.Doors.Door.prototype = new APP.General.FloorPlanElement();
APP.Build.Doors.Door.prototype.constructor = APP.Build.Doors.Door;
APP.Build.Doors.Door.prototype.category = "Door";

APP.Build.Doors.EntryDoor = function(x, y, width, height, parent) {
  this.initialize(x, y, width, height, parent);
};
APP.Build.Doors.EntryDoor.prototype = new APP.Build.Doors.Door();
APP.Build.Doors.EntryDoor.prototype.constructor = APP.Build.Doors.
EntryDoor;
APP.Build.Doors.EntryDoor.prototype.description = "Entry Door";
```

The `APP.Build.Doors.Door` constructor function specifies the previously defined `APP.General.FloorPlanElement` object as its prototype. The `APP.Build.Doors.Door` prototype overrides the value of the `category` property with the `"Door"` value. The `App.Build.Doors.Door` constructor function generates an object that represents an entry door; its prototype overrides the `description` property with the `"Entry Door"` value.

The following code declares two constructor functions: `Bed` and `FabricBed`. The code defines these constructor functions as properties of the `APP.Furnish.Bedroom.Beds` object:

```
var APP = APP || {};
APP.Furnish = APP.Furnish || {};
APP.Furnish.Bedroom = APP.Furnish.Bedroom || {};
APP.Furnish.Bedroom.Beds = APP.Furnish.Bedroom.Beds || {};
APP.Furnish.Bedroom.Beds.Bed = function() { };
APP.Furnish.Bedroom.Beds.Bed.prototype = new APP.General.
FloorPlanElement();
APP.Furnish.Bedroom.Beds.Bed.prototype.constructor = APP.Furnish.
Bedroom.Beds.Bed;
APP.Furnish.Bedroom.Beds.Bed.prototype.category = "Bed";
APP.Furnish.Bedroom.Beds.Bed.prototype.description = "Generic Bed";

APP.Furnish.Bedroom.Beds.FabricBed = function(x, y, width, height,
parent) {
  this.initialize(x, y, width, height, parent);
};
APP.Furnish.Bedroom.Beds.FabricBed.prototype = new APP.Furnish.
Bedroom.Beds.Bed();
APP.Furnish.Bedroom.Beds.FabricBed.prototype.constructor = APP.
Furnish.Bedroom.Beds.FabricBed;
APP.Furnish.Bedroom.Beds.FabricBed.prototype.description = "Fabric
Bed";
```

The `APP.Furnish.Bedroom.Beds.Bed` constructor function specifies the previously defined `APP.General.FloorPlanElement` object as its prototype. The `APP.Furnish.Bedroom.Beds.Bed` prototype overrides the value of both the `category` and `description` properties with the `"Bed"` and `"Generic Bed"` values. The `APP.Furnish.Bedroom.Beds.FabricBed` constructor function generates an object that represents a fabric bed; its prototype overrides the `description` property with the `"Fabric Bed"` value.

Working with nested objects that organize code

Now, we will write code that checks whether the previously defined objects that organized the code are defined. If they are defined, the following code creates objects with the previously defined constructor functions and calls the `draw` methods for all of the created objects:

```
if (!APP.Build.Rooms) {
  throw "Rooms objects not available.";
}
if (!APP.Build.Doors) {
  throw "Doors objects not available.";
}
if (!APP.Furnish.Bedroom.Beds) {
  throw "Beds objects not available.";
}

var room1 = new APP.Build.Rooms.SquareRoom(0, 0, 200, null);
var door1 = new APP.Build.Doors.EntryDoor(100, 1, 50, 5, room1);
var bedroom1 = new APP.Build.Rooms.SquareRoom(100, 200, 180, null);
var bed1 = new APP.Furnish.Bedroom.Beds.FabricBed(130, 230, 120, 110,
bedroom1);

room1.draw();
door1.draw();
bedroom1.draw();
bed1.draw();
```

The following lines show the output generated on the JavaScript console:

```
Room
Square room
X: 0, Y: 0. Width: 200, Height: 200.
Door
Entry Door
X: 100, Y: 1. Width: 50, Height: 5.
Room
Square room
X: 100, Y: 200. Width: 180, Height: 180.
Bed
Fabric Bed
X: 130, Y: 230. Width: 120, Height: 110.
```

Summary

In this chapter, you learned how to use all the features included in Python, C#, and JavaScript in order to organize complex object-oriented code. We took advantage of modules in Python, namespaces in C#, and nested objects in JavaScript. We organized multiple classes, interfaces, and constructor functions of a house floor plan layout application. If the basic features included in JavaScript to organize code aren't enough, we can use specialized libraries (such as the popular RequireJS).

Now that you have learned how to organize object-oriented code, we are ready to understand how to move forward to take advantage of all the things you learned so far in this book and use them in our real-world applications in Python, JavaScript, and C#, which is the topic of the next chapter.

8

Taking Full Advantage of Object-Oriented Programming

In this chapter, you will learn how to refactor existing code to take advantage of all the object-oriented programming techniques that you have learned so far. We will take advantage of all the different available features to refactor a piece of code and prepare it for future requirements in each of the three covered programming languages: Python, JavaScript, and C#. We will cover the following topics:

- Putting together all the pieces of the object-oriented puzzle
- Understanding the difference between writing object-oriented code from scratch and refactoring existing code
- Preparing object-oriented code for future requirements
- Refactoring existing code in Python
- Refactoring existing code in C#
- Refactoring existing code in JavaScript

Putting together all the pieces of the object-oriented puzzle

In *Chapter 1, Objects Everywhere*, you learned how to recognize objects from real-life situations. We understood that working with objects makes it easier to write code that is easier to understand and reuse. However, Python, C#, and JavaScript have different object-oriented approaches, and each programming language provides different features that allow you to generate and organize blueprints for objects. If we have the same goals for an application, we will end up with completely different object-oriented approaches in Python, C#, and JavaScript. It is not possible to use the same approach in these three languages.

In *Chapter 2, Classes and Instances*, you learned that in Python and C#, classes are the blueprints or building blocks that we can use to generate instances. Both the programming languages allow you to customize constructors and destructors. JavaScript has a different approach. We can easily create objects in JavaScript without any kind of blueprint. However, we can also take advantage of constructor functions and prototypes to group properties and methods that we can reuse to generate multiple objects using the same building blocks.

In *Chapter 3, Encapsulation of Data*, you learned about the different members of a class and how its different members are reflected in members of the instances generated from a class. We understood the possibility of protecting and hiding data and designed both mutable and immutable classes. Immutable classes are extremely useful when we work with concurrent code. Each programming language provides a different mechanism to protect and hide data. However, the three programming languages allow you to work with property getters and setters.

Python works with prefixes to indicate that we don't have to access specific members. C# is very strict and works with access modifiers to make it impossible for us to use members that we aren't supposed to access. In fact, if we try to access a member that isn't available for us to use, the code won't even compile. However, everything has a price, and C# adds an important amount of boilerplate code to provide these features.

In JavaScript, objects are extremely flexible and can easily mutate from the original form they acquired after we use a constructor function to create a new one. We can add members—such as methods and properties—on the fly. In fact, we can even change the prototype that is linked to an object and use all the members added to a prototype in the objects that we created before our changes. Bear in mind that JavaScript provides a mechanism that allows you to protect properties from being removed. We didn't take advantage of this feature in our examples.

In *Chapter 4, Inheritance and Specialization*, you learned about the different mechanisms provided by each programming language to specialize a blueprint. Python and C# work with inheritance; therefore, we work with classes that can become superclasses or base classes of a subclass or derived class. We worked with simple inheritance in both programming languages, performed methods and operators overriding, and took advantage of polymorphism. Also, we understood the power of overloading operators.

JavaScript works with prototype-based inheritance. We created objects that specialized behavior in this programming language. We also performed method overriding in JavaScript. We don't have to abuse large prototype chains in JavaScript because prototype-based inheritance can have a negative performance impact. We must take this into account, especially when we are used to taking full advantage of inheritance in other programming languages (Python and C#).

In *Chapter 5, Interfaces, Multiple Inheritance, and Composition*, you learned that C# works with interfaces in combination with classes. The only way to have multiple inheritance in C# is through the usage of interfaces. Interfaces are extremely useful, but they have a drawback, that is, they require us to write additional code. Luckily, there are tools included in all the modern IDEs. These IDEs allow you to easily and automatically generate an interface from a class without having to write all the code. We understood how we could use interfaces as the types required for arguments and that any instance of a class that implements the interface can be used as an argument.

Python allows you to work with multiple inheritance of classes; therefore, we can declare a class with more than one superclass. However, we should use multiple inheritances carefully to avoid generating a big mess. Python doesn't work with an interface, but works with a module that allows you to work with abstract base classes. It makes sense to use abstract base classes only in specific cases in Python.

We can work with composition in JavaScript to generate objects composed of many objects. This way, we can generate instances composed of objects created with diverse prototypes.

In *Chapter 6, Duck Typing and Generics*, you learned that both Python and JavaScript work with duck typing. We can add the necessary validation code to make sure that all the arguments have specific properties or belong to a specific type. However, the most common practice in both languages is to take advantage of duck typing.

C# uses interfaces in combination with generics to work with parametric polymorphism. We can declare classes that work with one or more constrained generic types. Generics are very important to maximize code reuse in C#.

In *Chapter 7, Organization of Object-Oriented Code*, you learned that Python allows you to easily organize source files in folders to define module hierarchies. C# works with namespaces, and we can easily match them with the location of all the source code files within folders in the project structure. We can declare a constructor function within objects in JavaScript and nest objects to organize code in JavaScript. However, if our code is complex and we want to use many files in different folders, we can use RequireJS, a popular code organization module.

Now, we will take our existing code and refactor it to take advantage of object-oriented programming.

Refactoring existing code in Python

Sometimes, we are extremely lucky and have the possibility to follow best practices as we kick off a project. If we start writing object-oriented code from scratch, we can take advantage of all the features that we have been using in our examples throughout the book. As the requirements evolve, we may need to further generalize or specialize all the blueprints. However, as we started our project with an object-oriented approach and organizing our code, it is easier to make adjustments to the code.

Most of the times, we aren't extremely lucky and have to work on projects that don't follow best practices. In the name of Agile, we generate pieces of code that perform similar tasks without a decent organization. Instead of following the same bad practices that generated error-prone, repetitive, and difficult to maintain code, we can use all the features provided by all the different IDEs and additional helper tools to refactor existing code and generate object-oriented code that promotes code reuse and allows you to reduce maintenance headaches.

For example, imagine that we have to develop an application that has to render 3D models on a 2D screen. The requirements specify that the first set of 3D models that we will have to render are a sphere and a cube. The application has to allow you to change parameters of a perspective camera in order to allow you to see a specific part of the 3D world rendered on the 2D screen (refer to *Figure 1* and *Figure 2*):

- The X, Y, and Z position
- The X, Y, and Z direction
- The X, Y, and Z up vector

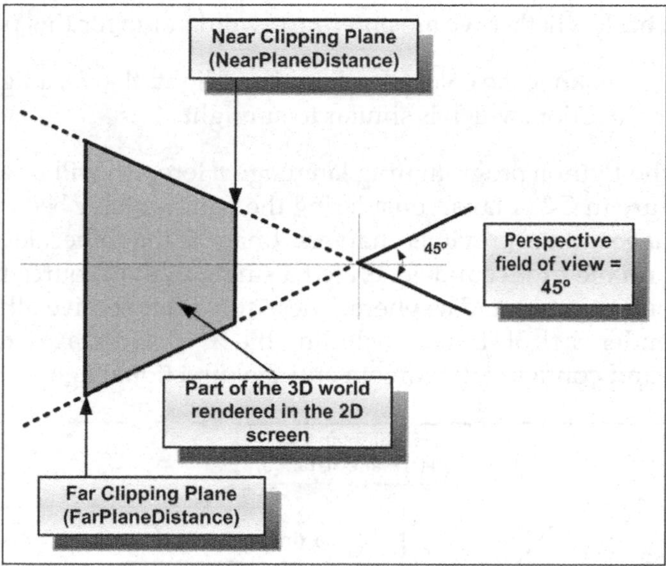

Figure 1

- **Perspective field of view in degrees**: This value determines the angle for the perspective camera's lens. A low value for this angle narrows the view. Thus, all the models will appear larger in the lens with a perspective field of a view of 45 degrees. A high value for this angle widens the view; therefore, all the models appear smaller in the visible part of the 3D world.

- **The near clipping plane**: The 3D region, which is visible on the 2D screen, is formed by a clipped pyramid called a frustum. This value controls the position of the plane that slices the top of the pyramid and determines the nearest part of the 3D world that the camera will render on the 2D screen. As the value is expressed taking into account the *Z* axis, it is a good idea to add code to check whether we are entering a valid value for this parameter.
- **The far clipping plane**: This value controls the position of the plane that slices the back of the pyramid and determines the more distant part of the 3D world that the camera will render on the 2D screen. The value is also expressed taking into account the *Z* axis; therefore, it is a good idea to add code to check whether we are entering a valid value for this parameter.

In addition, we can change the color of a directional light, that is, a light that casts light in a specific direction, which is similar to sunlight.

Let's start with the Python programming language. Here, we will be able to apply a similar procedure in C# or Java, considering the way we have been working with these languages in the previous chapters. Imagine that other developers started working on the project and generated a single Python source file with many functions that render a cube and a sphere. These functions receive all the necessary parameters to render each 3D figure, including the *X*, *Y*, and *Z* axes, determine the 3D figure's size, and configure the camera and the directional light:

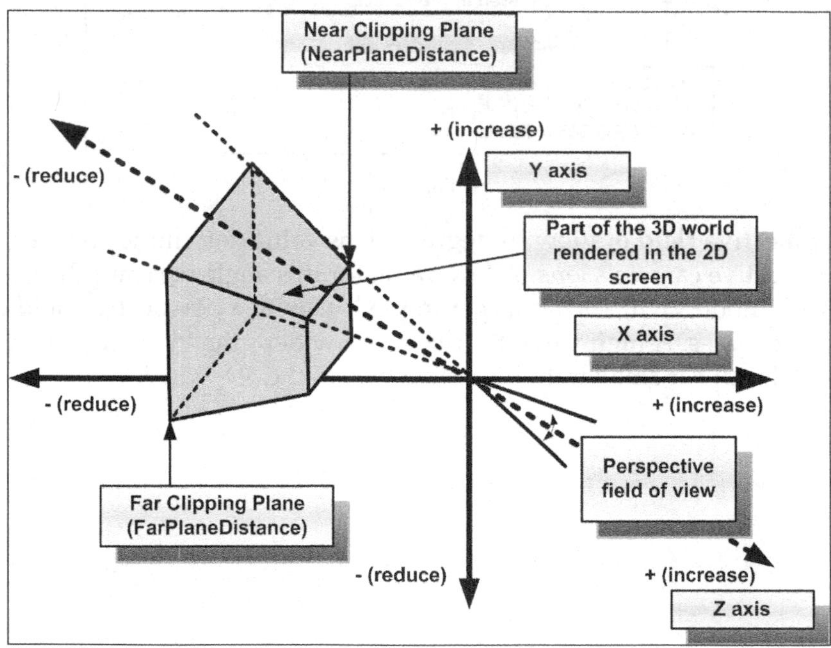

Figure 2

The following code shows an example of the declaration of the function that renders a sphere named `render_sphere` and the function that renders a cube named `render_cube`:

```
def render_sphere(x, y, z, radius, camera_x, camera_y, camera_z,
camera_direction_x, camera_direction_y, camera_direction_z, camera_
vector_x, camera_vector_y, camera_vector_z, camera_perspective_
field_of_view, camera_near_clipping_plane, camera_far_clipping_plane,
directional_light_x, directional_light_y, directional_light_z,
directional_light_color):
    pass


def render_cube(x, y, z, edge_length, camera_x, camera_y, camera_z,
camera_direction_x, camera_direction_y, camera_direction_z, camera_
vector_x, camera_vector_y, camera_vector_z, camera_perspective_field_
of_view, camera_near_clipping_plane, camera_far_clipping_plane,
directional_light_x, directional_light_y, directional_light_z,
directional_light_color):
    pass
```

Each function requires a huge number of parameters. Let's imagine that we have requirements to add code in order to render additional shapes and add different types of cameras and lights. The preceding code can easily become a really big mess, repetitive, and difficult to maintain.

The first thing we can change is to work with a `Vector3D` class instead of working with separate *X*, *Y*, and *Z* values. Then, we can create a class for each of the following elements:

- `SceneElement`: This class represents a 3D element that is part of a scene and has a location specified with the `Vector3D` class. It is the base class for all the scene elements that require a location in the 3D space.
- `Light`: This is a subclass of `SceneElement` and represents a 3D light. It is the base class for all the lights.
- `DirectionalLight`: This is a subclass of `Light` and represents a directional light. It adds the property of `color`. The property setter makes sure that we cannot specify invalid values for the underlying attribute.
- `Camera`: This is a subclass of `SceneElement` and represents a 3D camera. It is the base class for all the cameras.

- `PerspectiveCamera`: This is a subclass of `Camera` and represents a perspective camera. It adds the `Vector3D` attributes: `direction` and `vector`. In addition, the class adds the `field_of_view`, `near_clipping_plane`, and `far_clipping_plane` properties. The property setters make sure that we cannot specify invalid values for all the underlying attributes.
- `Shape`: This is a subclass of `SceneElement` and represents a 3D shape that has a location specified with a `Vector3D` instance. It is the base class for all the 3D shapes and defines an empty `Render` method that receives a `Camera` instance.
- `Sphere`: This is a subclass of `Shape` that adds a `radius` property and overrides the `Render` method defined in its superclass to render a sphere.
- `Cube`: This is a subclass of `Shape` that adds an `edge_length` property and overrides the `Render` method defined in its superclass to render a sphere.
- `Scene`: This class represents the scene to be rendered.

The `Scene` class defines an `active_camera` attribute that holds the `Camera` instance. The `lights` attribute is a list of `Light` instances, whereas all the shapes attributes is a list of `Shape` instances that compose a scene. The `add_light` method adds `Light` to the `lights` list. The `add_shape` method adds `Shape` to the shapes list. Finally, the `render` method calls the render method for each of the `Shape` instances included in the `shapes` list and passes the `active_camera` attribute and the `lights` list as arguments.

The following code shows the Python code that defines the previously explained classes. In this case, we will use attributes; we haven't added any validation code to keep the code as simples as possible. In addition, this code doesn't really render any shapes because it would require a huge number of lines of code. Also, don't forget to organize the code as you learned in the previous chapter:

```
class Vector3D:
    def __init__(self, x, y, z):
        self.x = x
        self.y = y
        self.z = z


class SceneElement:
    def __init__(self, location):
        self.location = location


class Light(SceneElement):
    def __init__(self, location):
```

```
        self.location = location


class DirectionalLight(Light):
    def __init__(self, location, color):
        super().__init__(location)
        self.color = color


class Camera(SceneElement):
    def __init__(self, location):
        super().__init__(location)


class PerspectiveCamera(Camera):
    def __init__(self, location, direction, vector, field_of_view,
near_clipping_plane, far_clipping_plane):
        super().__init__(location)
        self.direction = direction
        self.vector = vector
        self.field_of_view = field_of_view
        self.near_clipping_plane = near_clipping_plane
        self.far_clipping_plane = far_clipping_plane

class Shape(SceneElement):
    def __init__(self, location):
        super().__init__(location)

    def render(self, camera, lights):
        pass


class Sphere(Shape):
    def __init__(self, location, radius):
        super().__init__(location)
        self.radius = radius

    def render(self, camera, lights):
        print("Rendering a sphere.")

class Cube(Shape):
    def __init__(self, location, edge_length):
        super().__init__(location)
```

```
        self.edge_length = edge_length

    def render(self, camera, lights):
        print("Rendering a cube.")

class Scene:
    def __init__(self, initial_camera):
        self.active_camera = initial_camera
        self.shapes = []
        self.lights = []

    def add_light(self, light):
        self.lights.append(light)

    def add_shape(self, shape):
        self.shapes.append(shape)

    def render(self):
        for shape in self.shapes:
            shape.render(self.active_camera, self.lights)
```

After we create the previously shown classes, we can enter the following code in the `__main__` method:

```
if __name__ == '__main__':
    camera = PerspectiveCamera(Vector3D(30, 30, 30), Vector3D(50, 0,
0), Vector3D(4, 5, 2), 90, 20, 40)
    sphere = Sphere(Vector3D(20, 20, 20), 8)
    cube = Cube(Vector3D(10, 10, 10), 5)
    light = DirectionalLight(Vector3D(2, 2, 5), 235)
    scene = Scene(camera)
    scene.add_shape(sphere)
    scene.add_shape(cube)
    scene.add_light(light)
    scene.render()
```

The preceding code is very easy to understand and read. First, we created `PerspectiveCamera` with all the necessary parameters. Then, we created two shapes: a `Sphere` and a `Cube`. Finally, we created `DirectionalLight` with all the necessary parameters and `Scene` with the previously created `PerspectiveCamera` as the initial camera. Then, we added all the shapes and the light to the scene and called the render method to render the scene.

Now, compare the previous code with the following main method that calls the `render_sphere` and `render_cube` functions with more than a dozen parameters:

```
if __name__ == '__main__':
    render_sphere(20, 20, 20, 8, 30, 30, 30, 50, 0, 0, 4, 5, 2, 90,
20, 40, 2, 2, 5, 235)
    render_cube(10, 10, 10, 5, 30, 30, 30, 50, 0, 0, 4, 5, 2, 90, 20,
40, 2, 2, 5, 235)
```

The object-oriented version makes it easier to add parameters to any scene element. In addition, we can add the necessary light types, camera types, and shapes by specializing all the base classes. Whenever we find a behavior that is repeated in subclasses, we can generalize the code and move it to its base class. This way, we can reuse code and make future extensions to the application easier to code.

Refactoring existing code in C#

The following code shows an example of the declaration of the method that renders a sphere named `RenderSphere` and the method that renders a cube named `RenderCube` in C#:

```
public static void RenderSphere(
  int x, int y, int z, int radius,
  int cameraX, int cameraY, int cameraZ,
  int cameraDirectionX, int cameraDirectionY, int cameraDirectionZ,
  int cameraVectorX, int cameraVectorY, int cameraVvectorZ,
  int cameraPerspectiveFieldOfView,
  int cameraNearClippingPlane,
  int cameraFarClippingPlane,
  int directionalLightX, int directionalLightY, int directionalLightZ,
  int directionalLightColor)
{
}

public static void RenderCube(
  int x, int y, int z, int edgeLength,
  int cameraX, int cameraY, int cameraZ,
  int cameraDirectionX, int cameraDirectionY, int cameraDirectionZ,
  int cameraVectorX, int cameraVectorY, int cameraVvectorZ,
  int cameraPerspectiveFieldOfView,
  int cameraNearClippingPlane,
  int cameraFarClippingPlane,
  int directionalLightX, int directionalLightY, int directionalLightZ,
  int directionalLightColor)
{
}
```

Each function requires a huge number of parameters. Let's imagine that we have requirements to add code in order to render additional shapes and add different types of cameras and lights. The code can easily become a really big mess, repetitive, and difficult to maintain.

In *Chapter 3, Encapsulation of Data,* we worked with both mutable and immutable versions of the `Vector3D` class. Then, you learned how to overload operators in C#. The first thing we can change is to work with the `Vector3D` class instead of working with separate *X*, *Y*, and *Z* values. The following code shows a simple `Vector3D` class that uses auto-implemented properties. The code doesn't overload operators because we want to keep the example extremely simple:

```
public class Vector3D
{
  public int X { get; set; }
  public int Y { get; set; }
  public int Z { get; set; }

  public Vector3D(int x, int y, int z)
  {
    this.X = x;
    this.Y = y;
    this.Z = z;
  }
}
```

We will create a simple interface named `ISceneElement` to specify all the requirements for scene elements:

```
public interface ISceneElement
{
  Vector3D Location { get; set; }
}
```

The following code declares an abstract `SceneElement` class that implements the previously defined `ISceneElement` interface. The `SceneElement` class represents a 3D element. This element is part of a scene and has a location specified with `Vector3D`. It is the base class for all the scene elements that require a location in the 3D space:

```
public abstract class SceneElement : ISceneElement
{
  public Vector3D Location { get; set; }

  public SceneElement(Vector3D location)
  {
```

```
        this.Location = location;
    }
}
```

The following code declares another abstract class named `Light`. This is a subclass of the previously defined `SceneElement` class. This class represents a 3D light and is the base class for all the lights:

```
public abstract class Light : SceneElement
{
    public Light(Vector3D location)
        : base(location)
    {

    }
}
```

The following code declares a subclass of `Light` named `DirectionalLight`. The class represents a directional light and adds a `Color` property. In this case, we don't add validations for all the property setters just to make the example simple. However, we already know how to do it:

```
public class DirectionalLight : Light
{
    public int Color { get; set; }

    public DirectionalLight(Vector3D location, int color)
        : base(location)
    {
        this.Color = color;
    }
}
```

The following code declares an abstract class named `Camera` that inherits from `SceneElement`. The class represents a 3D camera. It is the base class for all the cameras:

```
public abstract class Camera : SceneElement
{
    public Camera(Vector3D location)
        : base(location)
    {
    }
}
```

The following code declares a subclass of `Camera` named `PerspectiveCamera`. The class represents a perspective camera and adds the `Direction` and `Vector` auto-implemented `Vector3D` properties. In addition, the class adds the `FieldOfView`, `NearClippingPlane`, and `FarClippingPlane` auto-implemented properties:

```
public class PerspectiveCamera : Camera
{
  public Vector3D Direction { get; set; }
  public Vector3D Vector { get; set; }
  public int FieldOfView { get; set; }
  public int NearClippingPlane { get; set; }
  public int FarClippingPlane { get; set; }

  public PerspectiveCamera(Vector3D location, Vector3D direction,
Vector3D vector, int fieldOfView, int nearClippingPlane, int
farClippingPlane)
    : base(location)
  {
    this.Direction = direction;
    this.Vector = vector;
    this.FieldOfView = fieldOfView;
    this.NearClippingPlane = nearClippingPlane;
    this.FarClippingPlane = farClippingPlane;
  }
}
```

The following code declares an abstract class named `Shape` that inherits from `SceneElement`. The class represents a 3D shape and is the base class for all the 3D shapes. The class defines an abstract `Render` method that receives the `Camera` instance and a list of `Light` instances:

```
public abstract class Shape: SceneElement
{
  public Shape(Vector3D location)
    : base(location)
  {
  }

  public abstract void Render(Camera camera, List<Light> lights);
}
```

The following code declares a `Sphere` class, a subclass of `Shape` that adds a `Radius` auto-implemented property and overrides the `Render` method defined in its abstract superclass to render a sphere:

```
public class Sphere : Shape
{
  public int Radius { get; set; }

  public Sphere(Vector3D location, int radius)
    : base(location)
  {
    this.Radius = radius;
  }

  public override void Render(Camera camera, List<Light> lights)
  {
    Console.WriteLine("Rendering a sphere.");
  }
}
```

The following code declares a `Cube` class, a subclass of `Shape` that adds an `EdgeLength` auto-implemented property and overrides the `Render` method defined in its abstract superclass to render a cube:

```
public class Cube : Shape
{
  public int EdgeLength { get; set; }

  public Cube(Vector3D location, int edgeLength)
    : base(location)
  {
    this.EdgeLength = edgeLength;
  }

  public override void Render(Camera camera, List<Light> lights)
  {
    Console.WriteLine("Rendering a cube.");
  }
}
```

Finally, the following code declares the `Scene` class that represents the scene to be rendered. The class defines an `_activeCamera` protected field that holds the `Camera` instance. The `_lights` protected field is a list of `Light` instances, and the `_shapes` protected field is a list of `Shape` instances that compose a scene. The `AddLight` method adds `Light` to the `_lights` list. The `AddShape` method adds `Shape` to the `_shapes` list. Finally, the `render` method calls the render method for each of the `Shape` instances included in the `_shapes` list and passes `_activeCamera` and `lights` list as arguments:

```
public class Scene
{
  protected List<Light> _lights;
  protected List<Shape> _shapes;
  protected Camera _activeCamera;

  public Scene(Camera initialCamera)
  {
    this._activeCamera = initialCamera;
    this._shapes = new List<Shape>();
    this._lights = new List<Light>();
  }

  public void AddLight(Light light)
  {
    this._lights.Add(light);
  }

  public void AddShape(Shape shape)
  {
    this._shapes.Add(shape);
  }

  public void Render()
  {
    foreach (var shape in this._shapes)
    {
      shape.Render(this._activeCamera, this._lights);
    }
  }
}
```

After we create the previously shown classes, we can enter the following code in the `Main` method of a Windows console application:

```
var camera = new PerspectiveCamera(
  new Vector3D(30, 30, 30),
  new Vector3D(50, 0, 0),
  new Vector3D(4, 5, 2),
  90, 20, 40);
var sphere = new Sphere(new Vector3D(20, 20, 20), 8);
var cube = new Cube(new Vector3D(10, 10, 10), 5);
var light = new DirectionalLight(new Vector3D(2, 2, 5), 235);
var scene = new Scene(camera);
scene.AddShape(sphere);
scene.AddShape(cube);
scene.AddLight(light);
scene.Render();

Console.ReadLine();
```

The preceding code is very easy to understand and read. First, we created a `PerspectiveCamera` instance with all the necessary parameters. Then we created two shapes: a `Sphere` and a `Cube`. Finally, we created `DirectionalLight` with all the necessary parameters and a `Scene` with the previously created `PerspectiveCamera` as the initial camera. Then, we added all the shapes and the light to the scene and called the `Render` method in order to render the scene.

Now, compare the previous code with the following code that call the `RenderSphere` and `RenderCube` methods with more than a dozen parameters:

```
RenderSphere(
  20, 20, 20,
  8, 30, 30,
  30, 50, 0,
  0, 4, 5,
  2, 90, 20,
  40, 2, 2,
  5, 235);
RenderCube(
  10, 10, 10,
  5, 30, 30,
  30, 50, 0,
  0, 4, 5,
  2, 90, 20,
  40, 2, 2,
  5, 235);
```

The object-oriented version requires a higher number of lines of code. However, it is easier to understand and expand based on future requirements. If you need to add a new type of light, a new shape, or a new type of camera, you know where to add the pieces of code, which classes to create, and the methods to change.

Refactoring existing code in JavaScript

The following code shows an example of the declaration of the function that renders a sphere named `renderSphere` and the function that renders a cube named `renderCube` in JavaScript:

```
function renderSphere(
  x, y, z, radius,
  cameraX, cameraY, cameraZ,
  cameraDirectionX, cameraDirectionY, cameraDirectionZ,
  cameraVectorX, cameraVectorY, cameraVvectorZ,
  cameraPerspectiveFieldOfView,
  cameraNearClippingPlane,
  cameraFarClippingPlane,
  directionalLightX, directionalLightY, directionalLightZ,
  directionalLightColor)
{

}

function renderCube(
  x, y, z, edgeLength,
  cameraX, cameraY, cameraZ,
  cameraDirectionX, cameraDirectionY, cameraDirectionZ,
  cameraVectorX, cameraVectorY, cameraVvectorZ,
  cameraPerspectiveFieldOfView,
  cameraNearClippingPlane,
  cameraFarClippingPlane,
  directionalLightX, directionalLightY, directionalLightZ,
  directionalLightColor)
{

}
```

Each function requires a huge number of parameters. Let's imagine that we have requirements to add code in order to render additional shapes and add different types of cameras and lights. The code can easily become a really big mess, repetitive, and difficult to maintain.

The first thing we can change is to define a `Vector3D` constructor function that provides the `x`, `y`, and `z` properties instead of working with separate *X*, *Y*, and *Z* values. The following code shows a very simple `APP.Math.Vector3D` constructor function:

```
var APP = APP || {};
APP.Math = APP.Math || {};
APP.Math.Vector3D = function(x, y, z) {
  this.x = x;
  this.y = y;
  this.z = z;
}
```

The following code declares an `APP.Scene.DirectionalLight` constructor function. This function generates objects that will represent a directional light. The constructor function defines the properties of `location` and `color`. We will use an `APP.Math.Vector3D` object for `location`:

```
var APP = APP || {};
APP.Scene = APP.Scene || {};
APP.Scene.DirectionalLight = function(location, color) {
  this.location = location;
  this.color = color;
}
```

The following code declares an `APP.Scene.PerspectiveCamera` constructor function. This function generates objects that represent a perspective camera. The constructor function defines the `location`, `direction`, and `Vector` properties that will hold the `APP.Math.Vector3D` object. In addition, this code declares and initializes the `fieldOfView`, `nearClippingPlane`, and `farClippingPlane` properties:

```
var APP = APP || {};
APP.Scene = APP.Scene || {};
APP.Scene.PerspectiveCamera = function(location, direction, vector,
fieldOfView, nearClippingPlane, farClippingPlane) {
  this.location = location;
  this.direction = direction;
  this.vector = vector;
  this.fieldOfView = fieldOfView;
  this.nearClippingPlane = nearClippingPlane;
  this.farClippingPlane = farClippingPlane;
}
```

The following code declares an `APP.Shape.Sphere` constructor function that receives `location` and `radius`. The code declares the location and radius properties with all its values received as arguments. The location property will hold an `APP.Math.Vector3D` object. The prototype defines a `render` method that prints a line, which simulates that it will render a sphere:

```
var APP = APP || {};
APP.Shape = APP.Shape || {};
APP.Shape.Sphere = function(location, radius) {
  this.location = location;
  this.radius = radius;
}
APP.Shape.Sphere.prototype.render = function(camera, lights) {
  console.log("Rendering a sphere");
}
```

The following code declares an `APP.Shape.Cube` constructor function that receives `location` and `edgeLength`. The code declares the location and `edgeLength` properties with all its values received as arguments. The location property will hold the `APP.Math.Vector3D` object. The prototype defines the `render` method that prints a line simulating that it will render a cube:

```
var APP = APP || {};
APP.Shape = APP.Shape || {};
APP.Shape.Cube = function(location, edgeLength) {
  this.location = location;
  this.edgeLength = edgeLength;
}
APP.Shape.Cube.prototype.render = function(camera, lights) {
  console.log("Rendering a cube");
}
```

Finally, the following code declares the `APP.Scene.Scene` constructor function. This function generates objects that represent the scene to be rendered. The constructor function receives an `initialCamera` argument that the code assigns to the `activeCamera` property. The `lights` property is an array that will hold `APP.Scene.DirectionalLight` objects. The `shapes` property is an array that will hold `APP.Shape.Sphere` or `APP.Shape.Cube` objects that compose a scene. The `addLight` method adds an `APP.Scene.DirectionalLight` object to the `lights` array. The `addShape` method adds either an `APP.Shape.Sphere` object or an `APP.Shape.Cube` object to the `shapes` array. Finally, the `render` method calls the render method for each of the elements in the `shape` array `Shape` instances included in the `_shapes` list and passes `_activeCamera` and the `lights` list as arguments:

```
var APP = APP || {};
```

```
APP.Scene = APP.Scene || {};
APP.Scene.Scene = function(initialCamera) {
  this.activeCamera = initialCamera;
  this.shapes = [];
  this.lights = [];
}
APP.Scene.Scene.prototype.addLight = function(light) {
  this.lights.push(light);
}
APP.Scene.Scene.prototype.addShape = function(shape) {
  this.shapes.push(shape);
}
APP.Scene.Scene.prototype.render = function() {
  this.shapes.forEach(function (shape) { shape.render(this.
activeCamera, this.lights); });
}
```

After we create the previously shown constructor functions and their prototypes, we can enter the following code on a JavaScript console:

```
var camera = new APP.Scene.PerspectiveCamera(
  new APP.Math.Vector3D(30, 30, 30),
  new APP.Math.Vector3D(50, 0, 0),
  new APP.Math.Vector3D(4, 5, 2),
  90, 20, 40);
var sphere = new APP.Shape.Sphere(new APP.Math.Vector3D(20, 20, 20),
8);
var cube = new APP.Shape.Cube(new APP.Math.Vector3D(10, 10, 10), 5);
var light = new APP.Scene.DirectionalLight(new APP.Math.Vector3D(2, 2,
5), 235);
var scene = new APP.Scene.Scene(camera);
scene.addShape(sphere);
scene.addShape(cube);
scene.addLight(light);
scene.render();
```

The preceding code is very easy to understand and read. We created an `APP.Scene.PerspectiveCamera` object with all the necessary parameters. Then, we created two shapes: `APP.Shape.Sphere` and `APP.Shape.Cube`. Finally, we created `APP.Scene.DirectionalLight` with all the necessary parameters and `APP.Scene.Scene` with the previously created `APP.Scene.PerspectiveCamera` as the initial camera. Then, we added all the shapes and the light to the scene and called the `render` method in order to render a scene.

Now, compare the previous code with the following code that calls the `renderSphere` and `renderCube` functions with more than a dozen parameters:

```
renderSphere(
  20, 20, 20,
  8, 30, 30,
  30, 50, 0,
  0, 4, 5,
  2, 90, 20,
  40, 2, 2,
  5, 235);
renderCube(
  10, 10, 10,
  5, 30, 30,
  30, 50, 0,
  0, 4, 5,
  2, 90, 20,
  40, 2, 2,
  5, 235);
```

The object-oriented version requires a higher number of lines of code. However, it is easier to understand and expand based on future requirements. We haven't included any kind of validations in order to keep the sample code as simple as possible and focus on the refactoring process. However, it is easy to make all the necessary changes to add the necessary validations as you learned in the previous chapters.

Summary

In this chapter, you learned how to use all the features included in Python, C#, and JavaScript in order to write simple and complex object-oriented code. We can even refactor existing code to take advantage of object-oriented programming in order to prepare the code for future requirements, reduce maintenance costs, and maximize code reuse.

Once you start working with object-oriented code and follow its best practices, it is difficult to stop writing code that works with objects. Objects are everywhere in real-life situations; therefore, it makes sense to code plenty of objects.

Now that you have learned to write object-oriented code, you are ready to use everything you learned in real-life applications that will not only rock, but also maximize code reuse and simplify maintenance.

Index

A

B

C

D

E

F

G

I

J

M

N

O

P

R

S

T

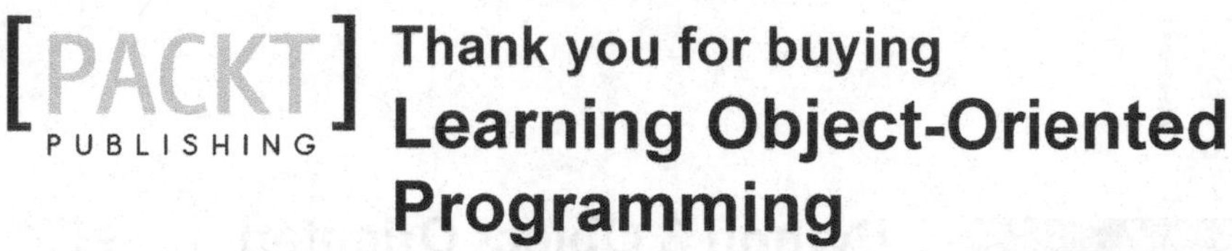

[PACKT]
PUBLISHING
Thank you for buying
Learning Object-Oriented
Programming

About Packt Publishing

Packt, pronounced 'packed', published its first book, *Mastering phpMyAdmin for Effective MySQL Management*, in April 2004, and subsequently continued to specialize in publishing highly focused books on specific technologies and solutions.

Our books and publications share the experiences of your fellow IT professionals in adapting and customizing today's systems, applications, and frameworks. Our solution-based books give you the knowledge and power to customize the software and technologies you're using to get the job done. Packt books are more specific and less general than the IT books you have seen in the past. Our unique business model allows us to bring you more focused information, giving you more of what you need to know, and less of what you don't.

Packt is a modern yet unique publishing company that focuses on producing quality, cutting-edge books for communities of developers, administrators, and newbies alike. For more information, please visit our website at `www.packtpub.com`.

Writing for Packt

We welcome all inquiries from people who are interested in authoring. Book proposals should be sent to `author@packtpub.com`. If your book idea is still at an early stage and you would like to discuss it first before writing a formal book proposal, then please contact us; one of our commissioning editors will get in touch with you.

We're not just looking for published authors; if you have strong technical skills but no writing experience, our experienced editors can help you develop a writing career, or simply get some additional reward for your expertise.

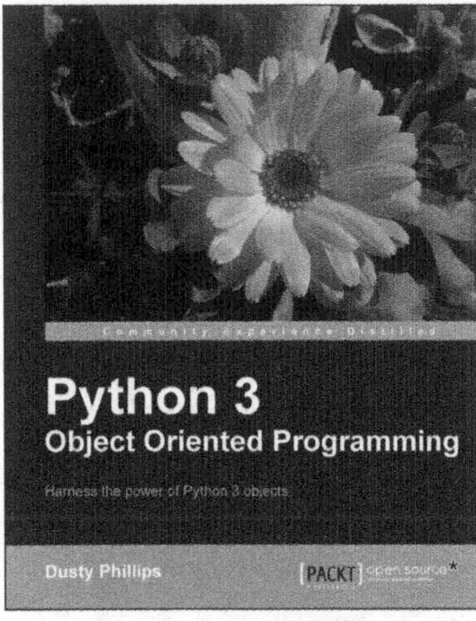

Python 3 Object Oriented Programming

ISBN: 978-1-84951-126-1 Paperback: 404 pages

Harness the power of Python 3 objects

1. Learn how to do Object Oriented Programming in Python using this step-by-step tutorial.
2. Design public interfaces using abstraction, encapsulation, and information hiding.
3. Turn your designs into working software by studying the Python syntax.
4. Raise, handle, define, and manipulate exceptions using special error objects.

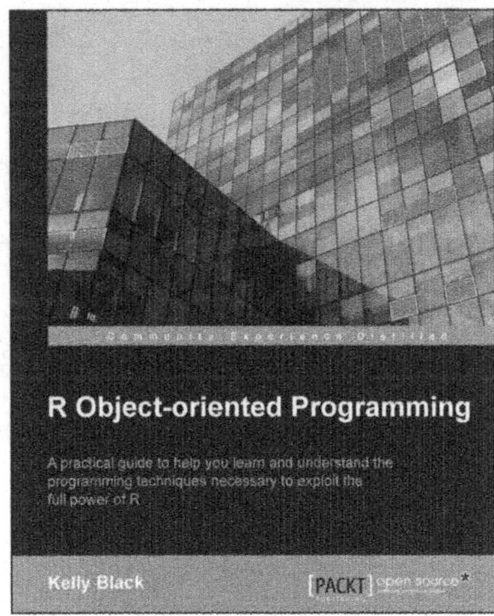

R Object-oriented Programming

ISBN: 978-1-78398-668-2 Paperback: 190 pages

A practical guide to help you learn and understand the programming techniques necessary to exploit the full power of R

1. Learn and understand the programming techniques necessary to solve specific problems and speed up development processes for statistical models and applications.
2. Explore the fundamentals of building objects and how they program individual aspects of larger data designs.
3. Step-by-step guide to understand how OOP can be applied to application and data models within R.

Please check **www.PacktPub.com** for information on our titles

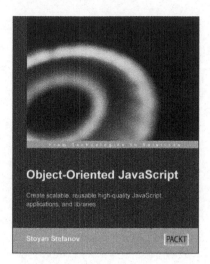

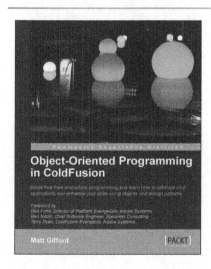

CPSIA information can be obtained
at www.ICGtesting.com
Printed in the USA
LVOW03s1929101115
461901LV00007B/243/P